W9-BXN-743

Choose
the
SOUTH

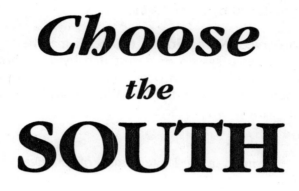

Choose
the
SOUTH

Retirement Discoveries for Every Budget

John Howells

GATEWAY
B O O K S

Printed in the United States of America

Gateway Books
Oakland, CA

Library of Congress Cataloging–in–Publication Data

Howells, John, 1928–
    Choose the South: retirement discoveries for every budget / John Howells.
        p. cm.
    Includes index.
    ISBN 0-933469-31-4
    1. Southern States—Guidebooks. 2. Retirement, Places of—Southern States—Guidebooks. 3. Cost and standard of living—Southern States. I. Title.

F207.3.H69 1997   97–44912
917.504′43—dc21   CIP

10 9 8 7 6 5 4 3 2 1

Contents

Introduction

My retirement planning guide, *Where to Retire* (Gateway Books, 1995), describes and recommends 150 communities throughout the United States as possible retirement choices. *Where to Retire* has received much praise as an overview of options around the nation. But because of the wide variety and large number of potential retirement locations, the amount of information on each listing in *Where to Retire* had to be kept to a minimum and some nice places were left out because of space limitations. Many readers find that when they narrow their choices to a certain section of the country, having more detailed information helps in making final decisions. Others already know where they want to retire and want to zero in on that particular area from the beginning.

To better inform folks who want to sharpen their focus on a particular region, Gateway Books decided to produce a series of regional retirement guides. This eases the job of a retirement writer, for it's far easier to present lots of information about a community than to make painful decisions as to what must be left unsaid. Therefore, this volume contains more in-depth information about previously discussed communities, plus descriptions of several new retirement locations—some places not covered in other publications. We've evaluated more than 75 towns in the southern states for your consideration, and by extension, many more places in surrounding localities.

In the 15 years since I began writing books on retirement, the scene has changed dramatically. For one thing, the average age of those leaving the workplace has decreased by more than five years. In addition to those normally reaching retirement age, millions of workers are being "downsized" or given "golden handshakes" (in plain English: fired). Whatever you call it, huge numbers of active, younger people are entering retirement whether they like it or not. Others, seeing the handwriting on the wall, are cashing in the equities in their homes, quitting the rat race and opting for early retirement.

The "baby boomers" are often the ones forced into early retirement as their generation begins crossing the 50-years-and-older bridge. According to a recent survey of boomers by retirement community developer Del Webb, 30 percent have plans to retire before age 60; more than a third of these retirees intend to move to another home for retirement and a large number plan on moving to another state.

Today's retirees are not only more youthful, but generally more affluent and clearly not ready to kick back with a cane fishing pole or watch soap operas all day long. They seek places where they can enjoy vigorous outdoor recreation and actively participate in community activities. People today like to consider themselves to be "relocating" rather than "retiring" and they often relocate within striking distance of the country's business concentrations—in case they want to keep their hand in the job market, on a consulting basis, if nothing else.

This demographic change in our working population is a major reason why southern states are climbing to the top of the graphs in numbers of out-of-state relocations. Because the vast majority of "downsizing" or "involuntary corporate outplacements" occurs in the immense industrial sections of the Northeast and Midwest, the involuntary retirees prefer to remain as close as possible to a source of part-time or full-time employment. Yet they also want to be as far as possible from frigid winters, expensive housing and high taxes. The movement is logically to the South. Not necessarily to Florida, as you might expect, but to those southern states with growing business and industry potentials. As a matter of fact, more Floridians relocate out of state than retirees from any other state.

At the same time businesses in the Northeast and Midwest are downsizing, southern states are wooing corporations, trying to entice them into relocating in the South. Companies are offered generous tax exemptions, plentiful labor and free land if they will only relocate their manufacturing plants. The strategy works. For example, industrial relocation has accelerated North Carolina's traditionally slow economy so that it is now the South's most industrialized state, with an unemployment rate of just 2 percent.

This flow of business and industry to the South creates an increased need for talented and skilled employees. This makes the South an even more attractive place for relocation, drawing steadily increasing numbers of folks from other states. And finally, this influx of northerners, midwesterners and northeasterners into the South is changing the traditional, introverted character of southern communities.

What is "The South"? A heavy question we wrestled with when we planned this book was: Exactly which states do we mean when we say the South? The "deep" southern states were obvious choices, but what about Florida? Isn't the Sunshine State part of "the South"? What about Texas? Virginia? One by one, we dealt with each state, omitting some and including others. We determined that Florida has a totally different culture from the rest of the South; as the saying goes, "Florida is the southernmost limit of Long Island." We decided that Texas is more "west" than "south." Virginia is below the Mason-Dixon Line and is generally considered "south," but it turns out that Virginia sends many more retirees out of state to retire than it takes in.

That left Kentucky. Technically, since Kentucky sits north of the Mason-Dixon Line and refrained from joining the Confederacy during the Civil War, it shouldn't be part of "Dixie." The biggest argument against including Kentucky is the state's northern climate. The northern edge of the state has weather little different from the northern states it touches—Illinois, Indiana and Ohio. After all, Cincinnati, which sits just across the river from Kentucky, isn't known for its balmy weather.

Eventually, we decided to include Kentucky, or at least southern Kentucky. Reason number one: many people from the North are actually retiring in Kentucky, and many more will be making that same decision. Number two: Kentucky is preferred by many who aren't wild about the idea of moving too far from their old neighborhood, friends and family. Just about anywhere in Kentucky that retirees might want to live is a reasonable, one-day drive to go back "home." And, the final reason: as we checked weather statistics for Kentucky, we realized that indeed the winters are somewhat milder than in most northern locations, at least in the lower third of the state. It isn't semitropical, that's true, but it also isn't arctic (the way I remember winters in Ohio and Illinois).

Of all sections of the United States, the easiest to describe is "the South." The term evokes images of magnolia blossoms and warm breezes. You think of weeping willows dipping their branches into lazy rivers, their surfaces swirling with bass and catfish. You picture easy living with the delicate scent of honeysuckle in the air. "The South" means gracious mansions with white columns, old, red brick and fresh, green ivy. You can almost taste the flowery extravaganza of spring and savor the warmth of lazy, relaxing summers. Brisk autumns and short, mild winters complete the weather menu. You probably anticipate gracious southern hospitality, delicious southern cooking and thick southern accents. And of course, there's always a low cost-of-living and affordable housing, and today, there are rolling golf courses interspersed with forests and modern lakeside subdivisions—golf courses where you can play four seasons a year. If this is your mental landscape of "the South," then we are on the same wavelength; that's the South we intend to describe here.

Weather in the South: Few would question that winters are far less severe in the South than in most northern, midwestern or northeastern states. Frigid weather is one big reason folks are happy to move south. Is southern weather perfect? Hardly. Many locations described in this book have snowfall in the winter—usually light, rarely sticking around for more than a few hours, or a day at the most. Residents in places like this boast of a "four-season climate" and point out that their golf courses stay open all winter. Other southern regions have no snowfall, but it does get chilly enough to wear a heavy sweater in the dead of winter. If you want a guarantee of warm winters, you're going to have to relocate to Florida or the Southwest.

What about summers? Aren't they hot, muggy and sweltering? Of course. But do you know *any* place in the North, Midwest or Northeast where it isn't beastly hot in the summer? If you want cool summers, you'll have to relocate to the West Coast. Oddly enough, summer temperatures in the South aren't much different from the North. The thing that makes southern summers seem hotter than they are is a slightly elevated relative humidity.

Take a look at the chart of selected cities below. Compare Memphis, Tennessee, with Wichita, Kansas. You'll see that they have approximately the same number of days over 90 degrees in the summer, and both have high humidity, but Wichita has almost twice as many days below freezing in the winter. Compare each of the sample cities and you'll see that the number of hot days are about the same for each pair and that the summer high and low temperatures are not much different. The big difference is in the number of below-freezing days, plus a few points of relative humidity. This extra moisture in the air, even though it isn't much, definitely makes it seem warm from mid-day on, although mornings and evenings are usually balmy and pleasant. The solution is to play golf or take your lakeside strolls in the morning and late afternoon, probably much the same as you did where you were living before relocation.

City, State	Average Humidity	Days 90 deg. +	Days 32 deg. -	July Avg. Hi	July Avg. Lo
Memphis, TN	69	64	59	88	72
Wichita, KS	66	62	114	87	70
Birmingham, AL	72	39	60	88	70
Kansas City, MO	69	40	106	83	69
Clarksville, TN	71	37	75	90	69
St. Louis, MO	70	37	107	85	69
Raleigh-Durham, NC	71	25	82	88	67
Chicago, IL	67	21	119	79	63
Atlanta, GA	70	19	59	86	69
Philadelphia, PA	67	19	101	86	67

Legend and Reality: Reality never precisely matches the ideal picture of the mind's eye. There are other images of the "the South" that aren't so idyllic. The news media of 30 years ago highlighted a dramatic struggle for civil rights, complete with violence and tragedy, as citizens of color fought for the right to vote and to be treated with dignity, as equals under the law. These impressions of conflict, social injustice and poverty were vivid and fade slowly.

This lingering bad press is unfortunate, because the South has undergone tremendous change over the past three decades, resulting in a 180-degree turnabout in the general conscience of the region. The younger generation today often expresses difficulty understanding just what the fighting was all about. Few can imagine a world where people should be prevented from participating in society because of skin color, or where they should drink from separate water fountains or sit in designated sections of buses and theaters.

Don't misunderstand: I'm not claiming that all southerners suddenly changed into color-blind liberals, totally free of racism and full of brotherly love. My point is that the overall southern attitude toward race relations has taken a dramatic turn for the better. From my perspective, I'm convinced that the South today harbors no more racism than the rest of the country.

(You might well accuse me of damning with faint praise, for we all know that some regions of our country harbor extremely racist organizations and militants dedicated to racial hatred. Ironically, it's usually northern and western states—like Michigan, Pennsylvania, Idaho and Montana—where extreme racist organizations have stoked fires of hatred. According to the Southern Poverty Law Center, racism in these places today is worse than the South *ever* was.)

In all, we've visited over a hundred communities in the South, and we were impressed by the gracious, genuine hospitality of the "retire-ment attraction" committees we worked with and how many of these committees included people of color. We spoke with African-American retirees who relocated to the South after working in other states. None reported problems with their new communities. One lady—a volun-teer with an Alabama chamber of commerce—said, "My husband and I were originally from New York, and we moved to California for careers in law enforcement. We'd never been in the South before. But we came here for a visit and fell in love with the area."

By chance, while doing our research in Alabama in the fall of 1996, the front page of Montgomery's daily newspaper carried a photo and story on former Alabama governor George Wallace about his presen-tation of the Lurene Wallace Prize for Courage to Vivian Malone Jones. (Ms. Jones was the black student whose intention of entering the University of Alabama inspired then-Governor Wallace's infamous "stand in the schoolhouse door.") As he presented the award, he asked for forgiveness for his actions back in those days of racial strife. In receiving the award, Ms. Jones said she was "happy to celebrate a change—a change of attitude, a change of feelings about what's happening in this state." On his behalf, Governor Wallace said, "Decades ago I stated publicly that my old views on segregation were, with 20-20 hindsight, wrong. Since that time, Alabamans of all colors have been able to foster new relationships and a radial harmony better than that of most other regions of the country." This is just one example of how things have changed in the South!

Admittedly, in some isolated areas in the South, people may cling stubbornly to traditions of intolerance, but certainly no more than their counterparts elsewhere in the country. However, folks who relocate from other states rarely choose to live in these "good ol' boy" environs in the first place. These islands of yesterday's mentality are typically rural, rustic communities where newcomers from outside the South find little to attract them.

Small-Town Syndrome: This brings up another point: While the South is abundantly stocked with delightful communities for retirement choices, some southern locations might seem totally inappropriate for "outsiders," no matter what your color, religion or politics. This can be true of isolated communities not only in the South, but in almost *any* rural area anywhere in the country—or anywhere in the world, for that matter. Unless you grew up in a small farm town, you might feel out of touch with your new neighbors. Don't misunderstand, rural southerners won't be unfriendly or make fun of you because you "talk funny"; on the contrary, your neighbors will shower you with obligatory southern hospitality. But unless you share at least a few common interests, you could feel left out and bored—particularly when conversations involve farm machinery, soybean prices or the best way to castrate hogs. Also, if your agricultural experience is limited to watering house plants, you might have few words of wisdom others care to hear. When your tastes in movies, music and food are considered weird, or if your political persuasion is at odds with the community's—or even worse, when you don't drive a pickup with a noisy muffler and a cracked windshield—you could feel like an alien. Again, communities like these aren't unique to the South; you'll find them in rural areas all over North America, in fact, throughout the world.

The bright side of the picture is: in the South you have your choice of any number of places that can match whatever level of sophistication and culture you care to maintain. We are firmly convinced that it's far easier to find compatible friends in the South than in similar towns elsewhere in the country. Therefore, all retirement locations described in this book are places where we—as Californians and "outsiders"—could feel comfortable in retirement. One criteria for selecting a community for evaluation was that it must have a number of "Yankee" retirees in residence who *like* living there. We interviewed these newcomers, with special interest as to their acceptance by townsfolk and the ease of making new friends. Without exception, we found they shared an unusually high level of enthusiasm, praise and pride for their new hometowns.

Obviously, the towns reviewed in this book are not the *only* nice retirement possibilities in the South. Many delightful and welcoming communities await your personal discovery.

Prime Rib and Pepsi-Cola: One southern idiosyncrasy may or may not affect you, but you should be aware of it. This is the custom of "local option" or "dry counties"—southern states allow counties to ban the sale of alcoholic beverages. If you don't drink, no problem. But, when dining out, if you happen to enjoy a glass of Cabernet Sauvignon with your prime rib instead of Pepsi Cola, you might feel deprived. Another point: Dry counties have a dearth of fine dinner houses, for the simple reason that it's the profits from liquor sales that pay for tasteful decor, interesting menus and gourmet chefs. So don't expect many gourmet restaurants in a dry county. If you have friends from out of state visiting your home—friends who enjoy an occasional cocktail or highball—you'll want to make sure to travel to the nearest "wet" county to stock up. Depending on where you live, that could mean a 100-mile round trip.

Once, when I mentioned prohibition as a drawback for attracting tourists and retirees, the mayor of a small Tennessee town disagreed with me, saying, "Why, buying alcohol's no problem here! We have plenty of bootleggers in our county. Believe me, you can buy anything you want, day or night, right here in town!" When asked why have laws against alcohol if enforcement is routinely ignored, he explained, "Well, you know how it is—the preachers want prohibition, and so do the bootleggers—yet folks like to drink. This way, everybody's happy."

Not to worry—if dining out and cocktails with dinner is part of your lifestyle, it isn't all that bleak. Most of the towns discussed in this book support private clubs or country clubs which are permitted to serve drinks—and they usually offer the best dinners in the area. People who seldom, if ever, play golf or tennis will join the country club just for the social and dining connections. When a club's major function is gregarious social activity, initiation fees and membership fees are often surprisingly reasonable. In many "country club communities," membership automatically goes with the home, and club dues are included in the property membership fees. You might make it a point to visit the local country club to see if you will "fit in" and whether it's worth the extra cost.

The South Welcomes You! It's nice to know you're wanted. And, of all the sectors of the United States, the South is by far the most welcoming toward retirees. In fact, folks here are downright *eager* to lure you into their midst. So much so that several southern states have established "retirement relocation programs" with personnel whose sole responsibility is to look for ways to attract and welcome newcomers to their state. Alabama was the first to inaugurate a retirement program, and Mississippi followed with a vigorous campaign, allocating half a million dollars a year for its retiree drive. Other southern states are considering financing a push for their share of retirees.

Why are they so interested in retirees? Because retirement is the South's newest and fastest-growing "industry." (It's called the "industry without smokestacks.") It's pollution-free and creates jobs without harmful ecological consequences. Furthermore, the state doesn't have to concede millions in tax exemptions and free land as it does with industry recruitment all too often. Plus, often after giving away land and tax breaks in recruiting industry, the community is dismayed when it turns out that the jobs created are filled by illegal aliens or by minimum wage workers without health care, who depend on welfare and food stamps, and who burden the school system with more children and low taxes.

According to Dr. Mark Fagan (a professor in Social Work at Alabama's Jacksonville State University), the impact of *one* retired couple moving into a community is economically equivalent to the creation of *three and a half* factory jobs! Many civic leaders are coming to the realization that it's a waste of resources to subsidize an industry to the tune of millions of dollars, just to create a hundred low-paying jobs. They're finding it's far easier to bring in 50 affluent retired couples who spend money and boost the economy to a much higher degree, who aren't dependent on welfare every time the factory lays off workers.

It turns out that the typical relocating couple brings an average of $300,000 in assets with them—from sale of their homes, stock investments, cash, CDs and so forth—to deposit in local banks and financial institutions. On the average, they enjoy an annual income in excess of $30,000, and more than 80 percent of their expenditures will be made in the community, greatly increasing money in circulation. They buy new cars, refrigerators and furniture, and they dine out frequently; they spend money on items that minimum-wage factory workers can't afford. So, instead of *taking* jobs, relocated couples *create* jobs, particularly in service, maintenance and construction industries. An additional benefit to the community is that these newcomers account for the vast majority of volunteer workers. Retirees from outside the state are usually among the most dedicated. This continuing flow of retirees from other states into the South is largely responsible for a dramatic upsurge in economic well-being and increasing levels of prosperity. Now you can see why southern states and communities are competing with one another for new retired couples. Yes, it's nice to be wanted!

Retirement Welcoming Committees: When visiting chambers of commerce in some states, particularly in popular retiree destinations such as Florida or California, we find the attitude: "Why the fuss over attracting retirees? They're coming here whether we want them or not!" So, when you move into a community where people are eager to have you as neighbors, you won't have to start off as a stranger and begin the process of making friends on your own. One way of speeding up this process is through local "retirement welcoming committees."

When you request retirement information from a typical southern chamber of commerce, your name and address will be entered into a database as a potential new resident. This is then turned over to the local welcoming committee. These committees consist of volunteer hometown boosters who are eager to attract outsiders and to share the bounty of their community. Ideally, volunteers are themselves from out of state—those who can best give you accurate information about relocation to their new hometowns. Don't be surprised if you receive a phone call from a committee member.

The volunteer might ask: "Made any final retirement decisions yet? Before you do, we'd love to show you our town. Be sure to give us a call when you get here, and my wife and I will take you on a tour." When this happens, by all means, take advantage of the offer. This is an excellent way to see the community through the eyes of insiders, especially if your hosts are retirees from some other state themselves. And you'll have a head start on meeting people and making friends should you decide to relocate there.

Typically, the retirement welcoming committee's involvement doesn't end with your making a decision. As you move into your new home, somebody will be there to make sure things are going okay and you'll be invited to social activities designed to integrate you into the community. The State of Mississippi, for example, insists that committees organize at least one activity each month for newcomers: a potluck, a dance, a home tour or any number of events designed to bring newcomers into contact with neighbors. We've visited towns where these activities are held weekly. (The southern-cooking potlucks were fantastic!) Not all towns support these committees, but those that do are particularly deserving of your consideration.

Quality of Life: Our travels have taken us through hundreds of communities and we've checked out many local conditions before making the final selections for this book. As pointed out earlier, because a town is *not* described here doesn't necessarily mean it wouldn't be a great place to retire. The bottom line is: there is no "best" place to retire for everyone. Selecting a place to relocate is a highly individual decision and depends on your personal lifestyle, future aspirations and, most importantly, what you consider to be an ideal quality of life.

The phrase "quality of life" means something different for every individual. When you ask Boston residents about their quality of life, you might hear them rave about the plethora of cultural events available to them. New Yorkers brag about their opera, stage plays and world-class restaurants. They can't live without jazz combos, museums and Fifth Avenue shopping. Big-city folks tell you they can't imagine life without all those exciting happenings that are characteristic of urban life.

When you ask the same question in a small southern town, "quality of life" might be defined in terms of peace and quiet, outdoor activities and low-keyed cultural activities. People here prize the high quality of the air they breathe, their sense of security, knowing what to expect from neighbors and a friendly community. Their quality of life is enhanced every time they're treated to the sight of a doe and her fawn grazing in a wooded glade. Miles of hiking and biking trails, top quality golf courses and world-class bass fishing replace opera, gourmet restaurants and museums. Hooking a trout on a hand-tied fly and watching it jump in a sparkling mountain stream substitutes for sitting in a stadium and watching the Cubs lose another game. It's a different quality of life.

Yet, southern retirement doesn't mean just outdoor activities. Many communities provide exciting cultural events and entertainment that rival those found in northern and eastern cities. Furthermore, southern urban centers such as Birmingham, Atlanta or Raleigh-Durham are usually a short drive from the preferred retirement communities, and they offer world-renowned entertainment, professional sports and museums. During a recent tour of Mississippi, we were treated to an exhibition from Russia's Catherine the Great collection—never before or since on display outside of Russia. As for good restaurants, we'll match those of Savannah, Charleston or New Orleans against those of San Francisco or Manhattan any day, not to mention the delightful specialty dishes of each southern region.

Southern Lifestyles: The South encompasses a wide variety of landscapes. You'll find everything from sandy beaches, rolling woodlands, rich agricultural countrysides and stalwart mountains of the Appalachians and the Ozarks—all of which offer a wide range of outdoor activities. All traditional open-air recreation can be enjoyed, including fishing, hunting, skiing, hiking, river rafting and more. Because southern winters are short and mild, you'll have longer seasons to enjoy the outdoors. Golf courses stay green the year round, and tennis courts receive constant use, save for an occasional few days of inclement weather.

Southern cities, towns and crossroad communities provide just about any kind of neighborhood you might wish for. The mix of rural, suburban and metropolitan settings produces a wide selection of lifestyles. You'll find something to fit any personality or appetite, and you'll find bountiful opportunities to acquire a taste for a new hobby, skill or whatever endeavor you'd care to try. During our research, we were continually surprised at the number of folks who relocated to the South after retirement and then decided to start or purchase a business. Remember, these guys are too young for rocking chairs.

"Southern Hospitality" is almost a cliche, yet there *is* such a thing and it's a definite tradition in the South. It's interesting to note how southerners interact with one another, as well as with strangers. You'll notice an open friendliness and sharing that differs from the general custom in other parts of the country. For example: it's surprising how often people drop by a friend's house for an unannounced visit. Sometimes a steady procession of acquaintances will be ringing the doorbell the whole day long. Close friends sometimes don't bother to knock; they just open the door and call out, "Anybody home?" They know they're always welcome for a chat. "Just passin' by," they'll explain, "so I thought I'd stop in to say hello." An extra cup of coffee is usually on the kitchen table before they can pull out a chair.

In other parts of the country, this would be unheard of. In my California neighborhood, before you visit someone other than a very close friend, you telephone first and see if it's okay to come over. In still other parts of the country, you either wait for an invitation or you suggest meeting for lunch at a nearby restaurant. For some folks, southern-style hospitality will take some getting used to. Some feel abused if casual acquaintances drop in and expect them to interrupt whatever they're doing to entertain them. Other folks love it.

It's our observation that southerners place a higher emphasis on entertaining and social obligations than do folks in other parts of the country. Life seems to be a continual round of luncheons, bridge tourneys, garden clubs, literary groups and dinner parties. Once invited, one must keep careful track of obligations and make sure invitations are reciprocated in proper time and order. Social etiquette is taken seriously. Failing to send a thank-you note to a host is considered rude, even though the occasion might have been considered insignificant in your hometown. When you receive an invitation to a social event, by all means accept it; this is where you begin to meet new people and make new friends. When you choose to retire in a town with an active relocation committee, you can be confident of receiving invitations.

Senior Centers: There's another interesting aspect about southern social life: the role of the local senior citizens' center. In many sections of the country, senior citizens' centers are dynamic places to visit, great places to socialize and *the* places to make friends. These centers are usually the focus of volunteer activity and the hub of community action. Not necessarily so in the South. With a few significant exceptions, the local senior center tends to be a dreary haven where low-income oldsters play cards or watch TV while waiting for the next free meal. Yet, we've run across a few delightful exceptions, where the senior community meets for lectures, concerts and plays, as well as the usual activities. A few inquiries will tell you whether it's worthwhile to seek out the local senior center.

In many southern towns, volunteer work and community action committees are coordinated by civic clubs like the Kiwanis or the Lions Club, rather than at the senior center. Often the local "garden club" (usually run by the town's social elite) spearheads committees for charitable or cultural campaigns.

Churches in the South: For many people, the role of a church is secondary, something that's an occasional issue in their lives. They might go to church for Christmas Eve or Easter services and whenever someone they know gets married or buried. Others never think about going to church; they're too busy catching up on weekend chores around the house.

But in the typical small southern town or city, churches are an integral part of everyday life. For many families the church is the center of their social lives. Spending an hour in church every Sunday is just as much a part of their weekly routine as mowing the lawn. People have friends they meet with every Sunday, but seldom see outside the church setting.

Something northerners aren't used to is that churches in the South are active politically. They can be surprisingly influential. When a congregation decides to pressure the local politicians, the message gets across; the congregation can muster votes. Church political clout is why so many small towns in the South are "dry." Some people aren't comfortable with this idea of church political action, but it's a way of life.

On the other hand churches can play a positive part in relocation by welcoming newcomers to a community. We've interviewed numerous retirees who seldom, if ever, went to church where they came from, but now are enthusiastic members of a congregation. One couple said, "When we showed up at church, everybody knew we were strangers. After the services we had a dozen people shaking our hands, asking where we were from and welcoming us to their town. We tried out several churches before selecting the one we attend now. Within a couple of months, it seemed like we knew everybody in town and were invited to join in all kinds of activities. The church was our doorway to the community."

Southern Accents: When television came upon the scene back in the 1950s, linguists were predicting the disappearance of regional accents. The assumption was that with standard American speech entering everyone's living room—bombarding people day and night—people would naturally begin to speak standard "Hollywood Television English." But that didn't happen.

After traveling through the South over the past years, we've become experts on accents. We can often tell not only which state a person comes from, but sometimes what section of the state. For example, southern Alabama seems to have a much thicker accent than the northern regions. South Carolina is different from North Carolina and the Appalachian regions of both states use yet a different accent. Louisiana has the most interesting collection of accents. The northern part of the state has an accent similar to the southern part of Arkansas, the middle of the state is distinct and New Orleans has its own patois. The most interesting of all is the Cajun accent, with its unique pronunciation and grammatical structure—both artifacts of the Cajuns' French heritage. For example, one might hear, "I'm going to dinner, me," or "Where Jeanne went, she?"

It takes a while, but you will become accustomed to southern accents, although you may have some mix-ups. One day while filling my gas tank at a service station, a man came to me and asked a question. I thought he said, "Ya' lock your car?" Bewildered, I replied, "Why should I lock my car? I'm just putting gasoline in it." He replied, "Well, ah got me a car just lock that one, 'cept it's a different color. And, I surely do lock it a lot!"

None of the Above: You may be one of those easy-to-please types whose interests are limited to television and gossiping with neighbors. We all know people who arrange their lives to fit the television schedule. Sunday is for sports or *60 Minutes*, Monday morning is for soap operas; Monday night is for Murphy Brown or Monday Night Football, and so on. Shopping trips to the supermarket, browsing the downtown stores and visiting neighbors have to fit into the space between programs.

While some folks would view a lifestyle like this as boring, others see it as a perfectly natural way to live; after all, this is the way they've lived all their lives. But when they had jobs, they couldn't afford the luxury of staying up late to watch David Letterman. And, since they worked during the daytime, soaps were something they heard others talk about. Now, when they can do anything they care to, they choose to indulge themselves with TV. However, I suspect these folks won't be reading this book—it doesn't make sense for them to move away for retirement since they have everything they need right where they live.

I would urge those who are thinking of moving when they retire to seriously consider the recreational and social facets of their new home base. Changing where you live is an opportunity to change your entire lifestyle. Your retirement can be a new beginning, not just a continuation of the same old groove (or maybe it's the same old rut).

Real Estate Prices: Throughout this book, I've tried to give the reader a flavor for approximate housing costs and real estate prices. Aside from the probability that my estimates will soon be outdated by inflation or unforeseen local circumstances, I've had doubts about the wisdom of including prices. They can be misleading in the extreme. Why? Because it's virtually impossible to truly convey an accurate picture of a housing market. It seems like it should be a simple job: just state the average sales price in a region, and let the reader extrapolate from there. You're either prepared to pay an average price for an average home, a more than average price for an above-average home, or a less than average price for a less-than-average home— whatever the pocketbook can stand. What's the problem?

Part of the problem is defining the term *average house* and the term *average sales price*. Suppose we agree that an *average house* is a 1,600-square-foot, three-bedroom, two-bath home in a comfortable neighborhood. That's the easy part. What's difficult is determining the *average sales price* of that average house. You see, statistics can indicate how many homes were sold in a given community, and how much money changed hands. Now if my junior high school math serves me correctly, we find the average sales price by dividing the total sales prices by the number of homes sold, thus we have the average sales price. But how many of those houses sold fit our definition of an average house?

Let's suppose we're looking at a community with a sudden boom in upscale housing. (That happens frequently in today's affluent retiree market.) Let's say a new, security-gated, country-club development (the only one in the area) is selling luxury homes at $500,000 each. At the same time, average homes in average neighborhoods aren't selling so well. Let's suppose 20 average houses sell for about $80,000 each, while ten $500,000 new homes are completed and sold. That brings the regional average sales price to about $175,000, yet we know full well that an average home costs less than half that amount in ordinary neighborhoods. At first glance, it would seem this community would be out of the question for many retirees who would love to relocate here, but couldn't afford a home costing over $80,000, when in fact a truly average house would cost about $80,000.

A further problem arises when a researcher interviews real estate agents about values of local property. Some brokers will quote the regional average sales price as the price of an average home. Other agents, realizing that the regional average sales price can be misleading, will estimate the cost of a truly average home. And others, anxious to entice buyers to the community, may exaggerate by quoting the lowest sales prices as if they were average prices.

In this book, I've tried to steer a center course between the tilts, but I'll be the first to admit that prices quoted here are quite subjective. Furthermore, there's always the chance that inflation could make these quotes obsolete long before this book is ready for its second edition. The long and short of the story is that you must do your own, on-the-spot research of real estate costs and availability.

Rental Homes, Apartments and Condominiums: In most smaller southern cities, condominiums and apartments are scarce. In fact, rentals of any kind are often hard to come by. That's because most housing is typically single-family, owner-occupied. The condo and apartment lifestyle seems out of place in smaller towns and cities in the South. There are a couple of reasons for this.

First of all, condos and apartments are a big-city solution to maximize living space, to squeeze as many people into an area as close to their jobs as possible and to minimize per-unit costs on expensive city property. But in small, laid-back southern cities, you can live on a farm outside the city and be at work in ten minutes. Another reason for condos is maintenance-free living for busy working people: someone else paints your house and there's no grass to mow. But when folks move to the country, they don't want to live cheek-by-jowl with neighbors. They *want* some lawn, shrubbery and landscaping. If retirees really don't want to mow the grass, they can afford small-town wages for someone to do it for them, or they can move to one of the many developments where landscaping is part of the membership fees.

But the major reason nice housing isn't readily available for rent is a more practical one. Owning rental property in a small town is not a profitable investment because high rents generally can't be charged. People in small towns who rent are generally lower-income people, who can't afford to buy and who are limited in what they can pay in rent. Apartments and rental homes can't return fair profits because in order to keep the units occupied, rents must be competitive (that means low!).

An exception to this condition can be found in college towns or near large military bases, where there is a substantial floating population that can afford to pay higher rents. So investors *can* make a profit by building apartment buildings, and regular homeowners, should they find it necessary to rent out their homes, can always find renters who can pay enough to cover the house payments.

Continuing Education: I just can't pass up the opportunity to climb on the soapbox and push an idea I'm enthusiastic about—something that grows more popular as time goes by: continuing education for seniors. Throughout the country, community colleges, adult education centers and universities are adding classes and programs expressly tailored to older adults' needs. More than two-thirds of U.S. colleges and universities offer reduced rates or even free tuition to older citizens. You'll no longer feel like the proverbial sore thumb in a setting where you have company your own age.

But continuing education for retirees is more than a pleasant learning experience; the classroom is a tool for retirement adjustment. Signing up for a class in Chinese cooking, fly-tying or rock polishing puts you in social contact with others from the community. An adult classroom is a great place to make friends with lively, stimulating people who share your interests, folks whose horizons are broader than Monday Night Football or tomorrow's Family Feud show. Taking classes is a quick, surefire way to readjust your lifestyle and become part of your new community.

Most schools have loads of fun classes, and many schools will allow you to audit the more serious courses—that is, take the class but not have to worry about quizzes, tests, finals or term papers. You get the benefit and fun out of a course without the tension of having to make the grade or participate in class discussions.

If you have a trade or special skill of some sort, an even faster way of getting known is to offer to teach a class. Community colleges and adult education programs are often strapped for cash to hire full-time teachers, and therefore welcome the opportunity to add classes with part-time or volunteer teachers. If your skills are needed, schools often don't require a teaching degree, just experience and the ability to communicate it to others.

Once, when my wife and I moved to a small city, I taught a couple of community college classes in freelance writing. Not for the money—which was almost nothing—but for the opportunity to meet townspeople with a common interest in writing. The class was a resounding success, for we made half a dozen friends and received an invitation to join a local writers' group. Our entrance into the town's social life was immediate and satisfying.

But, even if you have no intention of taking classes, a community college or university can be important to your lifestyle. Most schools provide the community-at-large with a wide selection of social and cultural activities, benefits which wouldn't exist without the school's presence. You don't have to be a registered student to attend advertised lectures and speeches (often free) given by famous scientists, politicians, visiting artists and other well-known personalities. Concerts, ranging from Beethoven to boogie-woogie, are presented by guest artists as well as universities' music departments. Stage plays, Broadway musicals and Shakespeare are produced by the drama departments, with season tickets often less than a single performance at a New York theater. Art exhibits, panel discussions and a well-stocked library are often available to the public. (You can't check out library books or magazines, but you're usually free to browse the stacks.) Some schools even make special provisions to allow seniors to use their recreational facilities.

What to Look for in Retirement

In interviewing and surveying retirees over the last 15 years, we've compiled the following list of requirements that most retirees consider essential in choosing a new hometown. Your needs may be different; feel free to add or subtract from the list, and then use the list to measure communities against your standards.

1: Safety. Can you walk through your neighborhood without fearful glances over your shoulder? Can you leave home for a few weeks' vacation without dreading a break-in? The majority of retirees feel that safety is the most important condition of all in selecting a new home. *Most southern communities boast of exceptionally low crime levels and high safety.*

2: Climate. Will temperatures and weather patterns match your lifestyle? Will you be tempted to go outdoors and exercise year round, or will harsh winters confine you to an easy chair in front of the television set? *Southern states enjoy mild winters and long springs and falls, and despite hot and muggy summers, year-round outdoor activities are possible.*

3: Housing. Is quality housing available at prices you're willing and able to pay? Is the area visually pleasing and free of pollution and traffic snarls? Will you feel proud to live in the neighborhood? *Most people relocating in the South upgrade their homes in size and quality,* *and they live in more upscale neighborhoods for less money than back home.*

4: Nourishment for Your Interests. Does your relocation choice offer opportunities and facilities for your favorite pastimes, cultural events and hobbies, be they hunting, fishing, adult education, art centers, or whatever? *Most southern communities have a full range of activities.*

5: Social Compatibility. Will you find common interests with your neighbors? Will you fit in and make friends easily? Will there be folks from your own cultural and social background and political orientation? Is there a "retirement welcoming committee" in place? What about continuing education programs at the local college? *Many southern towns have "retirement welcoming committees" to welcome you and make you feel part of your new community.*

6: Affordability. Are goods and services reasonable? Can you afford to hire help from time to time when you need to? Will your income be high enough to be significantly affected by state income taxes? Will taxes on your pension make a big difference? *Most southern states have significantly below-average costs-of-living, lower property taxes and many exempt pension income from taxes.*

7: Medical Care. Are local physicians accepting new patients? Does the area have a good hospital? Do you have a medical problem that requires a specialist? *Most southern communities have adequate medical care, but if you have special needs, be sure to check.*

8: Distance from Family and Friends. Are you going to be too far away, or in a location where nobody *wants* to visit? Or would you rather they *wouldn't* visit? (In that case, you'd do better even farther away.) Will your new location have attractions that will make grandchildren eager to come and see you? *Many people from the Midwest, North and Northeast are accustomed to traveling south for vacations, so it will be no problem for them to detour and visit your new location.*

9: Transportation. Does your new location have public transportation? Many small towns have none, which makes you totally dependent on an automobile or taxis. What about intercity bus connections? (When Greyhound took over Trailways bus system, many smaller towns were eliminated from service.) How far is the nearest airport with airline connections? Can friends and family visit without driving? *Some smaller southern towns have no city bus service, and occasionally no interstate bus or train service.*

10: Work—Volunteer or Paid. If you're an active person who wants to be involved in meaningful projects, will your new hometown have volunteer activities to keep you busy? If you want to work at your trade or profession on a part-time basis, will there be work opportunities in local business or industry? *Southern states actively encourage industries to relocate to the South, creating a demand for full or part-time positions for certain types of skills. Volunteerism and community service is a southern tradition.*

Scottsboro ●
Mentone ●
Guntersville ●
● Gadsen
Jasper ●   Anniston ●
Birmingham ●
● Pelham
Alexander City ●
Auburn ●

Eufaula ●

Evergreen ●
● Ozark
Enterprise ●   ● Dothan

Alabama

Alabama

When I first considered Alabama as a subject for retirement research, I must admit that my baggage was packed with preconceived notions and misconceptions. I was prepared to be disappointed. Not that Alabama was totally foreign to me. I'd frequently driven across Alabama's short Gulf Coast on the way to or from Florida. Also, when I was in my early twenties, I worked briefly for the Birmingham *Herald* and for an even shorter time for the Mobile *Press Register*. But that was years ago, when the thought of living permanently in Alabama—or anywhere for that matter—seldom occurred to me. Also, the low-rent neighborhoods in which I lived didn't leave me with a favorable impression of those cities.

Therefore, when the State of Alabama invited me to attend a Governor's Conference on Retirement, I attended with low expectations. I was in for a surprise. The conference was sponsored by a state agency called *Alabama Advantage* and was attended by delegates from all sections of Alabama and some from adjoining states. The

Alabama
The Cotton State, Heart of Dixie
Admitted to statehood:
December 14, 1819
State Capital: Montgomery
Population (1995): 4,252,982; rank, 22nd
Population Density: 83.1 per sq. mile: urban 67.4%
Geography: 30th state in size, with 52,237 square miles, including 1,487 square miles of water surface. Highest elevation: Cheaha Mountain, 2,405 feet. Lowest elevation: sea level, Gulf of Mexico. Average elevation: 500 feet.
State Flower: Camellia
State Bird: Yellowhammer
State Tree: Southern pine
State Song: *Alabama*

conference's purpose was to examine ways and means to attract out-of-state retirees from out of state, and how to convince them to relocate in the South. The delegates' sincerity and enthusiasm were contagious.

Before the conference was over, I had invitations to visit a dozen communities. Shelving all other plans, I set off on an odyssey through Alabama, visiting small towns and small cities all over the state. Surprises met me at every turn in the road: beautiful towns, lovely neighborhoods, friendly people. Retirement welcoming committees greeted me and proudly showed me around their hometowns. They each gave me an insider's view of what living there was all about. Significantly, the most enthusiastic boosters were those who themselves had moved in from other states.

After finding so many delightful towns in Alabama, I was surprised at how wrong my mental image had been. I resolved to return with my wife and look at the state of Alabama—and in fact the entire South—with a new way of looking for retirement destinations. That's when the idea for this book was born.

That was my introduction to the concept of "retirement attraction committees." Alabama seems to have pioneered this concept with *Alabama Advantage*. The program's success can be measured by the fact that since its inception, Alabama's share of retirees coming from other states climbed from 20th in the country to fifth.

Varied Landscape: Alabama is anything but the vast, flat farm country I had pictured. Northern Alabama varies from wooded hills to the Appalachian Mountains that extend into eastern parts of the state. Forests are thick here and the higher elevations produce a predictable yearly snowfall—not a lot, just enough to let you know there are four seasons.

The lower half of the state is a coastal plain of rich agricultural lands mantled with hardwood forests when not cultivated. The terrain varies from flat to gently rolling. The south-central part of the state is noted for its fertile, black soil, ideal for cotton production. The low hills are dotted with oak trees draped with Spanish moss and an occasional old plantation home set back from the road. Towns and cities tend to be modern, centered around an historic town center.

The state's southeastern portion is known as Wiregrass Country because of its native grass with wire-like roots. This land is excellent for peanuts and other crops. It's a place of small towns with old homes and shaded streets, as well as modern subdivisions, golf course communities and modern cities. This is a favorite relocation area for military retirees, partly because of the military bases and hospitals in the region.

Throughout the state, a series of dams create long lakes as the rivers are restrained for navigation and water power. With countless inlets, bays and coves, the lakes are bonanzas in recreation and scenic values. Thousands of miles of lakeshore provide home sites where residents dock boats, fish or just enjoy the luxury of a lakeside home. Owning a pontoon boat, a canoe or a fishing boat is as necessary as a second car for many Alabaman families. As if this weren't enough water variety, Alabama boasts its own "Riviera," a beautiful beach on the Gulf of Mexico. True, it isn't a very long stretch of sand, but it does add a finished touch to the state.

Weather: Alabama is a place of four distinct seasons. Spring begins early with white and pink dogwood blooms contrasting their colors with redbuds and rhododendrons, as if on a painter's canvas. Summers are long, languid and lazy. Fall brings another artist's canvas of yellows, oranges, browns and reds. Mild winter weather is all-important to most people considering relocation, and Alabama has what they're looking for. Even the coldest days in January find people on the golf courses or bicycling or strolling the hiking trails. In most regions, snow is a welcome rarity, something to be relished for its brief coloring of winter magic—not something to be cursed and shoveled.

Golfing Paradise: One strategy for increasing Alabama's retiree population meshes with a campaign for making tourism more attractive. The idea is: folks who vacation regularly in the same place tend to think of that place when retirement time rolls around. Since millions of tourists drive through Alabama on their way to their Florida vacations, the challenge is to lure travelers into pausing for a while.

The state's answer is a chain of golf courses known as the Robert Trent Jones Golf Trail. Seven championship golf courses were built, spaced from the foothills of the Appalachians all the way to the Gulf of Mexico. The concept is to provide the kind of championship courses normally found at private country clubs, yet with affordable daily greens fees, which range from $13 to $35. The beautifully designed clubhouses rival those found at expensive private clubs. Each club has something for every level of golfer, usually two par-72 courses and a par-three layout for the occasional golfer. Each stop on the Golf Trail is a unique challenge, and an invitation to stay a little longer in Alabama. Another tourist attraction is a series of fishing tournaments on the state's many great bass lakes. Folks tend to return year after year for the fun.

Safe and Affordable: Besides Alabama's great location and mild winters, crime rates are 20 percent below the national average, and Alabama combines quality living with one of the country's most favorable costs-of-living. Tax burdens are among lowest in the nation, with property taxes on a $100,000 home (way above the median sales price here) about $300—often less, depending on the community. No, that isn't $300 each *quarter*, or *month*; it's $300 for the *year*!

Real estate is affordable, with average new and resale home prices under $70,000. Other economic perks are: most pensions are exempt from taxes, fishing and hunting licenses are free for residents 65 and older, and Alabama's colleges and universities provide free or reduced tuition to residents 60 or over. Some private schools offer tuition discounts, special classes and access to recreation and cultural programs for retirees.

Variety of Communities: Alabama is more than just a low-cost place to live; it offers a wide variety of lifestyle choices and retirement opportunities. Small cities throughout the state tend to be prosperous looking, neat and welcoming. Residents are particularly proud of their old-fashioned downtowns. There's usually a town square, a county courthouse surrounded a large lawn and friendly shops and businesses. The residential neighborhoods are peaceful, with well-cared-for homes.

As more and more "outsiders" take up residence, the population becomes more cosmopolitan. You should have no difficulty finding a community where you "fit in." But what about places where you are the *only* "outsider"?

I interviewed George and Joan Merkel at their home on Highland Lake, Alabama, a delightful area in the hills north of Birmingham. They laughed as they recalled their children's reaction when they learned their parents were moving from Ohio to a remote, rustic area place in Alabama. "They stared at us in disbelief. After a moment of silence, our daughter said, 'You're going into a Witness Protection Program, aren't you?'" But when their children visited them in their new home, they fell in love with their parents' new hometown. Positioned on five acres of wooded, hilly land, their two-story home enjoys an expansive view of the lake and its own boat dock.

George and Joan are just about the only non-southern folks in the area. Curious as to their relationship with the community, I posed a question I always ask of Yankees who move into small southern communities: "How were you received by your neighbors?" By way of reply, George pointed out that he and Joan had received more invitations to join churches, social groups and clubs than they could possibly accept, and someone even suggested that he run for County Supervisor. He added, "We've made more friends here in two years than in 15 years living in Ohio."

Alabama Advantage for Retirees. We feel that the towns and cities that participate in Alabama's retirement attraction program deserve special mention as retirement destinations. Any community willing to put time and money into making you feel welcome is likely to be a pleasant place to live. By the way, the state publishes a free guide to retirement, with complete descriptions of the *Alabama Advantage* communities. (Write: Retiree Program, Alabama Department of Economic and Community Affairs, Montgomery, AL 36177-9985, or call (205) 284-8788.) Also, each Alabama community mentioned in this book has a welcoming committee to help newcomers assimilate into the social whirl of the town. While this won't ensure that you'll find successful retirement in Alabama, you know you'll be welcome and will not be a stranger.

Anniston

From the moment of its inception, Anniston was a planned, model city. Back in 1879 two entrepreneurs decided this is where they would build their textile mills and blast furnaces. They needed a town and commercial center to go with their enterprises, so they hired a team of well-known architects to design a company town. They insisted that the new town must be modern as well as pleasing to the eye. Of course, "modern" in those days meant "Victorian"—and that's what we see today. Most of these historic structures are still in use, well preserved and reflecting Anniston's rich heritage.

Anniston, with a population of 27,000, is the population center of Calhoun County. Immediately adjacent, the city of Oxford has another 10,000 residents. The two cities form the major shopping center for the surrounding area, which has a total population of 120,000. Thirteen miles away, not quite close enough to be considered an Anniston suburb, the town of Jacksonville provides a university setting. Including students, Jacksonville has a population of 11,000. Because Anniston is centrally located between Atlanta and Birmingham, the local slogan is: "Near Atlanta. Near Birmingham. Near Perfect."

We particularly liked Oxford as a retirement possibility. Originally it was called "Lick Skillet," but when time came to incorporate into a town, residents wanted a more dignified name. Can you get more dignified than "Oxford"? Essentially part of Anniston, Oxford has several unusually attractive neighborhoods which appear to be ideal for retirement living. Oxford's pride is its lake, which is circled by hiking trails, several tennis courts, a par-three golf course and a driving range. Nearby, a century-old cotton mill has been converted into an antique mall with more than 100 stores.

Sometimes a community's cultural values can be gauged by the way it invests tax dollars and what its citizens consider important. By spending millions of dollars to create the Anniston Museum of Natural History, the city of Anniston clearly stated its values; you get the picture of a community devoted to quality living. Uniquely designed, in the lovely Lagarde Park, the museum will captivate you with its amazing exhibits. This is worth a visit even if you aren't thinking about relocating in or around Anniston. At the museum you can go on an African safari, step back in time to the days of dinosaurs and witness a Pteranodon flying overhead, or explore underground worlds in a replica of an Alabama limestone cave, and more.

Adjacent to the museum is Fort McClellan, an army base occupying 15,000 acres of prime real estate, at least, until congressional cutbacks shut down the U.S. Army's basic training facility. At the moment, the federal government, the State of Alabama and the officials of the surrounding cities are trying to decide what to do with the valuable land. One purpose that seems fairly certain is to devote a percentage of the surplus property to retirement housing. A California-based, nonprofit company has proposed to convert some of the army post housing into upscale senior housing. With the post's golf course and recreational facilities, this might become a great possibility for retirement.

Anniston and nearby Gadsden both have enthusiastic retirement welcoming committees ready to assist newcomers. This helps immeasurably to get settled in your new hometown. The retirees we talked to were delighted about their decision to relocate in this part of Alabama. For example, Bert Smith—originally from San Francisco—said, "Most folks think when they retire, they have to go to either southern California or Florida. We tried both. We even lived in Costa Rica for a while, but we finally settled here in Anniston."

Recreation and Culture: Calhoun County boasts six golf courses, including one of the famous Robert Trent Jones layouts at Silver Lakes. The course features three championship nines plus a nine-hole short course. The layout was named by *Golf Digest's Places to Play* as one of the nation's Great Value Courses in the public category. In addition, Anniston has a municipal course with nine holes and a driving range.

Nearby Neely Henry Lake is a place where bass as large as 13 pounds have been landed. Other recreational activities in the region include waterskiing, boating, camping and swimming.

Jacksonville State University, Alabama's fourth largest university, advertises itself as "the friendliest campus in the South," and consistently comes up with quality entertainment ranging from theater to music to visual arts. The school's drama department presents a full season of entertainment, including a summer dinner-theater comedy. The university has continuing education programs and hosts Elderhostel programs for folks from all over the country.

Real Estate: The average sales price of three-bedroom homes in the Anniston area is about $65,000. Garden homes and town houses around the lake in Oxford cost between $70,000 and $80,000. Several exclusive areas, such as Golden Springs and Edgefield Farms, have beautiful homes that start at $250,000 and go as high as $450,000. Brentwood Terrace homes start at $100,000.

Medical Care: Calhoun County medical resources include more than 100 physicians, 45 dentists and three hospitals. Northeast Alabama Regional Medical Center has a 372-bed capacity and a staff of more than 900. Stringfellow Memorial Hospital is the next largest hospital with 125 beds and over 250 staff. Jacksonville Hospital, 13 miles away from Anniston, is an 89-bed general acute-care facility with modern diagnostic and surgical services.

When Grandkids Visit: There are so many grandkid-appropriate places here that it's difficult to make a decision. Of course you'll have to take them to the Museum of Natural History; that's a must. Another place, almost next door, is the Berman Museum—a mind-boggling collection of military treasures and artifacts. These were donated by Colonel Farley L. Berman after collecting rare weapons, sculptures and objets d'art for over 70 years. You'll see exquisite pieces, such as a Royal Persian Court Scimitar, Adolph Hitler's personal tea service and over 1,000 extraordinary bronze figures by such masters as Remington and Rodin.

Addresses and Connections

Chamber of Commerce: 1330 Quintard Avenue, Anniston, AL 36202. (205) 237-3536, (800) 489-1087.
Internet: (Anniston) http://www.buyersusa.com/nqc/cities/al/0060.htm (Silver Lakes) http://golf.jsu.edu/silver.html
Newspapers: *Anniston Star,* Box 189, Anniston, AL, 36202. (205) 236-1551.
Jacksonville News, 203 Pelham Rd., Jacksonville, AL 36265-2541. (205) 435-5021.
Airport: Gadsden Municipal Airport (30 miles) with shuttle service to air terminals in Birmingham (60 miles) or Atlanta (90 miles).
Bus/Train: Greyhound, Amtrak.

Anniston/Silver Lakes/Gadsden

	Jan:	April	July	Oct:	Rain	Snow
Daily Highs	62	75	91	74	48 in.	2 in.
Daily Lows	33	51	70	51		

Gadsden

Gadsden (pop. 47,000) is located in the southern foothills of the Appalachian Mountains, where Lookout Mountain and the Coosa River meet. This is probably Alabama's most successful city when it comes to recruiting out-of-state retirees. A few years ago, Gadsden realized that it was losing its industrial base and needed something to replace the disappearing factories, but didn't want to "chase smokestacks." Joining with several other cities in Etowah and Calhoun counties, Gadsden's retirement committee set a goal of attracting 50 retired couples a year. By 1994 they exceeded their goal; 63 couples moved to town that year. The next year 48 couples joined the party. In mid-1997, Gadsden's goal was already 14 couples ahead of schedule.

The impact of new residents on Gadsden's economy has been dramatic. It's a textbook example of how communities benefit from the influx of out-of-state retirees. Because of the newcomers, jobs were created for health care specialists, construction workers and retail businesses. Restaurants, motels and business services blossomed. These new jobs were of a clean, non-polluting, "smokeless-industry" nature and helped the area to free itself of dependency on a handful of manufacturing facilities. Since the program began in 1991, more than 4,000 people have moved to Gadsden—with the strongest growth from 1994–1997.

You definitely get the feeling that Gadsden is on the move. An important facet of its retirement program was a strong effort to make Gadsden a place where folks want to relocate. How did they decide what kind of changes to make? One of the community leaders told us, "We listen to the community and ask the residents what they *want*, instead of telling them what we are going to do."

As a result, the downtown is undergoing dynamic refurbishing and facelifting. Sidewalks on the main street have been widened, buildings remodeled, and trees planted. Every effort is being made to make the downtown seem like a park. As an example of Gadsden's forward thinking, a new public transportation system is scheduled to go into operation. Buses will run six days a week with route deviations during peak activity periods to larger employers, hospitals, the community college and special events. The service will offer a Birmingham Airport shuttle on a demand basis at an affordable fare.

All of this hard work has paid off. Gadsden was recently honored by a major national magazine as an "All-America City"—one of the nation's 50 best places in which to live. One factor in this award is Gadsden's low crime rates. Like most southern communities, crime rates are low, but here it has dropped to 20 percent below the national average.

The downtown's pride and joy is the huge 44,000-square-foot Gadsden Center for Cultural Arts. When a downtown department store closed its doors—a victim of strip mall syndrome—Gadsden decided to do something with the large multi-story building. Rather than allowing the edifice to disintegrate, they converted it into one of the most impressive monuments to rehabilitation we've seen. In its own way, the Center for Cultural Arts is as impressive as Anniston's Museum of Natural History. Besides housing a unique, hands-on museum and fantastic arts center, the facility has an exhibition hall, recital halls and a convention center. There's space for community meetings, private parties, concerts, proms and dances. (There are rooms where community organizations meet 300 days of the year.) The center has an experimental arts programs in which kids from a nearby housing project get paid to study art.

Rainbow City, Attalla and Southside: Two popular residential areas on Gadsden's outskirts are the towns of Attalla and Rainbow City. Attalla has a population of about 7,000 and a thriving commercial center. Much affordable housing is available here—Attalla was the bedroom community for employees of Gadsden's heavy industries before they closed some years ago. For a while, Attalla's downtown section all but died. Then city officials encouraged the establishment of antique shops and specialty boutiques, which seem to have turned the corner economically for Attalla, because folks come from miles around to shop, and storefronts are beginning to find tenants once again.

Rainbow City is slightly larger, with 8,000 inhabitants, and the residential areas are a bit more upscale. When Gadsden's industrial life was booming, this is where the white-collar and executive employees lived. Some exceptionally lovely homes are located here. Rainbow City and Attalla are both within minutes of downtown Gadsden.

Just below Rainbow City, the city of Southside has a population of about 6,000. Southside was so named because it sits on the south bank of the Coosa River and has many miles of river and lakeshore dotted with fine homes. The Southside area has the highest income per family in the county, yet housing isn't overpriced.

Silver Lakes: Silver Lakes is a gorgeous golf course development of rolling terrain and lakes near the edge of Talladega National Forest. Midway between Gadsden and Anniston, Silver Lakes serves as the official retirement information center for both towns. Silver Lakes is an experiment in retirement attraction, because this is the first time one of the Robert Trent Jones Golf Trail courses has ever been placed within a private development. This is a 36-hole, world-class golf complex and it's always open for public play.

Homes around the golf course are all new, well landscaped and as luxurious as you would expect from a golf course complex. Strict architectural guidelines ensure a high level of quality. Since the fairways belong to the state of Alabama, residents have no financial involvement in maintaining the facility. Yet, they have full access to the same low-cost greens fees charged the public.

Recreation and Culture: All the Gadsden area communities are within a short drive to mountains, rivers and lakes. Many homeowners can walk to lake or river; often their homes sit on the water. The Coosa River and its tributaries are famous for fishing, boating and other water sports. Two public golf courses in Gadsden as well as the public course at Silver Lakes are augmented by three country club courses. There are about 35 tennis courts in the area. Both Gadsden and Rainbow City have lighted walking/jogging tracks, and Gadsden features a walking trail through its wildlife preserve.

Gadsden State Community College, Alabama's largest two-year college, and the University of Alabama's Gadsden Center provide educational opportunities. If that's not enough, Jacksonville State University is about 18 miles away.

The Coosa River (more of a lake at this point) runs through Gadsden and its bank has been converted into a beautiful park. Every year residents hold a celebration called Riverfest, a three-day festival with top quality musical talent. Nationally acclaimed performers perform before crowds of 40,000 people in the park for the celebration.

Real Estate: Housing for relocation includes historic homes, urban condominiums and apartments, quiet subdivisions, country club living, river and lake homes, mountain cabins, rural houses with acreage and small farms. We found what we considered exceptional bargains in quality housing. The average price for a 2,000-square-foot home with three bedrooms, two baths, a family room and a two-car garage was around $70,000. A larger Victorian home might cost between $125,000 and $150,000.

Homes at Silver Lake are all recently constructed; garden homes (two-bedrooms) start around $80,000. Several models of homes range upwards with some deluxe places costing in the $300,000 range.

Medical Care: Gadsden is the regional center for specialized medical care of an 11-county area. The two major facilities are: Gadsden Regional Medical Center, with 346 beds, and Riverview Regional Medical Center, with 281 beds. Both offer 24-hour, physician-staffed emergency centers. There's also a Veterans' Administration outpatient center. There's a total of 645 hospital beds, 125 physicians and 58 dentists in the county. Also, an hour's drive by interstate takes you to the University of Alabama's Medical Center in Birmingham, recognized as one of the better hospitals in the nation.

When Grandkids Visit: They'll enjoy a cruise on the *Alabama Princess*, an authentic replica of the sternwheeler excursion boats that plied America's rivers in the last century. It has an enclosed main deck and serves snacks. The boat has an interesting history in that it once sailed on a lake in Texas; the owner dismantled it and brought the steamboat cross-country by truck to float in the Coosa River. Another must-see is spectacular Noccalula Falls, cascading over 90 feet into a natural rock gorge below.

Addresses and Connections

Chamber of Commerce: Retirement Development Office, P.O. Box 185, Gadsden, AL, 35902. (800) 238 6924.

Newspaper: *The Gadsden Times,* P. O. Box 188, Gadsden, AL, 35902. (205) 549-2000.

Airport: Gadsden Municipal Airport with connecting flights to Atlanta and Birmingham.

Bus/Train: Greyhound; Dial-A-Ride city transportation; Rural Area Transportation with scheduled routes and individualized pickups; Amtrak in Anniston (30 miles).

Lake Guntersville Area

North of Gadsden some 35 miles, a long network of lakes was created when the Tennessee Valley Authority constructed a series of 13 dams for power and navigation. The big dividend is a vast recreational water wonderland. Guntersville Lake is one of the largest, and is world-famous for trophy bass fishing, pleasure boating, waterskiing and sailing. Its 949 miles of winding shoreline is lush with forests, cabins, modern subdivisions, occasional scenic lakeside lots and breathtaking homes perched on river bluffs.

The city of Guntersville—almost entirely surrounded by lake water—takes full advantage of its 69,000-acre namesake. It is located in the rolling foothills of the Appalachian Mountains on the southernmost point of the Tennessee River.

With a population of less than 8,000, Guntersville is a mid-sized southern town with all of the advantages of a larger city. It enjoys a combination of beautiful natural settings, quality housing, an excellent medical complex, a prosperous business community and friendly people. One of the advantages of living in a small Alabama city like Guntersville is personal safety; it has one of the lowest crime rates in the country. The cost-of-living is similarly low. Also, Guntersville residents who qualify may have all or a significant portion of their property tax waived on request.

Like all Alabama towns mentioned in this book, Guntersville has an active relocation committee. The chamber of commerce and the committee sponsor get-togethers, such as barbeque dinners with square dancing, where newcomers and longtime residents meet and make new friends. People from all states and provinces enjoy relocation here, and military personnel love it because they have access to the commissary and exchange facilities of nearby military installations, including Huntsville's Redstone Arsenal.

Recreation and Culture: Touted as one of the finest sport-fishing lakes in America by the Bass Anglers Sportsmen's Society, Lake Guntersville often hosts the famous Bassmaster's Tournaments. Local boosters claim that once you've experienced the boating pleasure of Lake Guntersville, everything else will leave you high and dry. You'll find eight public launch areas and eight full-service marinas.

Lake Guntersville State Park, located on 5,600 acres, has an 18-hole championship golf course, a 322-site campground, a deluxe lodge and a convention center. Your camera may come in handy when on the lookout for American bald eagles that spend winters in the park. The park also boasts a nature center with a trained park naturalist and 31 miles of marked hiking trails.

The Guntersville Recreation Department offers an Olympic pool, lighted tennis courts, baseball-softball fields, a gym, meeting rooms, parks, playgrounds, lighted walking trails and a lighted bicycle trail.

Every April, Guntersville is home of the Art-on-the-Lake Festival, the nation's oldest event of its type. Local artists display their creations for exhibit and sale and there's a huge display of arts and crafts fostered by the Mountain Valley Arts Council. The city also brings nationally known plays to life through the Whole Backstage Theater and serves up over two tons of fresh delicacies from the Gulf of Mexico during the St. Williams Seafood Festival in August. Each winter the waters of Lake Guntersville sparkle and glitter to a multitude of colored lights during the annual "Parade of Lights" Boat Parade.

Real Estate: Whatever size or style home you desire, you'll find it in or around Guntersville. A custom-designed house, a Victorian home in a historic district or a sprawling farmhouse sitting on several acres—they're all available at below nationwide average prices. High quality homes average just over $80,000, with economical housing sometimes selling in the $50,000 range. Of course, the big attraction here is lakefront properties, with views and docks. The view properties have a wide price spread, with asking prices over $100,000. Lakefront property is rare, since the Tennessee Valley Authority controls most of the lakeshore.

Medical Care: The Guntersville-Arab Medical Center is a 92-bed hospital with a 24-hour emergency room. It's a primary care hospital with full medical and surgical services, staffed by 21 doctors offering a wide range of specialties.

The local health center is operated by the Marshall County Health Department. It provides such services as the Home Health Program, a prenatal care clinic, a TB X-ray clinic, Medicaid screening and cancer detection, along with immunization administration.

When Grandkids Visit: Your grandchildren will love to fish along the shoreline and catch a glimpse of the majestic American bald eagle at Lake Guntersville State Park Lodge. (Should the bald eagles fail to show up, just explain to the kiddies that when bald eagles wear toupees they look just like ducks. And they'll see plenty of ducks.) You don't have a boat? No problem. You can rent fishing boats, ski boats, pontoon boats, houseboats and sailboats by the hour, day or week.

Addresses and Connections

Chamber of Commerce: 200 Gunter Avenue, P.O. Box 577, Guntersville, AL 35976. (205) 582-3612, (800) 869-LAKE.

Internet: http://www.lakeguntersville.org
Newspaper: *Advertiser Gleam,* P.O. Box 190, Guntersville, AL 35976.
  (205) 582-3232.
Airport: Birmingham International Airport (90 minutes), Huntsville/Madison County Jetplex (45 minutes).
Bus/Train: The city has an on-demand public transportation system, with rides as low as $1 per trip.

Scottsboro

The wooded foothills of the Appalachian Mountains and the swelling Tennessee River provide a majestic backdrop for Scottsboro, another picture-book retirement town. Scottsboro's downtown offers both charm and convenience, centered around an old-fashioned town square and antique courthouse. Downtown is the hub of governmental, civic, business and professional activity. Stately older homes and churches with manicured lawns and shrubbery sit on beautiful tree-lined streets in the downtown area. In the spring dogwoods, azaleas and rhododendrons create a magical patchwork of color when their blossoms explode, tulips burst from the ground and flowering shrubbery flash color from every yard. (I first visited Scottsboro in the early days of spring, so I could have been overly impressed.)

Even though its population is only about 15,000, Scottsboro has ample shopping and facilities. In addition, it's convenient to several nearby larger cities for heavy shopping. Huntsville is a 45-minute drive, Chattanooga takes an hour and it's a three-hour drive to either Atlanta or Nashville.

An influx of people in the 1970s, a fairly common occurrence in the South, makes retirement in Scottsboro a comfortable possibility for those from out of state. It started when an industrial boom in the early '70s nearly doubled the size of Scottsboro. Along with their manufacturing equipment, the companies transplanted hundreds of employees to Alabama. People from the industrial North—and indeed the world—relocated here and provided the city with a healthy mixture of lifestyles and a diversity of ideas. These people—at first skeptical about moving to the South—now proudly call Scottsboro their hometown. When retirement time comes, most of these transplants choose to retire in "The Friendly City."

This increase in population not only created a cordial mixture of northern and southern neighbors, but it created a need for new housing. Throughout the town's wooded hills, new ranch-style homes of attractive brick were placed next to older, more traditional homes. This produced numerous pleasant neighborhoods with distinct personalities, places where neighbors are friends and where personal safety is exceptionally high.

An example of Scottsboro's progressive thinking is an ultra-modern community recreation center (known as the Rec-Com building), which serves a wide spectrum of citizens, from pre-school to elderly. Scottsboro voters didn't hesitate to allocate money for this impressive recreational and cultural complex during a time when voters around the country were refusing to pass school bonds or to fund libraries. The Olympic-size pool doubles as a training center for students as well as for senior citizen water aerobics. Rec-Com has a gymnasium, an indoor walking track, racquetball courts, handball courts and a game room, plus meeting rooms and hobby shops.

Another example of an event that reinforces Scottsboro's small-city feeling is a monthly happening called "First Monday Trade Day." Every first Sunday and Monday of non-winter months, the Old Courthouse lawn is transformed into a combination flea market/crafts fair extravaganza. Residents sell locally-grown produce, homemade jellies, antiques—anything that can be traded or sold. (Except livestock!) This tradition dates back 130 years, when circuit court was held only once a month at the courthouse.

Another unusual commercial enterprise is Scottsboro's "Unclaimed Baggage Center." This is where the major airlines' unclaimed luggage ends up. Between 75,000 and 100,000 pieces of luggage arrive here every year—to be sold to bargain hunters. So, if you want to find out what happened to your favorite silk blouse or to that Hawaiian shirt your husband liked so much, come here with credit card in hand; you might be able to buy it back.

The Shoals Area: To the west of Guntersville and Scottsboro, the Tennessee River runs along Alabama's northern edge forming Lake Wilson, which connects downstream with Guntersville Lake. A popular relocation area here, known as "the Shoals," consists of four cities: Florence, Tuscumbia, Sheffield and Mussel Shoals, all situated on or near Wilson Lake. Local fishermen claim to enjoy the best fishing in

Alabama on this part of the Tennessee River lake system. (However, every place I·visited in the state makes the same claim. I'd like to believe they are all correct.)

Florence is the largest of these towns, and is appreciated through-out the region for its four major hospitals that specialize in high-tech care services, some specifically designed for mature adults. A branch of the University of Alabama and a community college offer continuing education classes for a lifetime of learning.

Recreation and Culture: Outdoor enthusiasts immediately fall in love with Scottsboro. Strategically situated on the upper reaches of Guntersville Lake, where it narrows to an extra-wide river, residents find numerous opportunities for fishing, boating and other water sports. Hunting is great, with ducks, geese, dove, quail, turkey and deer in abundance. The limit on deer is "a buck a day," which is not only generous, but reflects on the large deer population in the region.

Golfers love the picturesque setting of the municipally-owned Goose Pond Colony Golf Course. Situated on the Tennessee River with mountains in the background, its 18-hole championship layout is consistently ranked among the Southeast's best public golf courses. Goose Pond, the largest and most complete of the area's 21 parks and recreational areas, offers camping facilities, a lakeside restaurant, a marina, cottages, meeting rooms and a paved hiking trail that meanders throughout the park at water's edge. The city also maintains eight tennis courts for daily public use at Veterans' Field Recreational Complex.

Plantain Pointe is the area's newest golf course, an 18-hole residential development that is semi-private. Despite being open only three years, the course has quickly become one of the more popular courses. The area's private club, Scottsboro Golf and Country Club, has a nine-hole course with swimming and tennis on the grounds as well.

Bass fishing is contagious here. You haven't lived until you see a bass tournament on the Guntersville Lake, with boats zooming away from the starting line to stake out claims on personal, secret hot-spots where prize-winning lunkers hide out. Contestants are said to reel in some of the biggest bass in the world. A great variety of other fish, such as white and black crappie, bluegill, catfish and white and yellow bass are also in the lake, waiting with bated breath for your baited hook.

Wonderful musicals and dramas regularly appear on the stage of Northeast Alabama State Community College. The theater welcomes volunteers to add to the fun with their outstanding productions. Scottsboro also has a community center, which hosts plays, planned senior activities and other events. The senior center, operated by the Council on Aging, is located by the lake's shore in Jackson Park. The center offers exercise and dance classes as well as classes in arts and crafts.

Real Estate: Scottsboro real estate makes the most of its blend of forested hills and lakeside woodlands. Residential areas show taste and charm in this setting, which enhances the quality of home ownership here. And the price is right too. Housing in the area can be as low as 22 percent below the national average. Some housing designed and reserved specifically for those over 55 are under construction. And of course Alabama property taxes are among the lowest in the nation, which helps make Scottsboro an outstanding retirement value.

Although some homes sell for well below $50,000, a nice home in an attractive neighborhood will run about $70,000, while executive homes on stately plots of landscaped ground can cost $300,000. Scottsboro also has condos, starting around $50,000 to the mid-$80,000s, complete with tennis courts and swimming pools.

Medical Care: Newly renovated Jackson County Hospital, recognized for its modern technology, is Scottsboro's pride and joy. With 170 beds and state-of-the-art equipment, the facility is superbly capable of handling the health needs of the region. Its staff of doctors specialize in a number of disciplines and it has an advanced on-site laboratory. The hospital also operates a branch facility about 30 minutes north of Scottsboro, in the town of Bridgeport.

When Grandkids Visit: When you have a lake full of fighting-mad bass, what else can you do but rent a boat and go after the rascals? If the kids don't like fishing, take them to one of the parks to feed the ducks. (Who knows, they might see a bald eagle.) An interesting nearby trip would be to the U.S. Space and Rocket Center in Huntsville. In addition to the world's largest collections of rocket and space exhibits, the Spacedome Theater projects films on a huge dome screen that surrounds the audience.

Addresses and Connections

Chamber of Commerce: 407 E. Willow St., Scottsboro, AL 35768. (205) 259-5500, (800) 259-5508.

(Florence) 104 S. Pine St., Florence, AL 35630. (205) 383-4704.
Internet: (Scottsboro) http://www.websun.com/sjcol
Newspapers: *The Daily Sentinel,* P.O. Box 220, Scottsboro, AL 35768.
  (205) 249-0845.
North Jackson Progress, 701 Veterans Drive, Scottsboro, AL 35768. (205)
  437-2395.
Airport: Huntsville International Airport (38 miles), commuter service.
Bus/Train: Greyhound.

Guntersville/Scottsboro

	Jan:	April	July	Oct:	Rain	Snow
Daily Highs	49	73	89	73	54 in.	3 in.
Daily Lows	31	50	69	49		

Alexander City/Lake Martin

Back in the mid-1920s, the Alabama Power Company decided to place a dam across the Tallapoosa River. Residents at that time were devastated—totally convinced that the rising waters would create swamps and breeding grounds for flotillas of mosquitoes and armies of bugs. Resigned to disaster, they sold out at five dollars to the acre, feeling lucky to get anything at all for such worthless land. Little did they realize! Lakeshore lots now go for a minimum of $25,000, up to more than $500,000! Also, travel writers now describe Lake Martin as one of the most beautiful recreational lakes in the South. It's become one of east-central Alabama's prime retirement destinations, having received numerous recommendations by retirement and relocation experts.

Scattered around the lake are nine or ten developments which range from relatively inexpensive places nestled among the woods to elegant gated communities with private golf courses. Almost 22,000 people make their homes on the 750 miles of shoreline—on sandy beaches, in secluded coves, or on rocky knolls with magnificent views. Officially designated one of Alabama's cleanest lakes, residents proudly refer to Lake Martin as "44,000 acres of pure drinking water." Residents rave about the quality of their new surroundings. Mrs. Sandy Underkofler, from California, said, "Retiring here has lowered my blood pressure, and the quality of our lives has quadrupled. Our reward for staying in California for 30 years was coming to Alabama."

With golf and water recreation as the central focus, newcomers have a wide choice of lifestyles, from exclusive golf course developments, where homes cost a small fortune, to mobile home parks with spaces that rent for $100 a month. However, don't expect super-bargains in real estate; after all, if you live on a lake as pretty as this, you'll pay for the privilege. Strict building codes ensure that the housing is high quality—no shacks or fish shanties are permitted.

Nearby Alexander City is an alternative for those who would like to be near the lake, but prefer more inexpensive housing in town. Alex City (as people here call it) is a charming place in its own right. The town owes its prosperity to the Russell Corporation, a local company that made good as a Fortune 500 textile giant. This hometown enterprise is one of the few manufacturers of athletic wear that decided not to abandon the United States and move to El Salvador or Vietnam in search of cheap labor. The Russell Corporation is not only staying in Alexander City, but is building new factories in the South.

Just 50 miles from the state capital of Montgomery and 30 miles from Auburn University, the Alexander City/Lake Martin area is conveniently located for the occasional big-city shopping and cultural fixes. Birmingham is a 70-mile drive via a superhighway.

An interesting concept in retiree banking is an innovative program started by a local bank, called "Prestige 55." Those over age 50 who open a new account at the bank ($10,000 or more) may join. (It used to be over 55, hence the name, but the lowering average age of retirees prompted a reduction in the age requirements.) Membership confers discounts with local merchants who participate in the plan, but the biggest benefits are seminars and social activities organized by the bank and other businesses. In addition to attending local events, Prestige 55 members go on trips, such as a tour of national parks, trips to Atlanta to watch big league sports and cruises to the Caribbean and Alaska. This 3,000-member program is so successful that other banks are imitating the program. Wherever you decide to relocate, it might be worth your while to join one of these banking programs.

Recreation and Culture: Quite naturally, recreation here centers around golf and water sports. Swimming, fishing, waterskiing and boating are favorites. Many residents keep powered pontoon boats tied at their lakefront homes, ready for fishing, loafing or a trip across the water to dine at a first-class restaurant. Wind Creek State Park, six miles from the center of Alexander City, is a popular place for fishing, camping and hiking. The lake communities support two sailing clubs, a waterskiing club, a Bassmaster's Club, a scuba-diving club and a rock and gem club.

The original championship golf course at Willow Point has 13 of its 18 fairways edging the lakeshore. Two other courses are similarly located on the water. Alexander City also has an 18-hole municipal golf course. Three of the famous Robert Trent Jones Golf Trail courses are nearby, with one less than an hour away, on Auburn's Lake Saughatchee.

The cultural and entertainment offerings of Montgomery and Birmingham are within an easy drive; Alexander City, however, provides its own entertainment. There's a little-theater group that stages several productions a year, and Alexander City Arts Council uses the Central Alabama Community College's facilities to bring plays, musicals and concerts to the community. The college also has special programs, free to students aged 60 and over.

Real Estate: Around the lake, housing choices range from moderately priced (not cheap) to very expensive. Some subdivisions have minimum square-footage requirements that ensure homes will be upscale. Two- and three-bedroom places in one golf complex can be found between $90,000 and $120,000, and in another from $115,000 to $150,000. In yet another development, building lots sell for $250,000 and up, so you can imagine the finished cost of a home. In Alexander City, real estate is comparable to that in similar southern locations, with acceptable homes starting in the high $60,000s.

Medical Care: Russell Hospital, in Alexander City, has a modern, 75-bed nonprofit hospital, with 24-hour acute-care facilities. In the last five years, 27 physicians have joined the hospital staff. The hospital maintains close ties with Birmingham's University of Alabama Hospital. For military retirees there's a regional hospital at Maxwell Air Force Base in Montgomery, about an hour's drive.

When Grandkids Visit: They'll enjoy Horseshoe Bend National Military Park. Just a few miles northeast of Alexander City is the battlefield where Andrew Jackson and the Tennessee militia defeated the Creek Indian nation in 1814. The kids can visit the museum to learn all about it and then picnic afterward under enormous oak trees, some of which probably were growing at the time of the battle.

Addresses and Connections

Chamber of Commerce: P.O. Box 926, Alexander City, AL 35011-0926. (205) 234-3451.
Internet: http://www.russell-lands.com/lakemap.htm
Newspaper: *The Daily Outlook,* 548 Cherokee Road, Alexander City, AL 35011. (205) 234-4281.
Airport: Montgomery's Dannelly Field (43 miles), Birmingham Municipal Airport (75 miles).
Bus/Train: A van service for seniors; Greyhound.

Alexander City/Lake Martin

	Jan:	April	July	Oct:	Rain	Snow
Daily Highs	56	76	91	77	58 in.	1 in.
Daily Lows	36	55	70	54		

Opelika/Auburn

Opelika and Auburn are pleasantly situated in the rolling hills and forests of eastern Alabama at the junction of the Piedmont Plateau and the Coastal Plains. This is a great location for retirement centered around continuing education.

Opelika is a friendly, quiet, yet active community of approximately 25,000 people. As the county seat of Lee County, Opelika has always been a gathering place for residents and visitors, and the recently renovated Courthouse Square is the perfect spot to meet friends and take in the sights of the historic downtown area. Next door is Auburn, with Alabama's largest university, with 22,000 students and 8,000 faculty and staff. These adjoining towns have a combined population of 57,000.

The small-town warmth and charm here are constantly enriched by neighbors from all over the country who are drawn here by Auburn University. In fact, a third of the residents in Auburn and Opelika, a large percentage of them retirees, come from other states. To this add the presence of an *Alabama Advantage* committee to welcome newcomers and you may have a winning combination.

A drive through the shaded streets of Opelika treats you to the sight of old homes being meticulously restored, a sure indication of the respect local residents have for history. Opelika is the quieter, residential side of the twin cities, with a chamber of commerce that recently won a Governor's award for the most active community in the state for recruiting retirees. This is also one of ten cities participating in the Alabama Historical Commission's Main Street Program, in an effort to revitalize downtown Opelika. The city has already received recognition for its accomplishments.

Auburn, just across an invisible boundary line, is the proud host of highly-respected Auburn University. Auburn's sprawling campus has a student population of 22,000. A National Science Foundation report ranks Auburn among the leading research universities in the nation, and *Changing Times* magazine recognizes the school as among the top universities, combining high academic standards with reasonable tuition costs.

In addition to the university, the area has a two-year school, Southern Union Jr. College, with about 1,400 students, and Opelika State Technical School with extended day programs. Because of the area's top-rated medical school and East Alabama Medical Center, health care here is superior. Nearby Fort Benning, Georgia, has a military medical facility for military retirees, as well as a commissary and post exchange.

Recreation and Culture: As you might imagine, football and basketball fevers are epidemic in each season. The only cure is to attend the university football stadium, which seats 80,000 fans, or the basketball arena, which accommodates 12,000.

Opelika is a golfers' paradise and is a stop on Alabama's Robert Trent Jones Golf Trail. This award-winning course, with a total of 54 holes, provides country-club quality golf at public golf course fees. Three other beautiful public courses and a private country-club course are also located in the Opelika/Auburn area, for a total of 126 holes of golf, plus a lighted par-three course.

Over 400 acres in city and county parks provide hiking trails, 20 tennis courts, swimming pools and picnic areas. Of course, the area's mild climate allows outdoor activities the year round. Great fishing is enjoyed at any number of sparkling lakes around the countryside, particularly at 130-acre Lee County Public Lake and 15 miles away on the Chattahoochee River.

Broadway musicals, Bolshoi Ballet, Boston Symphony are a few of the cultural activities presented recently by the Opelika Arts Association in the 1,200-capacity Performing Arata Center. Three other theaters in the immediate area are: Lee County Community Theater, Telfair Peet Theater at Auburn University and East Alabama Repertory Company. The Alabama Shakespeare Festival is in Montgomery, just 55 miles from Opelika and Auburn.

Real Estate: The average cost for a house in the area is approximately $88,000, which is on par with the state average and well below the national average. Prices range from $60,000 to $190,000. Besides the new housing available, Opelika has a beautiful section of older homes and Victorians which sometimes are available for purchase. There are a limited number of condos available, ranging from $55,000 to $65,000.

Medical Care: The East Alabama Medical Center, which is located in Opelika, is the regional medical facility for the eastern Alabama area. It has a 352-bed hospital with state-of-the-art facilities, including a new cardiology wing, cancer treatment center with radiation therapy and chemotherapy and every imaginable medical service. With over 118 physicians on staff and a medical arts complex, residents don't need to travel to get expert medical care. A Veterans' Administration hospital is 25 miles away, in Tuskegee.

When Grandkids Visit: Chewacla State Park, a few miles south of town, is a beautiful place with 696 acres of forest, campsites and hiking trails. There's a 23-acre lake for fishing and swimming, and boats are available to rent. Also, visit the Auburn University's aviary on campus and explain to the grandkids why the team mascot, a bald eagle, is named "Tiger." (Don't ask me, they're not my grandkids!)

Addresses and Connections

Chamber of Commerce: (Opelika) P.O. Box 2366, Opelika, AL 36803-2366. (800) OPELIKA.
(Auburn) 714 E. Glenn Ave., Auburn, AL 36831-1370. (334) 887-7011.
Internet: http://www.opelika.com/retire.htm
Newspaper: *Opelika-Auburn News*, P. O. Drawer 2208, Opelika, AL 36801. (334) 749-6271.
Airport: Columbus, GA airport (30 miles), Montgomery Airport (50 miles), Atlanta Hartsfield International Airport (90 miles).
Bus/Train: Greyhound.

Huntsville

	Jan:	April	July	Oct:	Rain	Snow
Daily Highs	49.4	73.0	89.4	73.4	54.7 in.	3.1 in.
Daily Lows	31.0	50.0	69.1	49.1		

Mentone, on Lookout Mountain

Alabama and western Georgia aren't generally noted for rugged mountains. The Appalachian chain does thrust its way into the northeastern part of Alabama, but by this point the mountains have begun to soften into rounded hills rather than sharp peaks. An exception is in the northeast corner of Alabama: the plateau of Lookout Mountain. Lookout Mountain's dramatic profile seems totally out of place in Alabama; the gently rolling countryside abruptly ends where rocky limestone cliffs jut upward, almost vertically, to end in a high plateau some 800 feet above the valley floor.

On the summit of Lookout Mountain Plateau we found a delightful little village set amidst a wooded wonderland—a town called Mentone. Although retirement possibilities here are just becoming known, seasonal retirement in Mentone has long been a tradition. In the late 1800s, people from Birmingham, Atlanta and from as far away as New Orleans were captivated by Lookout Mountain's tall pines, beautiful springs and cool summer weather. Trains brought city dwellers to the Valley Head station at the base of Lookout Mountain. Carriages then took the seasonal retirees up the winding road to Mentone, where hotels, houses and cottages awaited their stay. Since Lookout Mountain is the nearest true Appalachian environment to cities like Atlanta and Birmingham, it's no surprise that today people from the cities are interested in retirement here.

Mentone is reached via a steep road of switchback turns that climbs laboriously to the summit. The plateau features a pine forest, secluded lakes, log cabins and an occasional small farm. You'll feel as if you've been transported to another world. You can't really appreciate this until you stand on the precipice at Eagle Cliff and gaze down on the landscape far below.

The interesting thing about Lookout Mountain's geological formation is that the plateau is shaped like a shallow saucer. It catches rainfall and holds the water in numerous lakes, which make particularly popular places for retirement homes and weekend cabins. When the lakes fill up, they send water cascading into brooks and creeks to join the Little River's waterfalls and rapids.

At first glance, Lookout Mountain is an unlikely place to consider for retirement. Mentone is rustic, isolated and almost devoid of up-to-date services you might expect to find in ordinary retirement communities. But folks who've retired here say that's the charm. They can step back from the hustle and bustle of civilization, and enjoy a quiet lakeside home in the woods, yet be within a few minutes drive from the real world at the base of Lookout Mountain; the town of Valley Head is only a five-minute drive from the center of Mentone. Chattanooga is an hour away and Atlanta an hour and a quarter. However, Mentone isn't totally without amenities. It has churches, shopping and restaurants. Mentone even has its own newspaper, *The Groundhog*, published every month and eagerly awaited by residents.

Recreation and Culture: Cloudmont Resort on Lookout Mountain boasts Alabama's only ski facilities, and claims to be the most southern-most ski resort in the country. With snow not always dependable, the resort uses state-of-the-art snow-making equipment. There's snow throughout the season as long as nighttime temperatures drop below freezing to allow the machines to work. Saddle Rock Golf Course is also part of the 1,000-acre Cloudmont Resort complex.

Lake fishing is popular, and the lakes here don't need to be stocked. Hunting is ideal in a vast wilderness of lands that technically belong to lumber companies, but the woods are in the process of second-growth and open to all.

The village of Mentone celebrates three yearly events. First, the Rhododendron Festival happens in May, with live music, boat cruises, a beauty pageant and lots of good food. The second event is the Fall Colorfest in October, when Mentone residents celebrate with a costume ball, story telling and the *Groundhog Classic Run.* Finally there's the "Musical Mountain Christmas." Held about two weeks before Christmas, the residents celebrate with choir singing and a Santa Claus party.

Real Estate: Although the big attraction is peaceful isolation, plenty of elbow room and unspoiled wilderness, housing in and around Mentone is not just a collection of cabins. Historic hotels and Victorian homes of turn-of-the-century vintage are joined by contemporary houses, upscale estates designed to blend in with the forest and casual cottages that reflect their weekend or vacation function.

The countryside around Mentone is filled with small farms and acreages, and the village has numerous homes ranging from simple cabins to large two-story homes. Lakeside lots sell from $35,000 for three-acre, wooded plots. Without lake views, three acres sell for $10,000 to $15,000. An impressive lakefront development called "Lake on the Brow" has a collection of very plush homes, tastefully set in wooded acreage, starting in the mid-$150,000 range and going up to $250,000.

Medical Care: Living in backwoods, rustic villages always means a sacrifice of nearby medical care. However, from the village of Mentone, the nearest doctor is only five minutes or so away, at the base of the mountain abutment in the town of Valley Head. The hospital in Fort Payne is 15 miles away, not an uncommon distance in small-town living.

When Grandkids Visit: DeSoto State Park was named after the Spanish explorer who visited the region during his trek through the Southeast. The park contains 5,000 acres of wild and scenic wilderness area along the Little River. The scenery is breathtaking, with cascading waterfalls and hiking trails throughout the park. Little River Canyon, incidentally, is one of the deepest canyons east of the Mississippi River.

Addresses and Connections

Chamber of Commerce: P.O. Box 295, Mentone, AL 35984. (205) 634-4444.

Newspapers: *Fort Payne Times Journal,* Highway 11 N., Fort Payne, AL 35967. (205) 845-2550.

The Groundhog (monthly), P.O. Box 387, Mentone, AL 35984. (205) 634-4541.

Airport: Chattanooga.

Bus/Train: An automobile is essential.

Mentone

	Jan:	April	July	Oct:	Rain	Snow
Daily Highs	48	73	89	72	53 in.	6 in.
Daily Lows	29	47	68	48		

Alabama's Gulf Coast

At first glance at a map, you wouldn't expect Alabama to have any beach at all. Were it not for a narrow appendage of land that squeezes between Louisiana and the Florida Panhandle to reach the Gulf, the state of Alabama would be totally land-bound. The small parcel that does manage to reach salt water is split into a finger and thumb, separated by broad Mobile Bay.

But despite appearances, Alabama does have its "Riviera Coast." Visitors are flabbergasted at the quality and beauty of Alabama's 32 miles of sugary beach and sun-kissed emerald waters that lie between Pensacola and Mobile. In quality, if not quantity, the Alabama Coast matches anything Florida has to offer. Furthermore, it's peaceful and relatively uncrowded. An array of beach homes, year-round activities, fishing, golf and fresh gulf seafood are just some of the options retirees enjoy here.

Mobile, one of the Gulf's major ports, is a beautiful city, with many stately, old homes and streets arched over with live oak trees like green tunnels. We liked the looks of Mobile and were told that it's a great place for retirement. But with almost 200,000 inhabitants, it seems best like a town to visit, to take advantage of entertainment and cultural largess and then return to your nearby hometown.

There are many smaller towns in the Mobile area, with the traditional candidates for retirement being the towns of Fairhope and Daphne. But with success comes change: because the city of Mobile is just 15 miles or so away, these towns have become bedroom communities for those working in the city and for those wishing an upscale suburban atmosphere. As such, property has become more costly and the percentage of retirees has fallen off in recent years. This is why the focus has shifted to Alabama's Gulf Shore.

Gulf Shores/Orange Beach: The two small towns that comprise Alabama's "Riviera," Gulf Shores (pop. 5,000) and Orange Beach (pop. 3,000), are fast becoming choice destinations for relocation, particularly with golf nuts and surf fishermen. Traditionally a roost for thousands of "snow birds" each winter season, these communities entice winter visitors to become permanent residents when they retire. White-sand beaches, great fishing and friendly neighbors are persuasive amenities that entice retirees to stay on Alabama's Gulf Shore. Developers are building luxury retirement villages to accommodate more upscale newcomers. Pensacola, Florida, is just a 30-mile drive, and Mobile is about an hour away—both near enough for heavy duty shopping, but far enough away for you to feel like you're living in a small beach town.

An interesting diversity of retirees gives Gulf Shores and Orange Beach a cosmopolitan flavor not common in smaller resort towns. Because retirees come from all parts of the country, they bring a rich mixture of interests and talents. Also, the ratio of residents to tourists isn't nearly as askew as on some Florida Panhandle beaches to the east. Winter tourists, however, bring a blessing to gulf coast businesses; they create a demand for services. This means seasonal part-time jobs are available for those who want them, as well as nicer restaurants and services that might not be in place without tourist money.

Recreation and Culture: Orange Beach lays claim to the title of "Red Snapper Capital of the World." Nearly a hundred boats with experienced captains—the largest charter boat fleet on the gulf coast—are ready to take to deep blue for a half-day, day or overnight charter. Amberjack, cobia, grouper and mackerel, in addition to the snapper, are just a few of the other treasures of the deep you'll bring home from your expedition.

Great news for golfers: Championship courses by such designers as Jerry Pate, Arnold Palmer and Larry Nelson are making golf on the Gulf a challenging endeavor for players of every skill level. Seven golf courses are within a 20-minute drive or less.

Year-round residents love to participate in art shows, theater, concerts and other cultural pursuits. Mobile is near enough to visit for greyhound racing, theater and museums. Mobile's Mardi Gras, smaller and less known than the New Orleans fantasia, is said to be the oldest pre-Lenten celebration in the United States. Keep your calendar open for this carnival of carnivals.

Real Estate: Since one of the attractions here is golf, there's an emphasis on golfing communities. As one resident put it, "We're becoming a mini-Myrtle Beach—minus the traffic, noise and flash." One development, an upscale place called Craft Farm, offers patio-garden homes and condos from $115,000 to $150,000. According to the *Alabama Advantage Retiree Guide*, near the beach, a two-bedroom home can range in price from $45,000 to $75,000.

Medical Care: Even though the population is small, health care is adequate. Because of the number of elderly tourists each season, this area has an unusual number of paramedics, perhaps the highest per capita in the nation. A hospital is located in nearby Foley, just five miles from Gulf Shores. Foley, by the way, is a popular place because of its manufacturers' outlet stores, of the "shop-till-you-drop" genre.

When Grandkids Visit: The battleship USS *Alabama* is now retired near Mobile, and has its own 100-acre park as a dedication to Alabama war veterans. Its companion vessel, the submarine USS *Drum*, which participated with the USS *Alabama* in South Pacific sea battles during World Wart II, is also there, with 13 war missions to its credit. Also, on display are World War II fighter planes, a B-52 bomber, an A-12 Blackbird spy plane and a captured Iraqi tank.

Addresses and Connections

Chamber of Commerce: (Gulf Shores) P.O. Box 3869, Gulf Shores, AL
   36547. (334) 968-6904.
(Alabama Gulf Coast & Visitors' Bureau) P.O. Box 457, Gulf Shores, AL
   36547. (334) 968-7511, (800) 745-7263.
Internet: http://www.gulfshores.com/
http://www.e-board.com/gulfshr/gulfs01.htm
Newspaper: *Spot Light,* 641 Gulf Shores Pky., Gulf Shores, AL 36542-
   6425. (334) 968-5999.
Airport: Mobile, Pensacola.
Bus/Train: No city or intercity service; you need a car

Gulf Shores/Orange Beach

	Jan:	April	July	Oct:1	Rain	Snow
Daily Highs	61	78	91	79	64 in.	—
Daily Lows	41	58	73	56		

Shelby County

Birmingham, in north-central Alabama, is the center of a large industrial and technical complex. Skilled, technical and executive personnel are always in demand here, often on a consulting or part-time basis. For this reason, many of those forced into early retirement in the north and northeastern industrial areas look favorably toward the Birmingham area and its booming industrial environment.

However, retirees today tend to prefer smaller cities over a big metropolis like Birmingham. Therefore, we'll focus on a couple of towns near enough to take advantage of what the city offers, yet far enough away to avoid big-city living.

On Birmingham's southern flank, the hustle and bustle of a large population center fades away into busy suburbs, and finally disappears into a country-like atmosphere in Shelby County. Well, not really country, because you're within a half-hour's drive to Birmingham, with all its cultural and commercial amenities, but it's rare you'll need to drive to the city. The suburbs of Hoover, Pelham, Helena and Alabaster have shopping centers that would make most small cities envious. The crime rate in the county is one of the lowest in the state, and there are many middle-class to upper-class neighborhoods to choose from.

The most popular of relocation choices in Shelby County is Pelham, with a population of 15,000. The city of Hoover has a similar population and is also a desirable place to live. Other nearby suburbs offer more or less the same attractions as Pelham, so if you're thinking about exploring this area, Pelham might be a good starting place.

The *Wall Street Journal* recently listed this area among the country's top 20 fastest-growing, wealthiest, and most educated areas in the country. In 20 years the population has doubled, yet much of the growth isn't apparent. Many new homes are hidden in woodlands or on large lots with so many trees it's hard to see the houses. Developers are busy carving fancy developments into the steep foothills adjoining Oak Mountain State Park and clearing enough trees to place attractive homes. Although you'll find all kinds of housing—"from cottages to castles," as the chamber of commerce puts it—this is not an area with an abundance of economical housing.

Recreation and Culture: Golf is big in the Birmingham area and particularly so around Pelham, with three public golf courses and three private clubs. Since 1984, two PGA championships have been played here, plus a U.S. Amateur tournament at Shoal Creek Club and a Senior PGA tournament at Greystone Golf Club (both private clubs). The public 18-hole course at Oak Mountain State Park has an arrangement with some seniors who get unlimited free golf during the week in return for their weekend services. Within a short drive around the Birmingham area, there are at least a dozen golf courses.

Totally enclosed within Pelham city limits, the 10,000-acre Oak Mountain State Park is the largest in the state. The park has a 74-acre lake with a swimming beach, tennis courts, 35 miles of nature trails and a unique "tree-top nature trail" for bird watchers. Music lovers attend concerts at Oak Mountain Amphitheater. Nearby larger lakes and rivers have great boating and waterskiing, and some are well-stocked with rainbow trout, spotted bass and other game fish. Not far from Pelham is Black Warrior Hunting Preserve, the largest in the state. Because Alabama leads the nation in deer per acre, the hunting season is three months long with a generous limit of one deer per day.

Jefferson State Community College has a branch in Shelby County, a 20,000-square-foot facility located on 30 acres with 1,400 students. Also, the University of Montevallo is located in the county. Dating from 1896, the campus is known for its red brick streets and winding paths. Jefferson State maintains a year-round arts program that brings to the community a number of fine and performing arts productions. The college's concert and lecture series books many nationally known artists and lecturers.

Pelham's Civic Center hosts Broadway shows as well as performances by the Alabama Ballet and ice shows. Needless to say, the city of Birmingham presents a full slate of cultural offerings, and it's only a short drive away.

Real Estate: In 1996, the average price of a home sold in Shelby County was around $160,000. This isn't to say there aren't neighborhoods where housing is much less; there are just so many upscale places being sold that the average prices are pushed upward—homes in some of the more desirable locations start in the high $200,000 range.

Medical Care: Not only do Pelham residents have the advantage of Birmingham's excellent medical centers but they have a large medical complex right in their own backyard. The Shelby Baptist Medical Center includes a 210-bed hospital with a diagnostic center and a staff of more than 100 physicians.

When Grandkids Visit: Alabama's largest state park, Oak Mountain, is a great place for camping, hiking and canoeing. Paddle boats are for rent. One park feature is a wildlife center where caretakers keep injured animals and birds and nurse them back to health before returning them to the wild. The state of Alabama owns several sets of cabins on the lake and keeps the rents affordable. We spent a very pleasant time here, and are confident your grandkids would enjoy a mini-vacation here.

Addresses and Connections

Chamber of Commerce: P.O. Box 324, Pelham, AL 35124. (205) 663-4542.

Newspaper: *Birmingham News,* 2200 4th Ave., Birmingham, AL 35203-3802. (205) 325-2222.

Airport: Birmingham International Airport (20 miles from Pelham).

Bus/Train: Greyhound in Birmingham; Amtrak in Birmingham. No local bus transportation.

Jasper

A different retirement lifestyle on the opposite side of Birmingham, the small city of Jasper, with a population of 14,000, sits on a peaceful countryside of forested hills and small farms. Birmingham is just a 40-mile drive over Highway 78—and Corridor X is under construction, a high-speed superhighway that should trim the driving time to Birmingham to half an hour. Like Pelham, Jasper is sometimes described as a bedroom community for Birmingham, but on a more affordable scale. Jasper has traditionally been a blue-collar city, where coal mining was king until the black-gold mineral fell out of favor as an energy source, turning the region into a real estate buyer's paradise.

Like most small cities, Jasper's downtown suffers from strip-mall syndrome as shoppers patronize large malls and stores on the town's outskirts. As a result, the town center is quaint, quiet and laid back, a nice place for a stroll.

Jasper is working hard to bring more residents into its midst. One of the community's efforts to attract retirees is the "Newcomers' Club," which invites new residents to become acquainted with the community, to join in cultural and service programs and to make friendships through social gatherings. The Newcomers' Club holds monthly luncheon meetings to plan activities for the group. As an example of how out-of-state people are received: in a recent election for mayor of Jasper, voters chose Don Goetz, a "Yankee" who relocated here from Milwaukee.

One of the more upscale lifestyles in the Jasper area can be found on the shores of Lewis Smith Lake. A few miles outside Jasper, the lake is 35 miles long and has 500 miles of shoreline with a variety of scenic views, beaches, inlets, forests and rugged rock bluffs. Beautiful homes enhance some areas of the lake but most of its terrain has been left pristine and natural. Homes here are not cheap. Building lots are often priced at $75,000, and some boat docks are so elaborate they look as if they might cost as much as the homes they serve. Many of these fancy places are mere weekend places for doctors from Birmingham.

Recreation and Culture: Lewis Smith Lake is the place for boating, swimming and fishing. A boat ramp at Duncan Bridge is a well-known gathering spot for swimmers, fishermen and waterskiers during the summer months.

River's Edge 18-hole golf course, newly completed, is Jasper's pride and joy. Located minutes from town, it is the first and only public golf course in the county. Nestled on the bank of the Warrior River, River's Edge is one of the more scenic courses in Alabama. There's also a country club here with an 18-hole championship golf course and a fine tennis facility.

Jasper has two, two-year colleges, Walker College, a branch of the University of Alabama, and Bevill State Community College. Bevill has a program of continuing education which retired people take advantage of. Both credit and no-credit classes are offered to adult students. The Walker County Arts Council, established five years ago, works to bring a range of artistic and musical performances to Jasper.

Real Estate: While Jasper does have some areas of higher-cost homes, most housing consists of quiet residential neighborhoods with lots of trees and are priced a bit lower than typically low Alabama prices. In town, as well as on the outskirts, you'll find a few neighborhoods of stately, old homes—former residences of mine owners and supervisory personnel. Just a few minutes from the town center, newer subdivisions and wooded acreages are for sale at affordable prices.

Medical Care: Walker Baptist Medical Center, located in Jasper, provides northwest Alabama with up-to-date health care. A 267-bed hospital with 52 on-site physicians and 31 consulting physicians and staff, the hospital is connected with a state-wide system of 37 other cities to provide a comprehensive range of services to patients.

Community Health Systems (CHS) is headquartered in Jasper. A CHS project slated to be completed in 1997 is the Senior Life and Community Center. Its design allows for meeting and exercise rooms and banquet facilities for 1,000 people.

When Grandkids Visit: At one time, this region was famous for its productive coal mines, but today only two mines are working. The Alabama Mining Museum, in the nearby town of Dora, features an exhibit of how coal was mined during its heyday from 1890 to 1940. The museum depicts the development of the mines, and not only the methods and technical aspects of mining, but also a look into the life of the miner, above as well as below the ground.

Addresses and Connections

Chamber of Commerce: Newcomers Club of Jasper, P.O. Box 652, Jasper, AL 35502. (205) 384-4571.
Internet: http://www.perfectus.com/walker/jasper/#Jasper
Newspaper: *Daily Mountain Eagle,* 1301 Viking Dr., Jasper, AL 35501. (205) 221-2840.
Airport: Birmingham International (40 miles).
Bus/Train: Greyhound; Amtrak in Birmingham.

Birmingham and Environs

	Jan:	April	July	Oct:	Rain	Snow
Daily Highs	52	75	91	43	52 in.	2.2 in.
Daily Lows	33	51	70	51		

Eufaula

Before the Civil War, Eufaula was a prosperous river port and trading town for surrounding areas in Georgia and Alabama. Wealthy merchants and plantation owners created a showplace of beautiful homes in Eufaula that demonstrated their stature in the high society of the region.

Although Eufaula lost many soldiers during the Confederate-Union struggle, the town was never threatened by the ravages of war until the closing stages of the conflict. Suddenly, on April 29, 1865, a messenger galloped into town. He carried the news that the city of Montgomery had fallen to Federal troops. Four thousand Union cavalry were approaching. Fearing the worst, a delegation of citizens flying a flag of truce met the approaching troops hoping to negotiate. At that same time, another message arrived: the war was over! General J.E. Johnston had surrendered to General Sherman, and Robert E. Lee had presented his sword to General Grant at Appomattox.

To the town's great relief, the formidable band of warriors rode peacefully through town and crossed the river into Georgia. Just in the nick of time, Eufala's antebellum homes were spared for their later role as living museums of southern aristocratic living. Shortly after the war, Eufala regained much of its prosperity, whereupon another wave of extravagant building began in the 1880s to add a collection of wonderful Victorians to mix with the pre-war homes dating from the 1830s.

Eufaula occupies a site on the west bank of the Chattahoochee River Valley in the southeastern part of Alabama. With a population of 13,000, this is the largest town in Barbour County, which has a county-wide population of 25,417. Since the town is not far from either Fort Benning or Fort Rucker, Eufaula is convenient for military retirees: the base hospitals, post exchanges and clubs are an hour's drive away.

The town's main residential boulevard is shaded by gigantic oaks and colored by azaleas and flowering dogwood trees. Enormous antebellum homes and elegant Victorian homes line the boulevard in an opulent display of southern architecture. We visited Eufaula once in the springtime, and again in the fall. We can still visualize the colorful flowers, the freshness of sprouting leaves and the smell of spring, and later, the autumn hues of leaves drifting toward the ground and the smell of fall smoke.

Because of the mild climate, exquisite scenery, terrific fishing and other recreational opportunities, Eufaula has become home to numerous "Winter Eufaulians" who visit here during the mild winters and return to their "summer homes" after they've enjoyed a glorious spring.

People relocating to Eufaula are greeted by the Newcomers' Club. There is also an association of retirees who meet and socialize periodically. A few of the clubs and organizations that might appeal to newcomers are garden clubs, Bassmaster's, Rotary Club, Lions Club, Kiwanis International, literary clubs, the Optimists, Daughters of the American Revolution, Chattahoochee Sportsmen's Club, BPW, VFW, and more.

Recreation and Culture: Residents declare that Lake Eufaula is "The Big Bass Capital of the World." There may be something to this claim because Eufala hosts over 50 bass tournaments every year. In addition to providing outstanding fishing, the lake is well-used for swimming, waterskiing, boating, boat racing and jet-skiing. Hunters find the surrounding woods and fields productive for hunting deer and wild turkey.

Two state parks are nearby, Lakepoint Resort State Park and Blue Springs State Park, along with the Eufaula National Wildlife Refuge, an 11,200-acre preserve created to protect wildlife and habitat and provide a place to be enjoyed by visitors. The refuge is managed to preserve diverse species in greater numbers than the area could under natural conditions, by maintaining farmlands, grasslands, woodlands and wetlands.

Eufaula has three 18-hole golf courses: Lakepoint State Park (public), Country Club of Alabama (public) and Eufaula Country Club (private). There are also six lighted all-weather municipal tennis courts and swimming pools.

The Eufaula Little Theatre provides amateur thespians an opportunity to perform, and the Lake City Squares meet regularly for square dancing fun or to entertain at local events. In addition, Eufaula frequently hosts productions from nearby towns; a recent example was an appearance of Montgomery Ballet.

The Eufaula Concert Season began its 14th season in 1997 and features such programs as Floyd Cramer and "The Barber of Seville" by the National Opera Company. The Alabama Shakespeare Festival is only 90 miles away in Montgomery.

Eufaula is well served by Sparks State Technical College and the Bevill Center for Advanced Electronics. Senior citizens who are 60 and above can attend Sparks tuition-free (you must, however, pay "fees"). In addition, Sparks offers evening adult basic education classes.

The famous Eufaula Pilgrimage is held each year on the second weekend in April. This is Alabama's premier tour of old homes, an opportunity to experience southern hospitality at its finest. Grand antebellum and Victorian mansions are open to the public only during the pilgrimage. There are also many beautiful antebellum plantation houses scattered about the eastern part of the county that are included in the pilgrimage.

Real Estate: As in many small cities, rental properties are difficult to find. It's usually easier to find a house to buy than an apartment to rent. An average three-bedroom, two-bath home costs approximately $71,000 in an ordinary neighborhood. A really nice house in an expensive neighborhood can cost as much as $190,000. Occasionally one of the older antebellum or Victorians will appear on the market for even more.

Medical Care: Eufaula is proud of Lakeview Community Hospital which features an active medical staff as well as a dental clinic. Lakeview also provides a 24-hour emergency room physician. Many services are provided at Lakeview: respiratory therapy, physical therapy, home health, orthopedics, ICU/CCU, surgery (inpatient and outpatient), ENT specialists, hospice, etc. Emergency care is provided by the Eufaula Rescue Squad, a competent and highly qualified ambulance service.

When Grandkids Visit: We would definitely take grandkids to the Playground of Dreams located in Old Creek Town Park in Eufaula. After they've worn themselves out on the playground, they can cool off in Lake Eufaula only yards away.

Addresses and Connections

Chamber of Commerce: P.O. Box 697, Eufaula, AL 36072-0697. (334) 687-6664.

Newspaper: *Eufaula Tribune,* 514 East Barbour St., Eufaula, AL 36027. (334) 687-3506.

Airport: Columbus (48 miles), Dothan (52 miles), and Atlanta (164 miles).

Bus/Train: Greyhound.

Eufaula						
	Jan:	April	July	Oct:	Rain	Snow
Daily Highs	57	77	92	78	49 in.	0.3 in.
Daily Lows	36	53	72	53		

Evergreen

We would never have thought of visiting the little town of Evergreen, Alabama,—were it not for a friend who was showing us the better retirement locations in Alabama. Since he's in charge of the state's Retirement Attraction program, we took him at his word that Evergreen would be worth a stopover. "It's a small community," he explained, "but they've put more effort into their retirement attraction program than most places ten times the size of Evergreen." We were pleased that we did visit.

A delightfully rural community of 4,000 people, Evergreen sits in the south-central part of Alabama, about 40 miles from the Florida state line. It's surrounded by hills and forests, broken by an occasional farm and rolling fields. This is probably the least populated area in Alabama, yet the town is only a 90-minute drive to the beaches of Pensacola or Gulf Shores for saltwater recreation. Evergreen is also about halfway between Mobile and Montgomery for big-city shopping, a 75-minute drive in either direction.

Evergreen's business district is the essence of what small towns should be, and used to be. There's a thriving business section, with a traditional square, a railroad depot and the county courthouse. This is a comfortable downtown, a place where you might enjoy sitting on a bench to chat with neighbors. The old railroad depot—now called "Ye Olde Railway Emporium"—has been converted to a cooperative where local artisans (some retired) display and sell their beautiful handiwork. As we visited various parts of town, we were delighted with the lovely homes sitting on generous-sized lots with neat and well-cared-for landscaping—no matter what the price range. Speaking of prices, we found no better values on quality real estate anywhere else in the South.

It just so happened that our visit coincided with one of Evergreen's many town celebrations: an afternoon Halloween parade by costumed school children. It seemed like the entire town turned out, reinforcing our feeling of hometown America of yesteryear. We noticed that this wasn't an "all-white" celebration either, or one where people of color stayed to one side of the street and whites to the other. People not only mixed but joked, chatted amicably and reminded one another to bring their kids around for trick-or-treating. This answered one of our questions: we knew that folks in larger southern communities get along nowadays, but what about in small, isolated rural towns? We met several African-Americans, including the president and administrator of Reid State College, several members of the retirement attraction committee and a lady of color who had retired here from Oklahoma, and who was one of the most enthusiastic Evergreen boosters.

In order to ease the transition into retirement, Evergreen has a "Hospitality Team" to assist you. The group offers free services to help you find a home and aid you in financial, legal and health care matters. Most important, the team will introduce you to your new neighbors. Folks we interviewed attest to the friendliness of the community.

Retiree Al Burns said, "I'm from New Jersey but I worked in Boston and New York as a radio broadcaster. When I retired in New York, I couldn't afford to live there—just the taxes were enough to drive me away. When I moved here, I decided I needed something to do, so now I'm doing a regular program for Radio WPGG. I love it here!"

Camden: Located about 35 miles north of Evergreen (as the crow flies), the little town of Camden is a smaller alternative to Evergreen and also has a relocation committee eager to welcome newcomers. At one time, the nearby Alabama River was an important thoroughfare for steamboats; there were 200 riverboat landings along the river during the heyday of river transport. But all good things come to an end, as they say, and railroads and 14-wheeler trucks robbed the waterway of its commercial importance. This left Camden a sleepy, peaceful place, perfect for retirees. A series of dams has created a chain of lakes along the river, with fishing and recreation filling the vacuum left by the disappearance of steamboats. The lake formed by a dam at Miller's Ferry is a great place for fishing, boating and waterfowl hunting.

Camden is the seat of Wilcox County and its largest community (my guess is a population of about 2,000). If you're looking for a quiet, country setting among friendly neighbors, this might be the place.

Recreation and Culture: With more than three-quarters of the countryside covered in woodlands, outdoor recreation is popular here. Deer and turkey abound and bring hunters in from all over the region. (The nation's champion turkey caller lives here; he operates a business in Evergreen's business district.) There are many well-stocked ponds, which would typically be "well-kept secrets," but local folks are always happy to share their best fishing holes with you.

Evergreen has a private country club with a swimming pool and a 9-hole golf course. It isn't very fancy, but it isn't very expensive, either. It's a social center for clubs, dances and meetings.

A big event every year is the Castleberry Strawberry Festival, about 12 miles south of Evergreen. But the occasion that draws national attention is the Evergreen's annual "Fly-In Event." Several hundred vintage and experimental planes come roaring in every October to participate in an exciting display of flying machines. When we were there, a Boeing B-17 flew in, painted with the colors of the 398th Bomb Group, looking much the same as it did flying missions over Nazi Germany.

Although Reid State College is located in Evergreen, it is basically oriented toward vocational and business education. However Dr. Littles, its president, said the school is planning a series of continuing education courses that will be of interest to seniors.

Real Estate: In addition to a wide selection of older, pre-Civil War and Victorian homes waiting to be decorated to your taste, modern, conventional housing is readily available at competitive prices. For a three-bedroom, two-bath home, you can expect prices to start at $55,000. Custom homes can be built in subdivisions featuring golf and swimming, and large acreage tracts are waiting for the equestrian or the weekend gardener.

Medical Care: The Vaughan/Evergreen Medical Center is a 44-bed facility with a coronary care unit and respiratory therapy, as well as surgery and physical therapy units. At present, the hospital is constructing a 14-bed mental health crisis unit. The Conecuh County Health Center provides a well-rounded public program for health awareness.

When Grandkids Visit: They'll probably enjoy a visit to the Zee Donkey Farm, just out of town. The farm features zebras, donkeys and a combination of the two—which they call "Zee-Donks." Also, about six miles from town is Booker's Mill, an old homestead with rail fences, a waterfall, a water wheel, a log cabin built in 1887 and nature trails. It still looks how it did a hundred years ago. Curiously, much of the region hasn't changed all that much.

Addresses and Connections

Chamber of Commerce: (Evergreen) 100 Depot Square, Evergreen, AL 36401. (334) 578-1000.
(Camden) 110 Court St., Camden, AL 36726. (205) 682-4929.
Internet: http://evergreen.alabama-net.com
http://www.wiregrassarea.com/classifieds/evergreen.html
Newspapers: *Evergreen Courant,* Evergreen, AL 36401-2834. (334) 578-1492.
Conecuh Countian, Old Greenville Rd., Evergreen, AL 36401. (334) 578-1155.
Airport: Montgomery (65 miles).
Bus/Train: Amtrak at Atmore (39 miles).

		Evergreen			
	Jan:	April	July	Oct:	Rain	Snow
Daily Highs	57	77	92	78	54 in.	1 in.
Daily Lows	37	54	72	53		

Southeastern Alabama Towns

Before we discovered some of Alabama's better retirement locations, we kept hearing about a town called Dothan (pronounced *DOE-than*). Readers would ask, "Why don't you mention *Dothan* in your books?" We checked our Alabama road map and were puzzled why a place in the corner of southeast Alabama should have something special going for it. But we received so many inquiries, we decided to take a look for ourselves. We're glad we did.

Dothan and neighboring communities combine pleasant Alabama locations with unusually diverse retiree populations. Folks come from all over the world to settle here. This is partly due to nearby Fort Rucker, home of the world's largest helicopter training center; military families remember Dothan when making retirement plans, and post exchange privileges and access to military medical services make it convenient. Because Fort Rucker trains helicopter pilots from all over the world, military and civilian trainees from other countries remember the area when they retire, too.

Another source of Dothan's unusual diversity is a growing colony of civilian retirees from the Panama Canal Zone. Between 100 and 120 families have moved to Dothan to begin (or resume) their retirement careers. With the Canal due to be transferred to Panama in 1999, even more families will be on the way.

How did such an unlikely place as southeast Alabama become a mecca for folks who lived most of their lives in tropical Panama? It started some years back when one Canal Zone employee convinced his wife to retire in his home state of Alabama instead of staying in Panama, as most others did. When they returned to Panama for visits, they bragged so much about the charms and advantages of Dothan that others began visiting. Eventually they moved there. Then the treaty between Panama and the United States, which returned control over the canal to Panama, really started the ball rolling. With an unclear future ahead and no roots in any place outside Panama, many decided to look more closely into Dothan.

The city and its businesses sensed a trend, and, in an effort to draw as many retirees into the community as possible, sponsored emissaries to Panama to spread the word about the advantages of moving to Dothan. Obviously, it worked.

One lady said, "We have two excellent hospitals here, and any kind of business we need. We're only 90 minutes from Florida beaches. Another 90 minutes takes us to Tallahassee or Montgomery and four hours to Atlanta or Mobile." When asked how the local people accept outsiders, she replied, "All I know is that the mayor of Dothan keeps saying to our Panamanian Club, 'Bring us some more of those Panamanians!'"

Many of Dothan's new retirees were second- and third-generation residents of the Canal Zone; they went through the American school system there and graduated from Balboa High School before launching careers similar to their parents'—working for the Panama Canal Company. So many graduates of Balboa High School now live in Dothan that it seemed only natural to hold a class reunion here. Graduates came from all over the country and the world to attend.

However, the influx of retirees here is more than just an accident. The high quality of life, exhibited in the lovely neighborhoods throughout the area, draws people to Dothan. Quiet, tree-shaded streets with large lawns and elegant homes reflect well-kept neighborhoods and pride of ownership. The flowering trees in the spring and colorful leaves in the fall make changes of season a delight here. Visitors come every spring to follow the trail of pink along the annual Azalea-Dogwood Trail event.

Actually, our visit to Dothan wasn't exactly fair, because it was in February, a time when blossoming trees were exploding with color, birds were trilling songs of joy and the world was turning emerald green. Our travels through the neighborhoods there and in nearby Ozark and Enterprise were admittedly influenced by this early spring frenzy. Yet in neighborhood after neighborhood, even in the more humble places, we found quality housing and pride of ownership.

Ozark: Everything said about Dothan can be repeated about Enterprise (pop. 21,000) and Ozark (pop. 17,000). Of course, they are smaller, and those who value small-town qualities will adore Enterprise and Ozark. Why retire here? One retiree from Ozark put it this way:

"This area is the best of all worlds. We live far enough south to avoid winter cold, far enough away from the ocean to escape destructive humidity. We enjoy a small-town atmosphere, yet we're close to the Gulf Coast and great fishing. We're only minutes from Dothan."

The cost-of-living is always at least 10 percent below average, and property taxes are almost ridiculously low. For example: taxes on an owner-occupied home valued at $65,000 amount to $152.50 a year, but if the occupant is over 65 years of age, taxes drop to $136.25.

Ozark retirees appreciate the fact that they can drive all over the charming city with no traffic jams and few stoplights. A relatively inexpensive, full-service country club with a challenging 18-hole golf course is only two miles from the courthouse square in the center of town. Ozark recently converted Dale County Lake and the land surrounding it into a park for residents.

Enterprise: The closest town to Fort Rucker, Enterprise is a favorite retirement location of ex-military families. They remember the town with favor and think about it when retirement plans are discussed.

A wide variety of housing is available in Enterprise, and the town is continually expanding its inventory of homes. A recent development is a group of "garden" homes and townhouses. These are smaller, maintenance-free places for folks wishing to downsize their house size and their house chores. Always moving ahead, Enterprise is in the process of building a new park, with lots of walking trails and passive recreation.

Enterprise is also famous for an unusual landmark, a serious monument dedicated to an insect: the Boll Weevil. In the early part of this century many parts of the South went from the height of affluence to economic disaster because of the boll weevil. Within one season, the insects all but exterminated cotton, the crop responsible for the state's prosperity. But Enterprise/Ozark farmers didn't surrender to despair; they plowed under the cotton and planted peanuts. This change in tactics restored prosperity and then some. The relieved citizens decided to give credit where it was due, to the boll weevil, which forced them to make their communities even richer than before.

Enterprise is so proud of being a small town that one of its annual events is the "world's smallest St. Patrick's Day Parade." Parade officials elect a "designated Leprechaun" to march—only one marcher to a parade please, because more than one might permit some other town to stage a smaller procession and steal Enterprise's thunder! The parade's elected Grand Marshal is always in absentia; because obviously, if he attended the event, there would be more than one marcher. (I was told that my name might be put into nomination for Grand Marshal some day, since I live in California and wouldn't be likely to show up.) When the long-anticipated Saint Patrick's Day arrives, celebrants rendezvous at Tops Restaurant and drink Irish coffee while they wait for the designated Leprechaun to finish the journey. Since the parade route stretches only from Ouida Street to Tops's back door—a distance of approximately 50 feet—the wait isn't overwhelming. But the celebration is.

Enterprise is now the headquarters of a 13-county tourist and retirement association, whose office is coordinated with Enterprise's chamber of commerce.

Recreation and Culture: Recreational opportunities abound among these three cities. Within a short drive are five public golf courses, plus one of the famous 36-hole Robert Trent Jones courses. Strong recreation departments oversee 20 parks, six public swimming pools, 40 public tennis courts, four recreation centers, a softball complex and numerous organized team sports. The lure of fishing is available on nearby lakes or in the Gulf of Mexico, only 80 miles to the south.

The region has a surprising inventory of cultural events, including a symphony, ballet and a community theater. Wallace College offers a free tuition program for citizens 60 years or older who meet the admissions standards. Through the college's community services program, citizens, regardless of academic background, can take a wide variety of courses. Troy State University offers one course tuition-free to adults who have been out of school for at least 3 years and who qualify for admission to the university.

With seating for 3,200 persons, the Dothan Civic Center hosts a wide range of activities. The Dothan Opera House, a historic landmark built in 1903, opens its doors for theater productions, concerts and a host of other cultural events. Landmark Park, Alabama's state agricultural museum, the Wiregrass Museum of Art, Farley Nuclear Visitor's Center, and the U.S. Army Aviation Museum at nearby Fort Rucker all offer pleasant educational and cultural experiences.

Real Estate: As is the case in most of Alabama, housing is very affordable, with homes in quality neighborhoods ranging from $65,000 to more than $250,000. Something unusual in small Alabama cities: rentals are plentiful here, with more than 2,000 units available in private apartment complexes. This is partly due to the large number of military personnel who require temporary housing, partly due to high turn-overs. In the city of Dothan, the Housing Authority manages or subsidizes rents on over 1,200 housing units and manages Vaughn Towers, a 120-unit high-rise for senior citizens.

Medical Care: Among the three cities, there are four hospitals plus the medical facility at Fort Rucker. Ozark has Dale Medical Center, with 92 beds. The Enterprise Medical Center is a fully accredited hospital with 135 beds, and has recently added all the newest high-tech equipment. Dothan has two hospitals, Dothan Southeast and Flowers Hospitals.

When Grandkids Visit: You absolutely must take them to the Helicopter Museum at Fort Rucker. They'll see a complete collection of helicopters, starting with the first experimental machines to the enormous whirly birds that can carry a Sherman tank. A fascinating Vietnam exhibit shows the fighting helicopters as they were used in the war, with dramatic panoramas of battle scenes. This is an exhibit we've visited more than once, and wouldn't mind seeing again.

Addresses and Connections

Chambers of Commerce: (Ozark) 308 Painter St., Ozark, AL 36360. (334) 774-9321, (800) 582-8497.
(Enterprise) 553 Glover Ave, Enterprise, AL 36360. (334) 347-0581, (800) 235-4730.
(Dothan) 440 Honeysuckle Road, Dothan, AL 36302. (334) 792-5138.
Internet: (Ozark) http://alaweb.asc.edu/ala_tours/se2_att.html#7
(Dothan) http://www.snowhill.com/dothan/city/cityref.html
Newspapers: (Ozark) *Southern Star*, 428 E. Andrews, Ozark, AL 36320. (334) 774-2715, (334) 792-9330.
(Enterprise) *Enterprise Ledger,* 106 N. Edwards St., Enterprise, AL 36303. (205) 347-9533, (205) 347-0825.
(Dothan) *Dothan Eagle,* 227 N. Oates St., Dothan, AL 36303-4555. (334) 792-3141.
Airport: Dothan Airport.
Bus/Train: City bus, Dothan; Greyhound.

Dothan/Ozark/Enterprise

	Jan:	April	July	Oct:	Rain	Snow
Daily Highs	57.0	77.0	91.5	77.5	49.1 in.	0.3 in.
Daily Lows	36.4	53.3	71.8	53.1		

ALABAMA TAXES

Alabama Department of Revenue

50 North Ripley Street, Montgomery, AL 36104. (205) 242-1000

Alabama's tax bills rank 9th among the least expensive in the nation

Income Tax

Taxable Income	Rate	Taxable Income	Rate
First $500	2.0%	First $1,000	2.0%
Next $2,500	4.0%	Next $5,000	4.0%
Over $3,000	5.0%	Over $6,000	5.0%

General exemptions: $1,500 single, $3,000 married filing jointly, $300 each dependent. Additional for elderly: None.

Public/Private Pension Exclusion: Full exclusion.

Social Security/Railroad Retirement Benefits: Full exclusion.

Standard Deduction: $2,000 single*, $4,000 married filing jointly*

Medical and Dental Expense Deduction: Limited to amount in excess of 4% of adjusted gross income.

Federal Income Tax Deduction: Full exemption.

Other: Local earnings taxes are imposed by 11 cities at rates of 1% or 2%

*Alabama does not allow the additional standard deduction for people over 65 allowed for federal income tax purposes.

Sales Taxes

State 4.0%; **County** 1.0% - 3.5%; **City** 1.0% - 4.0%; **Special District:** 1.0% - 1.5%

Combined Rate in Selected Towns: Birmingham 7.0%; Huntsville 9.0%; Mobile 9.0% (10.0% food and drink)

General Coverage: Food is taxed, prescription drugs are exempt.

Property Taxes

Probably lowest in nation: Average assessment on a $100,000 home about $300 a year:
Alabama imposes state and local taxes on all real and personal property. Some intangibles are taxed. In relation to personal income, property tax collections are in the lowest third among the 50 states.

Homestead Credit: General exemptions: $4,000 assessed value on state taxes ($40,000 market value equivalent), $2,000 assessed value on local taxes, except those for school property ($20,000 market value equivalent).

Over 65 or disabled with AGI: Full exemption from state taxes, $5,000 of assessed value on local taxes ($50,000 market value equivalent).

Less than $7,500: Full exemption from state and local taxes.

Veterans: Full exemption from state and local taxes on VA-assisted homes.

Estate/Inheritance Taxes

Alabama does not impose an estate tax nor an inheritance tax. It imposes only a pick-up tax, which is a portion of the federal estate tax and does not increase the total tax owed.

Arkansas

If you could divide Arkansas into two states—by cutting diagonally from the northeast corner to the southwest corner—you would have two triangular-shaped territories so different from each other it's difficult to imagine they should be joined together as a state.

The southeastern triangle— defined by the Mississippi River running along its eastern side and Louisiana along the south—is flat as a football field and rich with black soil typical of the Gulf Coastal Plain. The region was settled early on by aristocratic cotton planters, slave owners who became enormously wealthy during cotton's reign. (These wealthy plantation owners kept to the flatlands of southeastern Arkansas; they considered the Ozarks, with their mountains and rocky hillsides, to be useless wilderness.) When the boll weevil doomed cotton, farmers were forced to shift to rice and other crops. Today, the southeastern triangle is still a rich agricultural region, great for farmers, but not particularly popular with retirees from out of state.

Arkansas
The Land of Opportunity, Razorback State
Admitted to statehood: June 15, 1836
State Capital: Little Rock
Population (1995): 2,483,769; rank, 21st
Population Density: 47.1 per sq. mile: urban 44.7%
Geography: 27th state in size, with 52,075 square miles, including 1,107 square miles of water surface. Highest elevation: Magazine Mountain, 2,753 feet. Lowest elevation: 55, Ouachita River. Average elevation: 650 feet.
State Flower: Apple blossom
State Bird: Mockingbird
State Tree: Pine
State Song: *Arkansas*

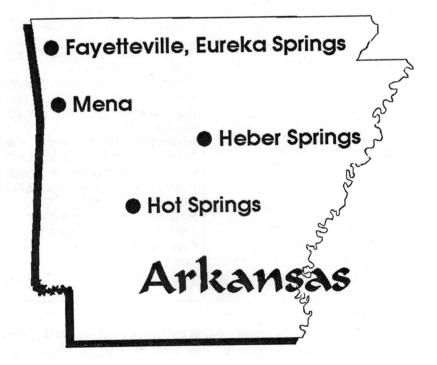

The part of Arkansas we're interested in for retirement and relocation is the northwestern triangle of land bordered by Oklahoma and Missouri. This region was settled by a different kind of people. They were neither rich planters nor slave owners. They were fiercely independent pioneers who journeyed here from the southern Appalachians. They came from the Blue Ridge and Smoky Mountains, from the Carolinas and from Tennessee and Georgia. The Ozark and Ouachita Mountains and forests, with maze-like valleys and steep wooded hills, suited their free spirits. Their Appalachian legends, music and folk art fit into the northwestern Arkansas mountains as if they had been made there. The Ozark Mountains were exactly what these settlers were looking for.

This northwestern section is where the Ozark Plateau joins the Ouachita Mountain Range. The fertile Arkansas River Valley barely separates them. The Boston Mountains are the highest part of the Ozark Plateau, with elevations of more than 2,000 feet. The Ouachita Mountains, on the south side of the Arkansas River, are the highest mountains in the state with summits reaching 2,700 feet above sea level. (By the way, please don't pronounce the word *Ouachita* the way it's spelled or you'll start people snickering. Say it this way: *WAH-shi-taw*.) Although geologists distinguish between the two mountain ranges (because the ridges of the Ouachitas run in a different compass direction than the Ozarks), local residents universally refer to their surroundings as "the Ozarks" no matter in which part they live.

History: Few people think of Arkansas as an early pioneer region, but western Arkansas was the original wild-west frontier. This was where the legends began; Arkansas' siege of lawlessness started back in 1828. Until then, western Arkansas had been the territory of several Indian tribes, including those Cherokees who had been forcibly removed from their homelands in the East by the U.S. government. After their forced march along the infamous "Trail of Tears," the Native Americans assumed they had a new homeland in the Ozarks. However, they were fated to be run out once again. The Treaty of 1828 moved the border of the "Indian Territory" farther west, to the present Oklahoma state line. Suddenly the Arkansas territory was open for unlimited settlement.

With almost no form of organized government, the region quickly became a haven for wild and woolly gunslingers and fugitives from the law. Outlaws such as Belle Starr, Jesse James, the Cole Younger gang and other legendary characters made their reputations here. In 1840 an easterner, newly arrived in Arkansas, wrote a letter home, describing Fayetteville this way: "This town is one of the most lawless and uncivilized places in all creation. Shooting, stabbing, knocking down and dragging out appear to be the order of the day. Almost everyone you see is armed to the teeth." This reputation for lawlessness lingered on after western emigration pushed the edge of civilization to the Pacific Coast. On the other side of the law, Judge Issac Parker, in his courtroom at Fort Smith, earned his reputation as Arkansas' "hanging judge" by dealing out death sentences right and left.

Safe and Affordable: Today, in stark contrast to the disorderly frontier days, Northwest Arkansas enjoys one of the lowest crime rates in the nation. People tell us they often don't bother locking their doors at night or when they go into town for shopping. Arkansas' mild, four-season climate, low taxes and personal safety make Arkansas popular for relocation. One thing retirees consistently mention about Arkansas is its affordable cost-of-living. Almost everything, from grocery items to property taxes, look like bargains to those moving into the state from the more expensive places to live. Arkansas' tax burden is about 30 percent below the national average. Depending on the community, housing costs are 10 to 20 percent below average. Inexpensive housing and friendly people draw retirees to the area, but the glorious Ozark environment, and a feeling of being on vacation the year round, makes people settle in Arkansas.

Enchanted Landscape: It's difficult to describe the Ozarks to someone who has never seen them. To this writer, these ancient mountains have an aura of enchantment, a magical fascination. As a youngster, growing up in suburban St. Louis, I eagerly looked forward to our annual vacations in the Ozark wonderland. There are mysterious woods to explore—of pine, oak and hickory, colored by flaming sumac and autumn leaves; crystal-clear springs of cold water mysteriously bubble up from limestone rocks or gush from deep caves. The only place I've seen that comes close to matching the

Ozark ambience is the Appalachians. Still, they never quite duplicate the enchantment for me. Every time I travel across the Midwest, I manipulate my route to detour through the Ozarks for a session of rejuvenation.

Many others must feel this way, because Arkansas is high on the list of states that attract out-of-state retirees. At least once in recent years, Arkansas surpassed Florida as a retirement destination. Again, most people relocate in the picturesque northwestern mountain areas rather than the flat farm country of the southeast. Some come here to retire, others to work. (Because of the state's healthy economy, unemployment figures are among the lowest in the nation.) But the majority of newcomers come to retire; according to one figure I've seen, 80 percent of Arkansas' incoming residents are over 60 years of age. They come from states like Illinois, Wisconsin, Minnesota and the Dakotas.

By no means are these newcomers jumping into unfamiliar territory; they've been vacationing here for years. They remember clear-running streams, crystal-clear air and lakes teeming with fish. Their retirement dreams include a home on the lake with a boat dock at the back door—lazy days of casting for bigmouth bass, bluegills or lake trout. Anyway, that's how the men might picture paradise. But women like Arkansas too; you needn't be a fishing enthusiast to enjoy the Ozarks.

Activities: Arkansas isn't all hunting, fishing and boating. Most communities where retirees choose to relocate have regular social and cultural events that bring people together. The state has a good system of colleges with continuing education programs. Of interest to seniors is the state policy on college education: schools waive general student fees for credit courses to persons age 60 and older, on a space available basis. State vocational and technical schools usually waive fees as well.

Newcomers from Minneapolis or Indianapolis make friends easily in Arkansas, not only because local people are friendly, but because their new neighbors often are transplants from the North and have similar interests, giving them things in common to talk about. One man told us, "Several of our neighbors are also from Chicago. Every time we get together we start talking about the Cubs." This works out fine, because believe it or not, many Arkansas natives have never even *heard* of the Chicago Cubs, much less spent time discussing the Cubs' pennant possibilities. Some might even giggle at the thought.

This influx of northerners into Arkansas has changed the makeup of the population. They've introduced new world views and made it easier for newcomers to "fit in." Without this outside influence, you could find yourself isolated among folks with whom you have little in common. Not that people would be anything but friendly and neighborly, but unless your cultural background is basically agricultural and small-town, you could have a difficult time adjusting without the out-of-staters.

The following are some northern Arkansas towns that we've visited and believe have potential for retirement. All have a significant number of non-natives. Some places are small, but none are isolated from medical and other important services. City transportation is sometimes a problem, something you'll have to look at if you don't drive.

Mena

Small towns have the reputation of being exceptionally low-crime areas. However, crime waves can strike anywhere, at any time. Recently, a serial auto thief struck the western Arkansas town of Mena. Faced with an emergency, Sheriff Mike Oglesby asked the local radio station to broadcast an emergency warning. The warning: "Don't leave your car keys in the ignition! Someone is stealing cars!" Fortunately the culprit was quickly apprehended—and turned out to be a high school student who liked joyriding. A good thing, too, because Mena citizens aren't used to heavy-duty crime waves. They probably wouldn't remember to remove their keys.

Mena is another retirement discovery that would have never come to our attention had it not been for the determined efforts of the town's retirement attraction committee. While speaking at a Southeastern Retirement Symposium in Tupelo, Mississippi, I was impressed by the large number of delegates from a place called "Mena, Arkansas." When I inquired what Mena had that might make it a good place for retirement, eight members of the team collared me and insisted on taking me to Mena. I protested that I hadn't time. I had to catch a plane the next afternoon. "No problem. We'll arrange for a private airplane to get you back in time to catch your flight." Seemed as if I had no choice—it was eight against one. After I arrived in Mena, I was delighted that I made the trip.

Sitting in a valley surrounded by western Arkansas' Ouachita Mountains, Mena is a pleasant town of 5,500 in a county of 17,000. It's near the Oklahoma border, about 77 miles west of Hot Springs, and 85 miles south of Fort Smith. Local boosters call their town "the pride of the Ouachitas." (Remember, say it this way: *WAH-shi-taw!*) Mena started out as a "railroad town" on the Kansas City, Pittsburgh and Gulf Railroad (later known as Kansas City Southern). The town was named after the wife of a Dutch coffee broker, Jan De Goeigen, who partially financed the railroad.

Arkansas' second highest peak, Rich Mountain, overlooks the town of Mena from its cloud-capped hideaway in the nearby mountains. In the late 1800s, the railroad built a resort hostelry up on the mountain. They named it the "Queen Wilhelmina Inn," in honor of the Netherlands's Queen and her impending visit. Residents are proud of this landmark, and love to take visitors there for lunch or a view of the sunset over a dinner of fine southern fare.

Mena is surprisingly prosperous looking, with several upscale neighborhoods where housing sells at scandalously low Arkansas prices. Another surprise—Mena is a college town. Students and faculty always brighten a community, adding a touch of energy and spirit. College influence shows in the way the downtown is still alive and breathing: The old railroad station, refurbished and restored, is now a museum and chamber of commerce office. Stores, businesses and restaurants are open and thriving, not boarded up and collecting cobwebs as in some small Arkansas towns.

Part of Mena's economic well-being is due to local industries that employ skilled workers, and consequently pay better-than-average wages. U.S. Motors, a division of Emerson Electric, provides a large number of jobs. Another skilled-worker employer is a large facility that repairs and maintains aircraft for major U.S. and Canadian airlines. Its technicians are all FAA qualified, and can work just about anywhere in the world they choose. But they like it here in Mena.

One man said, "We were looking for a good place to raise our children, and we couldn't find a better place than Mena."

Good wages have a multiplier effect on the economy—in precisely the same way as retired people's incomes do. When spent in the community, wages and incomes turn into profits and wages for other residents. They, in turn, have more money to spend, which benefits still others. The money goes 'round and 'round. Mena's community leaders see this very clearly. That's exactly why they are so enthused about sharing their community with retirees rather than going after marginal, minimum-wage–paying industries as many other Arkansas cities have done.

Recreation and Culture: Mena is surrounded by 1.5 million acres of the Ouachita National Forest, the South's oldest and largest national forest. There are 32 recreational areas in the forest where you can enjoy picnicking, camping, hiking, horseback riding, mountain biking, swimming fishing, hunting, and boating.

A network of trails twists and turns through the forest—from Talimena State Park in Oklahoma almost to Little Rock. Known as the Ouachita National Recreation Trails, they converge on Mena and are exceptionally popular throughout the region with ATV owners. (For those who don't know, ATV is an "All Terrain Vehicle," one of those three- or four-wheel motorcycle-type contraptions that can practically climb walls.) From as far as Texas and Florida, ATV enthusiasts travel to Mena to participate in contests and off-road races along the 50 miles of trails through breath-taking scenery. This is the country's only National Forest Service land where ATVs are permitted and encouraged.

For a small town, Mena surprised us by having two public golf courses as well as a private golf course at the local country club. Like most Arkansas small towns, Mena is in a dry county; however, for those who enjoy a glass of vintage grape with their steak, the local country club is allowed to serve. Also, the Oklahoma state line is less than 10 miles away. Ironically Oklahoma was one of the last states to permit legal sale of liquor, and now it's the first place people from neighboring states go to stock up their liquor cabinets.

Rich Mount, Mena's college, is a small school but has lots of get-up-and-go about it. The school's library has 20 computers, plus three computer labs, which the community is welcome to use between classes. Free tuition is offered to anyone over the age of 60, for either credit or audit. Many crafts and community service programs are presented at cost, with classes in everything from geology to watercolors.

Real Estate: Housing costs in Mena are pretty much standard for Arkansas. (That means very low.) The difference between Mena and the average Arkansas small city is a higher number of affluent neighborhoods than you'd normally expect. Older homes near the town center might sell for $45,000, and newer homes a few minutes away for $60,000. Exceptionally nice places—larger, and set on a lake or in a wooded subdivision—typically sell for $100,000 and up.

One couple I interviewed (retirees from Wisconsin) were absolutely delighted with their home—a three-bedroom, two-bath, modern log cabin sitting on nine acres of wooded property with a stream flowing through it. "We always wanted to live in a log cabin," they said, "and we absolutely fell in love with this one. When the seller told us he was only asking $65,000 for everything, we didn't even think about making a counteroffer. Then we found out taxes were only $300 a year!"

Medical Care: People here are determined to maintain and build upon the quality of their town. And naturally, quality health care is essential to this goal. The town's hospital, Mena Medical Center, was founded in 1950 and since its beginning, the community never hesitated to commit resources to maintain a high level of health care. The nearest full-service hospital is 45 miles away, so health care is essential. Therefore, when the hospital ran into financial difficulties a couple of years ago, Mena residents didn't hesitate. An overwhelming 80 percent majority voted for a sales tax increase to bail out the hospital and to add improvements. At the time of my visit, the sales tax was just about to expire, and the hospital was once again in great financial shape.

The 51-bed hospital has a staff of 17 physicians, covering specialties in cardiology, neurology, internal medicine, radiology, general surgery, urology, psychiatry and family practice. The hospital recently recruited an orthopedic surgeon. The facility also offers weekly clinics by visiting physicians in the areas of ENT, ophthalmology, dermatology and podiatry.

When Grandkids Visit: This is the time to back your three-wheeled all-terrain–vehicle out of the garage and take the grandkids for a spin through the forest. With unlimited miles of rugged trails ahead, you and the grandkids can zip along and enjoy the wind blowing through your hair as your ATV bounces and jolts along the rocky trail, splashing through creeks and climbing steep hills. An even better idea might be to set up a lawn chair beside Lake Mena and take a nap while the kids fish for catfish with a cane pole, earthworm, and a red-and-white bobber.

Addresses and Connections

Chamber of Commerce: 524 Sherwood, Mena, AR 71953. (501) 394-2912.
Newspaper: *Mena Star,* 501 Mena St., Mena, AR 71953-3337. (501) 394-1900.
Internet: http://www.mena-ark.com/index.htm
Airport: Ft. Smith (85 miles), Little Rock (135 miles).
Bus/Train: Greyhound; no local bus.

	Jan:	April	July	Oct:	Rain	Snow
Mena						
Daily Highs	48	74	93	76	40 in.	6.8 in.
Daily Lows	27	49	70	49		

Hot Springs

Long before white men set foot in this mysterious canyon of steam and gushing thermal springs, Indian tribes would journey long distances to enjoy the healing waters. Located in the lower part of the Oauchita Mountains, it was known as "Valley of the Vapors." Mystical steam rose from more than forty boiling springs on the side of a mountain. Indians considered it sacred, a place of peace. Historians say the first white person to visit the springs was the notorious Conquistador, Hernando DeSoto, who relentlessly searched the country for fabled gold and treasures. DeSoto and his soldiers encountered the springs back in 1541, but after a relaxing hot tub and massage, Hernando moved on—much to the relief of the Indians.

In 1832, Congress made history by designating Hot Springs as the first national reserve for public recreational use. Thus, Hot Springs was the forerunner of today's National Parks System. Around the turn of the century, Hot Springs developed into a world-famous spa. Hundreds of thousands came to enjoy the thermal waters, reputed to have great curative powers. Bathhouses, elegant hotels, and sophisticated housing accommodated visitors in proper style. During the 1930s through the 1960s, Hot Springs developed a reputation as a lively town with an exciting nightlife. Horse racing, roulette, blackjack and slot machines were just as popular as the hot springs. Big-name bands played in fancy nightclubs and glittering restaurants flourished in this mid-country, mid-century Riviera atmosphere. Wealthy and famous citizens rubbed elbows with ordinary people as well as crime syndicate bosses and Hollywood stars. Gambling, drinking and dancing the night away preceded health-restoring soakings in the hot springs the next morning. During its heyday, Hot Springs was considered as sumptuous a resort as Las Vegas or Palm Springs is today.

Casino gambling and nightclubs are just memories now. People come here to bathe in soothing waters and to enjoy the quiet atmosphere of the Oauchita Mountains. The bonus is fresh mountain air and the smell of pines and sassafras trees. After gambling was prohibited, the "old town," in the steepest part of the canyon, gradually fell into disrepair. Local shoppers abandoned downtown businesses in favor of shopping malls away from town. Things looked glum for Hot Springs.

However, once again, times are changing. A chamber of commerce campaign to revive tourism and retirement has paid off. Tourist interest in thermal springs and retiree discovery of the town as a great place to retire spawned a revival of the historic downtown. Once abandoned buildings now support fine restaurants, art galleries and quality shopping. Antique globe street lamps, Victorian trim, and horse-drawn carriages all emphasize the turn-of-the-century motif.

A new category of visitors comes to Hot Springs today; they bring retirement money instead of gambling money, and they tend to stay permanently. Hot Springs is now one of Arkansas' most attractive retirement possibilities. It combines the spirit of a 1920s resort with a small city of the 1990s. The charming downtown, the hot water bubbling from the springs, and the impressive architecture of the bathhouses constantly recall the town's rich history. Hot Springs is as different from other Arkansas towns as can be, and its rustic setting in the lower edge of the Ouachita Mountains provides scenic magic found only in Arkansas.

Part of Hot Springs' conversion from a gambling and entertainment economy was a successful campaign to relocate business, manufacturing, and medical services to the region. Abundant timber, clean water and mineral resources provided the necessary attraction to bring in several thriving industries. So the economy is just as strong as Hot Springs' scenic resources.

The old part of town sits in a canyon with buildings and homes clinging to the sloping-to-steep sides of the ravine. Most residential areas are located on higher levels where the land is rolling and hilly, but not steep—a good thing, because the canyon is subject to floods. A few years ago, a flash flood sent a six-foot wall of water crashing down the main business street, flooding stores and wreaking havoc. Hot Springs business people are used to this though. They cleaned out the mud and tidied up and, with little delay, the bathhouses, boutiques and restaurants were open for business.

Hot Springs Village: Hot Springs Village, one of the more impressive retirement complexes in Arkansas, is located 15 miles from the city. Unlike Hot Springs, with its last-century decor, however, the village is totally modern, almost like one of those Florida-style, self-contained and guarded enclaves. Opened in 1970, the village has grown into a community designed for recreation, vacations and full- or part-time living. To date, the complex has sold over 30,000 pieces of property, and has approximately 13,000 full-time residents living here full time.

Situated on 28,000 acres of rolling-to-steep Ouachita foothill wilderness, the property is covered with hardwood forest—oaks, hickories and a scattering of evergreens. Roughly one-third of the property has been converted into lakes and golf courses. As a resident, you automatically have privileges at either of the two country clubs and can play at any of the seven golf courses for green fees of only six dollars. The village also has 14 lighted tennis courts, hiking and jogging trails and swimming pools, both indoor and outdoor.

Hot Springs Village is not exclusively a retirement complex; people who work in the nearby city of Hot Springs also buy houses here. But since there are no schools (residents voted down a school tax to avoid having schools), families with younger children rarely purchase property. Thus the average age of residents is close to 60 years. Those choosing retirement here tend to come from large midwestern cities in Illinois, Missouri and Kansas.

Recreation and Culture. As part of the National Park System, Hot Springs is famous for its breathtaking mountain scenery. The city is bordered by Lake Hamilton and Lake Catherine, with more than 9,000 acres of land and 330 miles of shoreline. Lake Ouachita is only 30 minutes from downtown Hot Springs. Boating, fishing and waterskiing are enjoyed on all nearby lakes. Camping, fishing and hunting are available within minutes of town.

If it's golf you want, you've come to the right place. Hot Springs has two private country clubs with 63 holes of golf, and nearby planned communities offer five private golf courses, along with two public, daily-fee golf courses. Lake DeGray State Park also features a year-round 18-hole golf course. Hot Springs' city parks have 13 tennis courts, five of which are lighted for evening play. The country clubs also have tennis facilities.

The historic district has become the center for the development of the arts, with 14 fine art galleries displaying the work of local and national artists. The first Thursday and Friday of every month features a "Gallery Walk," when people from all over come to view the latest exhibits. Annual festivals include the Arkansas Celebration of the Arts, Hot Springs Documentary Film Festival, the Hot Springs Jazz Festival and Hot Springs Music Festival.

Real Estate: Residential neighborhoods fall into two distinct categories: Victorian and modern. The older sections have ample yards and large homes—often with beautiful landscaping and large shade trees. These are pleasant neighborhoods, full of nostalgia, peace and quiet. Farther from the town center, neighborhoods are more modern, with conventional bungalows, duplexes and low-profile apartment buildings. There are several new, high-quality senior citizens developments and some surprisingly upscale mobile home parks. Several golf course communities are set in scenic locations away from town, with upscale housing, right on the greens or tucked away among the trees. One features 24-hour security, an 18-hole PGA golf course, an Olympic size swimming pool, and everything you'd expect to find in a similar Florida development.

The local newspaper lists typical prices for homes in nice neighborhoods (two- and three-bedrooms) for $70,000 and up. In less fancy neighborhoods, homes can be found for less than $60,000. Some lakefront properties are being offered for as low as $100,000.

There appear to be more apartments than usual for a town of Hot Springs' size, probably because of the seasonal tourist invasions which encourage temporary housing. Since the demise of gambling and the subsequent tourism decline, apartment owners have been forced to become competitive with rents.

Property in Hot Springs Village is not inexpensive, at least not for Arkansas, but it is certainly first class and returns full value for the money. The average new home constructed in the village is approximately 1,800 square feet and costs $130,000. Prices of existing homes range from $70,000 to $400,000. Town homes in the village range in price from $60,000 to $150,000.

Medical Care. From pre-historic times, visitors came to Hot Springs for the legendary curing power of the water. In this sense, Hot Springs has a long history of medical care, and it continues the tradition today. Hot Springs boasts no less than three major hospitals, with a total of 572 beds and the latest high-tech equipment. There are 128 practicing physicians, as well as 28 clinics and seven nursing homes in the vicinity. The major medical facilities are: Levi Hospital, National Park Medical Center and St. Joseph's Regional Health Care Center.

When Grandkids Visit: Now mind you, I've never been to it, but I see a very interesting listing for an alligator farm and petting zoo. Maybe your grandkids would like to pet an alligator. (Better get their parents' permission first. If the grandkids's behavior has been bad lately, maybe they'll consent.) An alternative would be the Hot Springs National Park visitor's center. This historic, palace-like building of marble and mosaic will give you a feel for what the bathhouses must have been like during their prime. There are exhibits and, as I recall, an interesting movie about the history of the region.

Addresses and Connections

Chamber of Commerce: 659 Ouachita, Hot Springs, AR 71902. (501) 321-1700.
Newspaper: *Sentinel-Record,* P.O. Box 580, Hot Springs, AR 71902-0580. (501) 623-7711.
Internet: (Hot Springs) http://hotsprings.dina.org
http://www.ci.hot-springs.ar.us./index.html
(Hot Springs Village) http://www.hsnp.com/5seasons
Airport: Hot Springs Airport.
Bus/Train: City bus (Hot Springs); Greyhound.

Hot Springs/Hot Springs Village

	Jan.	April	July	Oct.	Rain	Snow
Daily Highs	52	75	93	77	55 in.	3 in.
Daily Lows	31	52	71	53		

Fayetteville

Up in the northwest corner of Arkansas' Ozark Mountains, two great candidates for senior relocation await your consideration. On either side of 28,000-acre Beaver Lake, Eureka Springs and Fayetteville have both received favorable publicity as great places for relocation. Between them is the small city of Rogers, and to the north of Fayetteville is one of the earliest planned developments in Arkansas, Bella Vista.

Fayetteville is the largest, a city of about 50,000 people plus almost 15,000 students at the University of Arkansas. It is located in Washington County, whose population exceeds 120,000, one of the fastest-growing sections of the state. This part of Arkansas also shares in some of the most beautiful Ozark scenery in the entire region. It starts just a few miles from downtown Fayetteville.

One way you can tell you're in a college town: look for a collection of off-beat gourmet restaurants. Fayetteville has 'em all. Besides a tempting selection of Japanese, Mexican and barbecue restaurants, downtown Fayetteville offers esoteric eating establishments with names designed to grab your attention, such as: Gumbo Joe's Cajun Grill, Penguin Ed's, Armadillo Grill and Schlegel's Bagels. I can't imagine a restaurant named "Penguin Ed's" in a farm town in flatland Arkansas. The chef would be arrested and handcuffed by the local sheriff before the first penguin-on-rye sandwich ever left the grill. (Armadillo, they might accept—if served with red-eye gravy and biscuits.) When Bill Clinton was first running for Congress back in 1974, he and his campaign committee used to meet at a popular place in Fayetteville called the D-Lux Café. (Now doesn't D-Lux Café sound more like down-home Arkansas?)

The University of Arkansas is Fayetteville's heart and soul. Without intentionally doing so, the school, its students and professors add excitement and vigor to the city. To fully savor the magnetism of the student-resident community you must visit Dickson Street, near the campus. This colorful, entertaining street is filled with bistros, restaurants and art galleries. It's a place to dance the night away to your favorite music. (Doesn't sound like Arkansas, does it?) Dickson street is also home to the splendid Walton Arts Center.

Fayetteville has a history of educational values. The original university building, Old Main, is the oldest existing educational building in the state, and the campus' pride and joy. It was completed in 1875 and is now home to the Fulbright College of Arts and Sciences. The university is ranked as one of the top schools in the country in the number of chief executives produced for major U.S. companies. (And Bill Clinton taught law at the university before he entered politics.) The nearby town of Rogers is the home of Northwest Arkansas Community College, with 2,600 students to add to the educational scene.

Fayetteville's downtown is a delightful combination of a healthy business sector combined with a well-preserved historic district, which local residents refer to as "the Square." Commercial and residential buildings have been lovingly restored to their 19th-century glory. They contrast nicely with contemporary architecture containing shops and offices. Local farmers and craftspeople are encouraged to bring their wares to the laid-back farmers' market on the square, three times every week. A tourist trolley provides free transportation for shoppers and visitors to move around Fayetteville's downtown on their leisurely errands.

Bella Vista. About 20 miles north of Fayetteville is the planned community of Bella Vista. One of the earlier experiments in Ozark developments, Bella Vista started 30 years ago and now has over 11,000 year-round residents and thousands of seasonal residents. It was created by the same developers as Hot Springs Village, employing the same concepts, although it's older. Originally intended as a retirement and vacation resort, it became popular with commuters to Fayetteville who didn't mind the drive over the new four-lane highway. When you buy into Bella Vista, you automatically belong to four country clubs and recreational complexes. Residents have access to tennis courts, swimming pools, eight lakes and seven golf courses.

Recreation and Culture: The surrounding mountain ranges encourage hiking, camping, spelunking (caving) and outdoor recreational activities for all ages. Several major state and national park areas, including the famous Ozark Highlands Trail, are nearby. Regional lakes and rivers are justifiably famous for bass and trout yields. Golf and tennis are readily available, with five public courses and two private golf clubs.

The University Theater and North Arkansas Symphony regularly present drama and concerts. The Walton Arts Center near downtown Fayetteville provides a top-drawer venue for the performing arts and is the center of a rebirth of the Dickson Street area.

Fayetteville has a potpourri of activities during every month of the year. The season festivals, SpringFest and AutumnFest, bring large crowds to Fayetteville. One of the world's largest arts and craft events, the War Eagle Fair, is just a short drive away.

Real Estate: Homes around the Fayetteville historic district are very much in demand, with potential buyers asking to have their names placed on a waiting list. Most homes have been completely renovated, and are large, from 2,500 to 4,000 square feet. Downtown historic homes sell for as much as $300,000. By way of contrast, a few blocks away is Wilson Park, a safe, homey neighborhood with houses built in the 1950s and '60s, with much lower price tags—starting in the $75,000 range. Some acceptable neighborhoods have homes selling for as little as $50,000, and other, more elaborate developments have building lots that cost more than that. In short, the range of real estate is wide here, from Arkansas-inexpensive to more than you'd like to pay.

A dozen attractive areas around town, farther away from the city center, offer affordable housing in secure-feeling neighborhoods. Seven upscale developments are in place. One of these is a golf course subdivision, with residents' back yards touching the greens. There's at least one "secured neighborhood" with a security gate and homes starting at $175,000. If you can't find something suitable in Fayetteville, you can try Rogers, Beaver Lake, or half a dozen small towns within a 20-minute drive of Fayetteville's Square.

In Bella Vista, the older homes and townhomes near the center of town are about 1,200 square feet and sell for as little as $50,000. Homes on the lakes or golf courses start in the low $100,000 range and go on up to $500,000.

Medical Care: Washington Regional Medical Center is a not-for-profit, acute medical hospital as well as a teaching hospital. Its 294-bed medical center offers a complete range of services, including cancer care, cardiac care and cardiac surgery, kidney dialysis and much more. Specialties include 24-hour emergency/trauma, hospice care, radiology, renal dialysis and general surgery. Fayetteville City Hospital is the area's main geriatric center and source for home health care, and the Veterans' Affairs Medical Center offers clinics in numerous specialties.

Bates Medical Center, in Bentonville, takes care of immediate health needs of Bella Vista. It is a 63-bed acute-care facility with an intensive care and coronary unit, as well as other services.

When Grandkids Visit: The Arkansas Air Museum is one of many choices to entertain the little ones. The aircraft here aren't merely exhibits, they actually fly. From world-famous racing planes of the 1920s and 30s to an early airliner, the planes are maintained in flying condition. There's a collection of military and commercial aircraft, including open cockpit biplanes and closed cabin mono-planes that carried pioneering airmen and women into the skies of the nation over an 80-year time span. There's a hands-on flight simulator and a walk-in workshop where you can watch restoration in progress.

Addresses and Connections

Chamber of Commerce: P.O. Box 4216, Fayetteville, AR, 72702-4216. (501) 521-1710
Internet: http://cavern.uark.edu/depts/wathinfo/fayette.html
http://www.uark.edu/ALADDIN/fffinfo/profile1.html
Newspapers: *Northwest Arkansas Times,* 212 North East Ave., Fayetteville, AR 72701. (501) 442-6242.
The Morning News, 203 N. College, Fayetteville, AR 72701. (501) 444-6397.
Airport: Drake Field, commuter connections. A new regional airport for northwest Arkansas under construction.
Bus/Train: Greyhound; local bus transportation.

Fayetteville/Eureka Springs

	Jan.	April	July	Oct.	Rain	Snow
Daily Highs	48	73	93	75	39.9 in.	6.8 in.
Daily Lows	26	49	70	49		

Eureka Springs

This delightful town sits in a primeval Ozark setting just 45 miles from Fayetteville and 35 miles from the town of Rogers. Eureka Springs is truly a small town, with fewer than 2,000 residents, yet its downtown looks like it belongs to a small city of the 1890s. It's a place where time seems to stand still—if you want it to. The word Eureka means "I have found it," and this is how many visitors felt when they decided to convert their vacation visits into permanent retirement. For the past 110 years, a continual stream of outsiders has been re-discovering Eureka Springs. They first come as tourists; many return to retire.

Tourists and retirees discovered Eureka Springs in the late 19th century. The attraction was the "magic" healing quality of the spring waters that flow from the canyon's grottoes. Perhaps the mineral water helped, but getting away from the crowds and squalor of the city, breathing the pure mountain air and seeing the lovely Ozark surroundings probably had more than a little to do with the miracle cures.

Newcomers began arriving in large numbers in the 1870s, when the Frisco Railroad ran a line into town to carry visitors from Chicago, St. Louis and Kansas City. Several large and luxurious hotels were built to accommodate the crowds. Wealthy families from the big cities built ambitious Victorian mansions that duplicated their residences in their home cities. Before long, the town's winding streets were lined with homes, hotels and commercial buildings, displaying fancy gingerbread styles of that era.

Then, during the First World War, folks stopped coming to Eureka Springs. The town's bonanza was put on hold; its popularity declined as residents moved away or died. Lovely homes were boarded up and forgotten as absentee owners lost interest in the town. The Great Depression was the final blow; Eureka Springs almost became a ghost town. At the time, townsfolk must have viewed this abandonment as extreme misfortune, but today's residents see it as a stroke of luck. This temporary loss of popularity created a virtual time capsule of Victorian architecture. Otherwise, Eureka Springs would have suffered from modernization, with the old buildings gradually replaced with modern structures.

Your first glimpse of the Eureka Springs is a guaranteed surprise. Solid limestone and brick buildings, wrought-iron fancy work and gracefully styled mansions with winding carriageways make the town a fascinating window into yesterday. The entire town was placed on the National Register of Historic Places in the early 1970s. Boutiques, restaurants, art galleries and other businesses occupy the downtown's street-level stores with second- and third-floor apartments for those who live downtown. Spring Street, which encircles the town in a steep embrace, looks much the same as it did at the turn of the century—trolleys and all. It's no wonder the community has traditionally drawn talented artists and their patrons to Eureka Springs.

A walk along Eureka Springs' narrow, curving streets will lead you up steep hills and down even steeper ones. The idea of walking around town isn't necessarily to get somewhere in particular, but rather an opportunity for serendipitous discovery. Regal Victorian buildings line the twisting streets, some looking down on the business district near the canyon floor, others viewing the Ozark forested hills.

This incredible collection of Victorians rivals and perhaps surpasses the finest San Francisco has to offer. Some homes have fluted columns rising three stories in front of dignified brick facades and wrought-iron balconies—homes that look as if they belong on a *Gone with the Wind* movie set. It's difficult to describe Eureka Springs without slipping into clichés because the entire town *is* a cliché, a magic peek at yesterday.

The town and environs offer all the amenities many retirees seek: good medical facilities, a quaint, artistic cultural atmosphere, friendly neighbors, recreational opportunities and inexpensive real estate. Eureka Springs has become both a retirement mecca and an artist colony—a great place to live.

Holiday Island. A five-mile drive from Eureka Springs takes you to an ambitious golf/country-club resort known as Holiday Island. Located on Table Rock Lake, the resort is set on 4,300 acres of natural beauty. The lake is narrow at this point, following the twists and turns of an old river bed, thus creating a large number of lakefront lots. Two golf courses (one 18-hole and one nine-hole layout), a number of tennis courts, two swimming pools and most of the facilities expected of a resort community are in place. There's little question about the lake's popularity as a place for relocation; 90 percent of the residents are from other states, mostly from Illinois, Missouri and Texas.

Beaver Lake. About eight miles from Eureka Springs, Beaver Lake used to be a no-nonsense place for cabins and lakeside homes, without the fancy facilities of a resort or high resort prices. Mobile homes are permitted in some lakeside areas, although they are fewer in number than conventional homes. However, today high-quality homes are popping up all over. There's at least one gated community of upper-echelon places, with lots selling for $65,000 and up. The inexpensive places are gradually being replaced by higher-quality housing. The lake offers 28,000 acres of fishing, skiing, sailing and swimming. Residents claim they catch black bass, white bass, stripers, catfish, pan fish, trout—apparently everything but sailfish and tuna.

Recreation and Culture: The nearest public golf course to Eureka Springs is in Berryville, a 10-mile drive down the road. But nearby Holiday Island has excellent golf courses, so enthusiastic

golfers purchase inexpensive lots and pay the $283 annual assess-
ment for unlimited use of the courses. Owners of lots also have the
right to stay in the development's campground and use all the
facilities. Most non-residents use their membership just for the golf
courses.

Lake fishing tops the outdoor recreation menu; it's a year-round
hobby here. Table Rock Lake, six miles north of Eureka Springs, has
52,000 acres of fishing fun. Beaver Lake is another favorite place for
angling, swimming and boating. For river fishing, the White River is
seven miles from town, with trout and walleye fishing. Canoeing is
popular here, with rentals available.

During the entire month of May, Eureka Springs hosts a festival
celebrating the "Art of the Ozarks." Every day, especially on week-
ends, there is something "arty" going on. A favorite: gallery walks at
14 of Eureka Springs' fine arts galleries, where you can hobnob with
local artists and fine craftspeople. You visit workshops where artists
are working, perhaps learn their techniques first-hand, take a peek
at their studios and their up-and-coming work. Visitors and residents
also enjoy walking tours, stopping in at historic inns and lodgings
for tea and crumpets as they visit with local artists and musicians.
Violin music is enjoyed in the park in the afternoon and a full
orchestra in the evening. There's a poetry walk, a kite exhibit, dance,
theater, and more. And nearly all of these events are free.

Real Estate: An interesting aspect of Eureka Springs is that you
often can buy a historic Victorian home for about what you'd pay
for an ordinary tract home in most parts of the country, or even less.
Recent offerings were a Victorian cottage for $59,000 and a large
Victorian with a separate apartment on the second floor for
$108,000. Several retired couples have converted their spacious old
mansions into delightful bed-and-breakfasts.

In the old days, not all Victorian homes were mansions. Ordinary folks lived in modest-sized houses just as they do today. These
places are exceptional bargains, and conventional housing on the
town's outskirts are similarly priced well below the national average.

At nearby Holiday Island, houses and condos are reasonably
priced, considering the amenities of the development. Recently a
three-bedroom, two-bath place on a big lot was offered for $66,000
(advertised by a private party; it would cost more through the sales

office). Condos sell in the $60,000 range, and large homes, on or near the golf courses, have asking prices at $100,000 and more. Lot prices begin at $3,000 (as low as $1,500 from private sellers) and can go as high as $50,000.

Medical Care: Eureka Springs Hospital is a small, acute-care and surgical facility, capable of taking care of the needs of Eureka Springs and nearby Holiday Island. The facility has several good doctors on staff. A larger hospital, Berryville Carroll Regional, is located ten miles to the east in Berryville.

When Grandkids Visit: Take a ride on the Eureka Springs and North Arkansas Railway. You can catch the train at the town's original train depot on Main Street. The ride takes 45 minutes aboard a genuine steam train. One of the highlights is an animal conservatory where the kids can view lions, tigers, bears and other animals. There's also a petting zoo, but don't let 'em pet the lions and tigers. Better not bother the bears either.

Addresses and Connections

Chamber of Commerce: 81 Kings Highway, Eureka Springs, AR 72632. (501) 253-8737.
Internet: http://www.pimps.com/eureka.html
Newspaper: *Eureka Springs Chronicle,* Hwy 23 S., Eureka Springs, AR 72632. (501) 253-9719.
Airport: Fayetteville (46 miles).
Bus/Train: Greyhound.

Eureka Springs\Holiday Island

	Jan.	April	July	Oct.	Rain	Snow
Daily Highs	45	69	89	16	44 in.	6 in.
Daily Lows	23	46	68	47		

Greers Ferry Lake

A few years ago in north-central Arkansas, where the Ozarks begin, retirees from St. Louis, Kansas City and Chicago "discovered" a new retirement location. It's called Greers Ferry Lake—about 60 miles north of Little Rock. Retirees liked the area because of lake recreation, exceptionally low housing costs and because it's close enough to their grandchildren and old friends that they can go home for a visit whenever they please.

Greers Ferry Lake has become something of a legend in Arkansas retirement success stories. This is one of the first places where economists tracked the economic benefits of bringing well-heeled retirees into the locality. The region changed from a dormant, passive group of crossroad communities into a dynamic and progressive area. The lake made it possible, but the newcomers made it happen.

Three towns share in this success story—Heber Springs, Greers Ferry and Fairfield Bay. All three communities are located on or near the 40,000-acre man-made reservoir, one of a series created by the Army Corps of Engineers. Completed just over thirty years ago, the lake has consistently ranked among the top 20 most popular Army Corps of Engineers lakes in the nation. (President Kennedy's last official act was to dedicate Greers Ferry Dam, on his way to Dallas in November 1962.) Visitors who flock to the Greers Ferry and the Little Red River areas each year recognize the lake as one of the cleanest and most beautiful lake areas in the region.

The lake, filled with bass, stripers, walleye, catfish and lunker-sized trout, catches the attention of tourists and fishermen as well as folks considering an Ozark retirement. Its 300 miles of wooded shoreline provide a scenic background for recreation as well as wooded lots for retirement homes. Inexpensive property, low taxes, a four-season climate and an almost nonexistent crime rate add to the attraction of retirement here.

With the influx of retirees, Heber Springs—the largest of the communities—zoomed from a population of 2,500 to well over 6,000. The vast majority of newcomers were retired couples. Their pension money and savings pumped up bank deposits more than 20-fold and the extra purchasing power boosted retail sales, created jobs and generated tax money for local improvements. Townspeople readily admit that this new prosperity is largely due to their new neighbors who put pension dollars, stock dividends and Social Security money to work for the community good.

Home building activity continues today, with lovely new neighborhoods materializing in low-density clusters, hidden in wooded, lakeshore settings. Many small neighborhoods are located *outside* town limits, nestled in forested glades, often invisible from roads and highways. Typically, a development consists of a grouping of from 10 to 50 homes, sometimes with lake views. This arrangement cuts the expense of utility installation as well as construction costs. There could be as many as 200 of these mini-neighborhoods scattered throughout the forest. Although building lots are often half an acre or more, the setting creates a sense of closeness and neighborhood among the homeowners. "We never worry about leaving our home vacant during the winter," remarked one resident, "because our friends watch the place for us."

In the newer developments (and most are new) quality is excellent; most homes are brick and tastefully placed on wooded lots. Low labor costs make possible high construction standards at lower selling prices. Properties with lake views are naturally priced higher, but not remarkably so. This is because a "lake view" home is never a "lakefront" home. The Army Corps of Engineers prohibits ownership of land directly on the shore beyond a determined high-water line. This means no boat docks or direct access, and no immediate advantage to being next to the water. Lakeside homes enjoy the view, but so do places set farther back. Unlimited water access is provided by public docks, ramps and marinas.

Sky Point Estates is a unique development that appeals to those who fly small planes. Instead of having a home next to a golf fairway or green, people here build their homes next to an air strip. In addition to a two-car garage, they'll build a small hangar to house their airplane. When they're ready to go somewhere, they roll the plane from the hangar, taxi onto the runway and say goodbye.

Heber Springs is not far from Little Rock, an hour's drive away. With a metropolitan area of nearly 250,000, Little Rock provides health services that smaller towns cannot. Its libraries, museums and other cultural attractions fill a void for those who are used to larger cities. Little Rock is also the closest place to stock up on wine, beer and scotch to serve your guests, for like most smaller Arkansas towns, we're talking dry county.

Greers Ferry: The small community of Greers Ferry sits invitingly on the other side of the lake, on a peninsula, almost surrounded by water. This is truly a small town with fewer than 800 residents. But folks point out that this figure is a bit misleading. A large number of people choose to relocate outside Greers Ferry's town limits.

The community provides all the basic services needed for day-to-day living, yet it's so small and uncongested that it doesn't require traffic lights. Greers Ferry has grocery stores, craft shops, and three branch banks. As a consideration for retirees' health care, the community has two full-time doctors and provides free ambulance service to Heber Springs' Cleburne Hospital.

People who've moved here from out of state say it's very easy to become acquainted and to make friends. This is understandable, considering how many residents themselves come from other areas of the country. Heber Springs has a Newcomers' Club to help you get acquainted.

Fairfield Bay: *Better Homes and Gardens* magazine once nominated Fairfield Bay as one of America's 50 Best Family Resorts—and with good reason. The pristine setting contains some of the most beautiful scenery in the Ozark foothills on the resort's 14,000 acres. The crown jewel of the development is the panoramic view of magnificent Greers Ferry Lake.

Fairfield Bay, at the far end of the lake, is for those who prefer a more upscale setting, where they can own a home near or next to one of the development's golf courses. This resort/retirement community features round-the-clock security and all the advantages of an exclusive, gated complex. The Bay's own 50,000-square-foot shopping center has more than 30 retail stores, including a full supermarket, pharmacy, banks, medical clinic, library, food and gifts. There's even a bowling alley.

Fairfield Bay offers two championship golf courses, tennis courts, lake and river activities, a convention center, shopping and businesses. The development is one of several built around the country, always with the name "Fairfield" connected with it. The resorts are always well planned and attractive. (A sister development, Fairfield Glade, near Crossville, Tennessee, is described in this book under the section on Tennessee.)

Recreation and Culture: Fishing, of course, is the most popular outdoor recreation here. This is one of the few places in the country where it's possible to fish for bass, walleye and trout in the same day. One great thing about fishing in Arkansas is the season never closes. Largemouth bass, in the 15-pound plus range, have been taken from Greers Ferry Lake along with the state-record walleye that weighed in at over 22 pounds (just under the world record). Hybrid stripers, spotted bass, and smallmouth are also targets of sportsmen. Summer night fishing is a legal as well as popular way to spend an evening.

The Little Red River, known as a smallmouth bass stream before Greers Ferry was built, has become a nationally famous trout stream because of the cold water flowing from under the dam, from the lake bottom. Most rainbow trout catches are in the one to four pound range. However, five- to 12-pounders are not uncommon. In fact, the Little Red River yielded the world-record German brown trout; it weighed over 40 pounds!

In and near Heber Springs, four golf courses are open for public play, even though two are at membership country clubs. These are Lost Creek Golf Club, Red Apple Inn at Eden Isle, Riverland and Thunderbird Country Club. Fairfield Bay has two public golf courses, Mountain Ranch and Indian Hills.

At Fairfield Bay Tennis Center you'll find a lighted ten-court complex. Pro shops and lessons are available. For more family fun there are three outdoor pools, miniature golf, volleyball, shuffle-board and horse shoes—plus picnic areas with grills.

The Cleburne County Arts Council, located in Heber Springs, sponsors plays, art shows and musical entertainment on a regular basis. A series of popular festivals are staged in Heber Springs, including the Ozark Frontier Trail Festival and Craft Show. One of the year's most anticipated events is the "Great Cardboard Boat Race." Contestants race boats constructed solely of cardboard; the winners are the last ones to sink.

Any of the Greers Ferry Lake communities are within an hour's drive of Hot Springs, with many popular cultural activities. There you'll enjoy presentations by the Arkansas Repertory Theater, the Arkansas Arts Center and the Arkansas Symphony.

Real Estate: Housing prices here have risen along with the improving economy, but prices and quality are remarkably better than where most retirees come from. A typical remark by new residents is, "Our new home is twice the size as the one we sold back home, and it cost half the money." Property taxes come as a pleasant shock when new residents receive tax bills that are just a fraction of what they paid back home. This isn't to say there aren't some extravagant and lavish homes to be found here, but the views are worth it.

Local real estate professionals assure us that a plentiful supply of housing is available for all income groups. One third of the homes sold recently went for $60,000 or less. Another third sold for $100,000 or more. Moderately priced homes, with 1,600 to 1,800 square feet, average $80,000; executive homes with 2,500 square feet and more start at $125,000. New home construction is booming, and there are several restricted subdivisions within a five-mile area with lots for building high-quality homes.

Medical Care: The Cleburne Memorial Hospital is a 49-bed facility with modern surgical services. The hospital provides one-day outpatient surgery, and has a four-bed coronary unit. The emergency room services are available on a 24-hour basis. The hospital has 37 doctors on staff. Recent improvements include a $53,000 expansion for the nuclear medicine facility and an emergency room waiting area.

When Grandkids Visit: Take them to Blanchard Springs Caverns, where you'll see one of the most spectacular and carefully developed caves anywhere. This is a "living" cave where glistening crystalline formations hang from the ceiling to meet their counterparts rising from the floor. Before entering you are treated to a movie, "The Amazing World Below," which will set your mood for exploring. You can stroll through large, beautifully lighted rooms with paved trails for comfortable walking.

Addresses and Connections

Chamber of Commerce: (Heber Springs) 1001 W. Main, Heber Springs, AR 72543. (501) 362-2444.
(Fairfield Bay) P.O. Box 1159, Fairfield Bay, AR 72088. (501) 884-3324.
(Greers Ferry) P.O. Box 354, Greers Ferry, AR 72067-0354. (501) 825-7188
Newspapers: *The Sun-Times,* 107 North 4th St., Heber Springs, AR 72543. (501) 362-2425
Cleburne Herald Tribune, 510 W. Main, #2, Heber Springs, AR 72543. (501) 362-4040.
Internet: http://www.btnet.com/hscham.htm

Airport: Little Rock (75 minutes).
Bus/Train: Greyhound, in Searcy (30 minutes).

Heber Springs/Greers Ferry Lake

	Jan.	April	July	Oct.	Rain	Snow
Daily Highs	50	72	92	73	49 in.	4 in.
Daily Lows	29	49	69	50		

Mountain Home and Bull Shoals

On the northern border of Arkansas, where the state touches Missouri, one of Arkansas' Ozark treasures has been luring both tourists and retirees for years. Two enormous man-made lakes, with serpentine fingers, crooks and bends, spread through the region. One of them, Bull Shoals, eventually reaches up into Missouri and connects with the Table Rock Lake system. Bull Shoals Lake is the largest, stretching and twisting for 100 miles. Norfork Lake is the twin to Bull Shoals. Together they create more than a thousand miles of forested Ozark shoreline. Water-skiers, scuba divers, sailboaters, houseboaters and swimmers come from miles around to enjoy the abundant, clear water.

Three towns in the lake region consistently receive praise from travel and retirement writers. Positioned midway between the two lakes, Mountain Home is the largest, with a population of 10,000. The smaller communities of Bull Shoals and Lakeview have a total of 4,000 residents and sit right on the shores of Bull Shoals Lake.

The transition from vacation to retirement occurs quite naturally in the Mountain Home-Bull Shoals area. Families come to vacation every year; then gradually their vacation retreats change into retirement homes. Because new residents come from all imaginable parts of the country, the Bull Shoals-Norfork Lake complex has become a miniature melting pot. We were surprised at how many people we met who had relocated here from traditional retirement states like California and Florida. They came here to take advantage of an exceptionally low crime rate, inexpensive living and gorgeous Ozark living. More than a third of the area's residents are over 60 years old.

According to legend, Mountain Home received its name back before the Civil War. Plantation owners from southern Arkansas and

Tennessee would come here to escape the lowland humidity and avoid the yellow-fever-carrying mosquitoes. Even then, the region was considered a summer resort. The aristocrats brought their favorite slaves, who were always delighted to escape the drudgery of cotton cultivation and harsh plantation life. The slaves referred to this favorite place as our "mountain home."

Mountain Home has a true downtown district that includes a picture-book, old-fashioned town square. But, as usual, many shopping and consumer businesses have moved to the highway on the edge of town. Yet downtown Mountain Home manages to retain a sense of low-keyed success, with thriving shops, offices and restaurants. Mountain Home services the surrounding region of 30,000 people, and its businesses and stores are able to provide all the consumer goods and services anyone could reasonably ask for. If they don't have it in Mountain Home, it could be illegal.

Which brings up another subject: In many Arkansas communities—most, in fact—the sale of beer, wine and liquor is illegal. People from nearby counties have to travel to Mountain Home to stock their liquor cabinets and wine cellars. Curiously, liquor stores are legal in Mountain Home, but restaurants are prohibited from selling alcoholic beverages by the drink; only private clubs may do so.

According to couples who've relocated in the Mountain Home-Bull Shoals area, the major attractions are mild winters and low living costs. One couple from just north of Chicago said, "We cut our property taxes by $2,000 a year by coming here, and we cut our heating bills by more than half. The money we save makes the difference between struggling to stay within our budget and having money to spend for luxuries."

Bull Shoals. Surrounded on three sides by Bull Shoals Lake, the towns of Bull Shoals and Lakeview are quiet and residential. The communities are about 15 miles from Mountain Home, over a pleasant highway that winds and twists through picturesque Ozark woods.

Home buyers have their choice of places snuggled among pines and oak trees or lake-view properties. The lake's deep blue waters are legendary among bass fishermen. The rivers and streams feeding the lake are considered premier for rainbow trout fishing. This lakeside community presents a peaceful, quiet contrast to Mountain Home's commercial, medical and cultural largess.

The shores of both lakes are off-limit to construction and boat docks; the water's edge comes under the jurisdiction of the Army Corps of Engineers. These restrictions protect the lake's pristine quality and keep it from being cluttered with sagging docks and scruffy-looking fish shacks. The shoreline always looks clean and natural. The public, however, has free access to both lakes and rivers for fishing, boating and swimming. Public marinas will house your boat for less than $400 a year, so you don't have to keep pulling your boat out of the water after every fishing trip.

Recreation and Culture: Nineteen parks around the lake were developed through cooperative efforts of local, state and federal agencies for public use and enjoyment. They have camping and picnic facilities with tables and grills, but the focus is on fishing, particularly bass fishing. Four state-record bass catches have come from these waters. The record striper weighed in at 53 pounds and a white bass at 51 pounds.

The world famous White and North Fork Rivers, which issue respectively from Bull Shoals and Norfork Dams, draw anglers from around the world in search of trophy rainbow and brown trout. You'll find resorts, outfitters and plenty of guides to help you find the best fishing spots. And best of all, fishing is a year-round activity.

Bull Shoals has an 18-hole golf course, situated on the scenic White River and open all year. The fairways stretch up the mountain's slope, providing great exercise for the golf enthusiast and probably some frustration, as well. Mountain Home also has an 18-hole golf course, as well as driving ranges, public tennis courts and fitness trails.

Among other interests, virtually every water sport is available on Bull Shoals Lake, including swimming, boating, waterskiing, parasailing, windsurfing, sailing, scuba diving, snorkeling and fishing.

Arkansas State University at Mountain Home is a community college at present but is in the process of becoming a four-year school. The downtown college campus encourages seniors to attend tuition-free. Several courses are specially tailored for mature adults.

Both the school and Mountain Home's Committee on Performing Arts present drama and musical performances throughout the year.

Real Estate: The range of housing is broad enough to fit any budget. Your choices can be lakeside or riverside, on mountain slopes or small farms, or in town. According to local real estate people, the average selling price of a house in Mountain Home is $81,000. But acceptable three-bedroom places can be found starting at $55,000. A three-bedroom two-bath mobile home on two acres was recently offered at $25,000—including a 20-foot by 22-foot garage and a covered, screened deck. The most expensive listing we looked at was $185,000, but that was for a good-sized brick home on 74 acres.

A small home in Bull Shoals, on a city lot, might sell for less than $60,000, with taxes around $450 per year. Higher quality homes, with 2,000 square feet, run around $110,000, with taxes around $900. Building costs range between $45 to $55 per square foot.

Recently a four-acre mini-ranch was advertised as having: lush green pasture with a corral for horses, a three-bedroom home, a horse barn and outbuildings for $85,500. We were told this was a reasonable price. (That would be a reasonable price for a garage in some areas of the country.)

Medical Care: Mountain Home's Baxter County Regional Hospital functions as a medical center for the residents of Bull Shoals and surrounding communities, even as far as Missouri. Hospital services include a 24-hour emergency department, physical therapy, radiation and outpatient surgery. A paramedic station is connected with the hospital, proud of their ambulance response time of five minutes.

When Grandkids Visit: An Ozark float trip might be in order. The cold waters of the White River below Bull Shoals Dam offer some of the best trout fishing in the Ozarks. One of the best ways to fish this river is from a comfortable deck chair as your drift boat glides leisurely down stream. The 20-foot drift boats are equipped with personal fishing guides, born and raised on the river, who know every secret hiding place of the rainbow, brown and cutthroat trout. The record here is 33 pounds, but most are pan-sized. The guide shows the grandkids how to hook and land trout; if they don't catch any fish, it won't be your fault, and they'll have fun anyway.

Addresses and Connections

Chamber of Commerce: (Mountain Home) 1023 Hwy. 62, Mountain Home, AK 72653. (501) 425-5111.

(Bull Shoals) P.O. Box 354, Bull Shoals, AK 72619. (501) 445-4443, (800) 447-1290.

Newspapers: *Baxter Bulletin,* 16 W. 6th St., Mountain Home, AR 72653-3508. (501) 425-3134.

Daily News, Hwy 62E, Mountain Home, AR 72653. (501) 425-6301.

Internet: http://www.mtnhome.net

Airport: Baxter County Airport, between Mountain Home and Bull Shoals (commuter flights).

Bus/Train: The Area Agency on Aging operates a local bus service. Greyhound in Mountain Home.

Mountain Home/Bull Shoals

	Jan.	April	July	Oct.	Rain	Snow
Daily Highs	45	69	91	73	54 in.	7 in.
Daily Lows	29	48	68	49		

ARKANSAS TAXES

Arkansas Department of Revenue

P.O. Box 3628, Revenue Office, 7th and Wolf, Little Rock, AR 72203

Ph. (501) 682-7250

Arkansas' tax bills rank 19th among the least expensive in the nation

Income Tax

First $2,999	1.0%	Next $6,000	4.5%
Next $3,000	2.5%	Next $10,000	6.0%
Next $3,000	3.5%	$25,000 or over	7.0%

General exemptions: $20 tax credit, single $40 tax credit, married; $20 tax credit, dependents.

Additional for disabled : $20 tax credit, blind or deaf.

Additional for elderly: $20 tax credit, 65 or over $6,000

Private Pension Exclusion: $6,000.

Social Security/Railroad Retirement Benefits: Full exclusion.

Standard Deduction: 10% of gross income to maximum of $1,000.

Medical and Dental Expense Deduction: Federal amount.

Federal Income Tax Deduction: None.

Other: Cash rebate for property taxes on homestead, depending on income level, for people over 62.

Sales Taxes

State 4.5%: County 0.0% - 2.0%: City 0.0% - 2.0%

Combined Rate in Selected Towns: **Little Rock:** 5.5%; **Fort Smith:** 6.5%; **Pine Bluff:** 5.5%

General Coverage: Food is taxed, prescription drugs are exempt

Property Taxes

Average assessment on a $80,000 home about $730 a year.

State and local taxes are imposed on real and personal property, including intangibles. In relation to personal income, property tax collections are in the lowest third among the 50 states.

Income ceiling: $15,000 (WWI veterans and their widows exclude Social Security and retirement income)

Maximum benefit: $250 for incomes below $7,000

Homestead Credit: Disabled veterans, surviving spouses not remarried, and minor dependent children: Full exemption from state property not taxes up to 80 rural acres and 1/4 acre in city.

Estate/Inheritance Taxes

Arkansas does not impose an estate tax nor an inheritance tax. It imposes only a pick-up tax, which is a portion of the federal estate tax and does not increase the total tax owed.

Georgia

Georgia is the largest state east of the Mississippi. It stretches from the golden beaches of the Atlantic and the rivers of South Carolina on the east to Alabama on the west. The north of Georgia is marked by the Blue Ridge Mountains, part of the Appalachian chain, where Georgia adjoins Tennessee and North Carolina. Florida borders Georgia's southern edge. The landscape varies from rich farmlands and wooded hills and mountains to saltwater marshes and barrier islands. The famous Okefenokee Swamp, of Pogo and Albert Alligator fame, is also in Georgia. (If you don't remember Pogo, you are too young to retire.) Georgia has sophisticated metropolitan · clusters, small towns and small cities, and offers many, many retirement choices.

Georgia is widely known as "the Peach State." However, its production of pecans and peanuts and

> **Georgia**
> The Empire State, Peach State
> Admitted to statehood: January 2, 1788
> **State Capital:** Atlanta
> **Population (1995):** 7,200,882; rank, 10th
> **Population Density:** 121.8 per sq. mile: urban 67.7%
> **Geography:** 24th state in size, with 58,977 square miles, including 1,058 square miles of water surface. Highest elevation: Brasstown Bald, 4,784 feet. Lowest elevation: Sea level, Gulf of Mexico. Average elevation: 600 feet.
> **State Flower:** Cherokee rose
> **State Bird:** Brown thrasher
> **State Tree:** Live oak
> **State Song:** Georgia On My Mind

peaches probably bring in more money than peaches. Therefore, Georgia also calls itself "the Pecan State," and sometimes "the Peanut State." And on occasion, it uses its official nickname: "The Empire State of the South." It will probably come as no surprise that the state song is "Georgia On My Mind."

Although agriculture is important in Georgia, industry and trade have become even more significant in today's world. Like other

Habersham
County ● ● Rabin County

● Athens

● Atlanta

Georgia

Savannah ●

● Moultrie
Golden Isles ●

● Thomasville   ● Valdosta

southern states, Georgia has welcomed many northern business enterprises that elected to relocate away from the crowded cities and frigid winters of the northern industrial belt. Georgia's gross domestic production ranks among the nation's top dozen states.

Along with their production facilities and equipment, these relocating companies bring their prized employees to Georgia. Naturally, when retirement rolls around, most of these displaced northerners choose to stay right where they are; they retire in Georgia. They are being joined by retirees from northern, midwestern and eastern states, people who see Georgia as a great place for a new beginning.

The State of Georgia lists 65 communities it feels should qualify as top places to retire. However, in this book we narrow our focus to look at just three regions that are by far the most popular and well-known places for retirement.

The first is the mountainous region of the Appalachian Plateau where the Blue Ridge Mountains, Middle Mountains and the Appalachian Ridge create spectacular views and scenic tranquility. This area always draws nationwide publicity as a quality place for retirement.

The second region we'll look at is Georgia's Colonial Coast, home to some of the nation's most fascinating history, with beautiful beaches, golden marshes, swamps and natural wildlife. For over a century, Georgia's coast has been a popular place for retirement.

The third and last region isn't quite as well known as the first two, but we feel it has great possibilities. It's rightfully called the "Plantation Trace" because it contains the largest number of plantations in the South, some still in operation. The Trace also has traditions of tourism and retirement going back over a hundred years; northerners have been coming here for its warm, year-round climate and outdoor recreational adventures.

The Blue Ridge Mountains

Northern Georgia is blessed with a band of the Appalachian Plateau that reaches into north-central and northeastern Georgia, rising to the state's highest elevations. With a total land mass of 1,400 square miles, this five-county area has only 71,000 residents. Average annual rainfall is a generous 60 inches that sustains the roaring rivers, streams and waterfalls that crisscross its terrain. The famous Appalachian Trail, the goal of all serious hikers, starts in northwest Georgia.

Georgia's primary rivers originate in this northern mountain area. The state's eastern border with South Carolina is marked by the Chattooga River, which eventually becomes the Savannah River and empties into the Atlantic. The Chattahoochee River flows from the edge of the Blue Ridge Mountains to the lower Alabama-Georgia boundary. All the major rivers are navigable below the fall line (an imaginary line dividing uplands and lowlands), and present many recreational opportunities on their way to the sea.

Several counties in this mountainous section of Georgia make up the state's best known retirement region. Rabun, Habersham and Lumpkin counties draw the most attention. Several towns here consistently receive top ratings from retirement writers as great places to relocate.

The region's four-season climate plays host to mild winters with occasional light snowfalls and moderate summers that are tempered by cool mountain breezes. Crisp winter days, sometimes touched with brief snows, give way to an explosion of spring wildflowers. Then, lush, green summers keep streams and lakes cool even in the height of the season. Fall is marked by shows of fiery colors in autumn brilliance. Lifestyles here revolve around the seasons. Because the extremes in weather are so mild, outdoor recreation is possible year-round.

Rabun, Lumpkin and Habersham

This three-county region, up in the northeast corner of Georgia—where North and South Carolina join—has enjoyed much media publicity as one of Georgia's choice relocation areas. It's easy to see why. With lovely mountain scenery everywhere, you're never far from lakes, rivers and three state parks. The Chattooga Wild and Scenic River is nearby, with dramatic waterfalls and spectacular rapids and other natural beauties. Deep canyons like the 1,200-foot chasm of Tallulah Gorge, high peaks like the 3,600-foot Blue Ridge Crest and the spectacular 729-foot plume of Amicalola Falls all combine to create some of the most dramatic and stirring scenery of the Appalachian chain. The famous Appalachian Trail traverses the counties. All this wilderness thrives here, yet is 90 miles or less from Atlanta. South of here, the Blue Ridge Mountains dwindle into foothills and finally change into gentle hill country as you approach the fringes of metropolitan Atlanta.

Successful publicity has taken its toll in northeast Georgia because of the numbers of people who've decided to relocate here. Although not overwhelming, the influx of newcomers to a sparsely settled area naturally pushed up real estate prices. Once at bargain basement levels, it's no longer a buyer's market here, especially in Rabun County. In fact, the campaign to attract retirees was so successful that the Clayton Chamber of Commerce was besieged with so many requests for relocation packets, they had to start charging money to send them out—printing costs, postage and handling got out of hand. But this doesn't mean homes are expensive, just not cheap any longer.

Rabun, Lumpkin and Habersham counties have several delightful towns suitable for retirement. Clayton, in Rabun County, has attracted the most attention, probably because it's one of the more picturesque of Blue Ridge Mountain country. Other locations—such as Clarkesville, Demorest, Helen and Dahlonega—haven't achieved quite the popularity. To date the demand for homes in these locales hasn't quite reached the level in Clayton. The terrain around these latter towns can be more accurately described as Blue Ridge foothills rather than Blue Ridge Mountains, but this doesn't distract from their charm.

None of the dozen locales that make up this region are very large. Clayton, with a population of 1,700, is the largest town in the high-mountain region of Chattahoochee National Forest. Dahlonega is the largest in the three-county area, with a population of 3,100. Many places here are mere villages; Helen, for example, has only 300 year-round residents. For this reason, folks hereabouts don't think in terms of towns; when you ask where they live, they'll reply "Rabun County," or "Habersham County" rather than mention a specific locality. But the commercial districts in these towns are larger than one would expect because they serve customers from the surrounding countryside. For example: Clayton is the commercial center for the Rabun County's 11,648 residents; as such, it provides an unusually good selection of shopping, business and medical services.

An example of a natural getaway near the town of Clayton is an area called Sylvan Falls. Next to the Chattahoochee National Forest, about 600 homes are tucked away in the forest here, some with lookout vantage points from a 2,500-foot-high ridge. Not all homes are blessed with such breathtaking views, but each enjoys its own little natural paradise of rustic beauty. I once visited a couple, retired here from New Orleans, who live on the apex of the ridge. As we gazed out over the view, Marjorie said: "We feel like we're on the edge of Heaven here in the Blue Ridge Mountains of northeast Georgia. It has to be one of the most beautiful spots in the country!"

On the county's eastern edge, Lake Burton supports a lakefront settlement of upscale retirement homes as well as weekend hide-aways for affluent Atlanta citizens. The lake is owned by Georgia Power Company, and the lots are leased, rather than sold. In fact, deeded lake lots are the exception around here because the power company controls so much land.

One feature all residents point out proudly is their four-season weather. As local boosters say, "This is where spring spends the summer." Flowering trees in the spring, delightful summers and fall colors keep you aware of the seasons, yet comfortable enough to enjoy them.

Few communities the size of Clayton can support a senior citizens' center, and here is no exception. As an excellent substitute, the chamber of commerce organized a club called the Silver Eagles. About 200 enthusiastic members hold monthly meetings, elect officers, arrange social activities and tours, and share their expertise with others in the community. The camaraderie developed among the members is contagious. This is the place for newcomers to come and meet their new neighbors and forge all-important community connections. The program is such a success that it's being emulated in other parts of the country.

Clarkesville (pop. 1,400), the county seat of Habersham County, is another town often praised by retirement writers. A tourist brochure claims it is just an hour's drive from Atlanta, but I'd hesitate a long while before getting into a car with anyone who makes the 75-mile drive in an hour! The countryside here is made up of rolling hills rather than low mountains, and while not as picturesque as Clayton, it has a rural charm about it.

Another major retirement destination is Dahlonega, the location of the United States' first full-blown gold strike. Gold was discovered here in 1828 and can still be panned today. Dahlonega boomed, until gold was discovered in California in 1849. Suddenly the local miners deserted their claims en masse and hotfooted it out West. The restored county courthouse now has a gold museum.

Recreation and Culture: Outdoor recreational opportunities are tops in Rabun County, partly because of the lakes, rivers and forest, and partly because so much of the land belongs to the public. Without going very far from home you can enjoy world-class trout fishing in the Chattahoochee's headwaters and whitewater rafting on the Chattooga. Georgia's only ski lift is located in nearby Sky Valley. Rabun County Country Club has a nine-hole golf course, and Sky Valley has an 18-hole championship layout that's open to the public. Clayton has a municipal golf course and tennis courts.

For continuing education, there's North Georgia Technical Institute near Clarkesville, with several credit and non-credit classes, and senior citizens do not have to pay tuition fees. Piedmont College in Demorest is another community college with courses of interest to seniors.

Real Estate: Surprisingly, housing costs here are not as inexpensive as you might expect in a sparsely-settled, forested countryside. It turns out that a large percentage of the land is U.S. Forest Service property and Georgia Power owns another large chunk, including some of the bigger lakes. So it can be a seller's market when it comes to purchasing that building lot. According to Rabun County Chamber of Commerce, the median price for a two- or three-bedroom home is $75,000. Since this area is in a rural setting, condos and apartments aren't overly abundant, so inexpensive rentals are not easy to come by.

Medical Care: Two hospitals with a total of 88 beds and 21 medical doctors offer 24-hour staffed emergency rooms and deliver a wide range of health care services. There are both county and city ambulance services, equipped for trauma care, and a county-wide volunteer rescue service.

When Grandkids Visit: Give 'em the thrill of discovering a bonanza. In Old Dahlonega and Crisson Mines, they can try their luck at panning for gold. This area was the top gold producer in the nation until the California Gold Rush of 1849 drew miners out west.

Gold from Dahlonega was used to gold leaf the State Capitol building in Atlanta.

Addresses and Connections

Chamber of Commerce: P.O. Box 750B (Highway 441 North), Clayton, GA 30525. (706) 782-4812.
Internet: http://ngeorgia.com/cgi-bin/links/county/rabun
http://www.gamountains.com/rec.html
http://www.hartcom.net/lowe/Habersham.html
Newspapers: *Clayton Tribune,* North Main, Clayton, GA 30525. (706) 782-3312.
Forsythe County News, 121 Dahlonega Rd., Cumming, GA 30130-2405. (770) 887-3126.
Airport: Atlanta (127 miles); Greenville, SC (95 miles); Athens, GA (83 miles); Asheville, NC (96 miles).
Bus/Train: Greyhound. Amtrak, Toccoa (28 miles from Clayton).

Rabun County/Clarkesville

	Jan.	April	July	Oct.	Rain	Snow
Daily Highs	68	86	92	82	60 in.	10 in.
Daily Lows	15	30	55	39		

Georgia's Colonial Coast

The Atlantic seaboard from Myrtle Beach, South Carolina, down to the Florida state line is known as the "Low Country" (sometimes spelled "Lowcountry"). The name is descriptive of the flat landscape of meandering creeks framed by peninsulas and coves of moss-laden live oaks and palmettos, where the silence is broken by the melodious songs of meadow larks and the lazy "kraannk" of the blue heron or the cry of a gull. Bordered on the west by sandhill ridges and on the east by the ocean, this band of Low Country is sparsely settled and is famous for its variety of birdlife.

Because of the region's fabulous history, Georgia's 112 miles of Atlantic coastline are proudly referred to as the "Colonial Coast." The region is among the most beautiful, unspoiled lowlands in the eastern United States. The wild salt marshes, swamps and pine forests; the barrier islands with moss-draped oaks and magnificently preserved

Colonial towns bring to life historical mysteries and afford satisfying retirementlifestyles.

The high water table and marshy lands of the Low Country were perfect for rice plantations. When rice was king, elaborate estates like Laurel Hill Plantation were picture-book images of the Old South. For some reason, rice is no longer grown, and little remains of these magnificent old homes. The old plantations have found new service as wildlife preserves and habitat for waterfowl and wading birds.

Barrier Islands. All along the Colonial Coast, from the bottom of Georgia north to Charleston, a well-developed chain of barrier islands sits just offshore, protecting the salt marshes, tidal creeks and mainland from wave erosion and storms. The early Spanish explorers along this coast called them the "Golden Isles." The protective islands make it possible for the marshes, inlets and bays to become nurseries for shrimp, oysters, crabs, striped bass and other tasty commercial seafood.

Most of the islands are uninhabited; they're set aside as wildlife refuges or wilderness areas. But a handful of islands are developed, some spectacularly so. The popularity of the islands is due to the picturesque combination of beaches, semitropical wilderness, and beautiful homes positioned midst woods of oak and magnolia. Spanish moss hanging from tree limbs lends a touch of mystery to the scene. Adding to the attraction are marvelous recreational facilities. The variety of lifestyles for retirement seem endless here.

Spanish explorers liked the Colonial Coast well enough to found a colony here 400 years ago, in hopes of finding gold in the Brunswick and Golden Isles region. After a short stay, most of the Spaniards abandoned the islands. They felt discouraged after finding no gold, and they failed to understand the potential of the Golden Isles for golf course development. (It isn't fair to ridicule the Spanish for that oversight; nobody told them that golf wouldn't become popular in Georgia for another three hundred years.)

The region is like a living history book. Flags of five nations have fluttered at different times over public buildings and Colonial military installations. Perfectly preserved buildings, some dating from as early as 1720, are constant reminders of the region's fascinating centuries of European colonization. You'll see Colonial churches, fortifications and battlefields where armed militia confronted Spanish, British and

Union Army invaders. On display are ruins of antebellum plantations and slave quarters. British colonists found this region perfect for growing rice and cotton, two of the South's most profitable export crops. They imported slaves from what was known as the Windward Rice Coast of West Africa because of their expertise with rice and cotton. Today, descendants of those African tribesmen speak an interesting mixture of tribal language and English, called Gullah.

Georgia's Colonial Coast provides a wide variety of lifestyle possibilities, recreational opportunities and home choices. Living arrangements range from historic homes to conventional subdivisions of ranch-style houses, from modest cottages to opulent homes that couldn't be duplicated with today's construction methods and includes gated communities with private golf courses and ocean views.

Brunswick

Known as the "Gateway to the Golden Isles," Brunswick is a quaint port city named for the German ancestral home of King George II, who issued Georgia's first land charter. The quiet streets and squares were laid out long before the American Revolution and their names, like Newcastle, Norwich, Prince, Dartmouth and Gloucester, convey Brunswick's historical atmosphere and give it a decidedly English flavor. It's interesting that Brunswick didn't rename the streets after the American Revolution, as many towns did in a fever of patriotism. An authentic flavor of the South can be tasted here as well, for this is the home of the world-famous Brunswick Stew. The seafood's great, too.

Compared with the upscale communities on the islands, Brunswick is a rather ordinary town of 20,000 inhabitants, but there's a charm about the place that money can't buy. The Old Town historic district delights visitors with antebellum and fine Victorian architecture, including several historic bed-and-breakfast establishments. Claiming to be the Shrimp Capital of the World, the city's waterfront district hosts an armada of shrimp boats that supply the Georgia Colonial Coast's restaurants and seafood shippers for the East Coast. Watching the shrimpers unload their catches is fascinating—best done in late afternoons during shrimping season, which runs from early June to the end of February.

Property here is reasonable (if not downright cheap), and most older homes are well kept. Streets are sheltered by overhanging oak trees draped with Spanish moss—quiet and peaceful. Classic southern homes with columns and balconies grace the side streets, mixed with modern bungalows and cottages. However, most neighborhoods immediately surrounding the town center don't appear to be suitable for retirement. Most people choose either to relocate either in the Old Town historic district or away from the center in newer subdivisions, or better yet on one of the islands. The islands are connected to the mainland by toll causeways from Brunswick.

St. Simons Island

Named "San Simeon" by 16th-century Spanish colonists, St. Simons is the largest of Georgia's fabled Golden Isles. Britain entered the scene in 1736, when General James Oglethorpe established Georgia's first military outpost here at Fort Frederica. In 1742, Oglethorpe's troops defeated Spanish insurgents at the Battle of Bloody Marsh and determined British control of the region.

The island flourished under British authority as rice, indigo and cotton plantations expanded. Later, islanders actively participated in the revolution against British rule. The revolutionary warship U.S.S. *Constitution*, better known as Old Ironsides, was clad with iron-hard planks from live oak trees cut on St. Simons Island. The mid-19th-century saw dozens of sprawling antebellum plantations covering the island, their ruins an enduring reminder of an era now long past.

The plantations have become beautiful residential areas, golf courses, tennis courts and quaint commercial areas with countless shops and restaurants. Instead of rice or cotton, the major harvest today is tourists. They come here year-round to swim and sail along St. Simons' miles of lovely beaches, to challenge its 81 holes of golf and to dine in gourmet restaurants. The island's original town center is called the Village, a quaint district at the island's southern tip. The Village includes a 200-year-old working lighthouse, a great fishing pier, shops, boutiques and a coastal history museum. Many handsome homes, both large Victorians and cute cottages, sit within walking distance from the Village.

The hauntingly beautiful Christ Church, built in 1736, is near the island's northern end, with a wooded cemetery where many of the island's earliest settlers are buried. John Wesley, the father of Methodism, first preached on these grounds. The land between Christ Church and the Village has many attractive homes, often set back from the road under spreading oak trees festooned with Spanish moss.

The northern portion of St. Simons Island is less crowded, with homes set on wooded acreage along the lightly traveled road. Several developments are underway here, with upscale housing set among oaks and palmettos.

St. Simons residents manage quite well coexisting with tourists. Several shopping areas hide behind shrubbery, partially hidden from view from the main road that curves along the beach side of the island. Several miles of fine public beach make excellent places for picnics.

Sea Island

Reached by causeway from St. Simons Island, Sea Island is home of the internationally acclaimed five-star resort, The Cloister. The Cloister was established in the 1920s by industrialist Howard E. Coffin, noted as the inventor of the Hudson automobile. (If you can't remember the Hudson, you aren't old enough to retire.) Sea Island became an exclusive retreat for the nation's super-wealthy. The barons of industry and finance constructed enormous mansions in the style of the Roaring 20s, reminiscent of what the Great Gatsby would have adored. These gorgeous homes are the island's hallmark, but since the end of World War II, some less ambitious homes have made their appearance—less ambitious, perhaps, but not inexpensive.

Jekyll Island

A hundred years ago—when being a millionaire meant more than having equity in an above-average Connecticut home—millionaires from all over the country converged upon Jekyll Island to develop their own private winter retreats. Only club members were permitted to live on the island, making this one of the most exclusive resorts in the entire world. They named it the "Jekyll Island Club." It was a compound of elaborate, two- and three-story Victorian homes (they called them "cottages") and they established a huge clubhouse-restaurant complex. The Rockefellers, Morgans, Vanderbilts, Pulitzers and others—reputed to control one-sixth of the world's wealth—convened here to escape the rigors of northern winters, and to decide the fate of U.S. politics and the world economy.

The Jekyll Island Club closed at the beginning of the World War II, never to reopen. Later, the island was purchased by the state of Georgia and made into a state park. The island's Historic District has become a popular tourist attraction. The original clubhouse is now a turn-of-the-century hotel, and some of the elaborate "cottages" have been restored and opened to the public for tours.

The fact that all of the island's land belongs to the state of Georgia creates an interesting situation. All of the lovely homes here sit on state-owned property; the land must be leased from the state of Georgia. Apparently this doesn't affect the homeowners to any great degree. While they don't pay property taxes (after all, they don't own the property), their lease payments for the land equal what their taxes would be. Technically a real estate transaction on Jekyll Island involves buying a lease instead of a deed. But this doesn't affect the price, since the cost of the lease is equal to the value of a home on a conventional piece of land.

Jekyll Island, once a haven for America's aristocracy, now beckons to all. Recreation on the island encompasses miles of beautiful, white-sand Atlantic Ocean beaches, four championship golf courses with 63 holes, two tennis complexes with indoor and outdoor play, a water fun park, a fishing pier, marinas, dining, shopping, and an outdoor amphitheater with seasonal musical events. What more can you ask for?

Recreation and Culture: "Living here is like being on permanent vacation—there are so many things to do," said a woman who retired to St. Simons Island from Kansas City. As you might expect, golf is the biggest sports attraction, with courses scattered about like confetti at a New Year's party. In fact, Jekyll Island is the site of Georgia's largest public golf resort: 63 holes on three 18-hole layouts and one 9-hole course. Jekyll Island Tennis Center has 13 clay courts, and is ranked with the best facilities in the country. Brunswick has three public and one private golf course; St. Simons Island has four courses with 81 holes. The area's total is 216 holes of golf!

Area beaches invite sunbathing, swimming and beachcombing. Miles of biking and hiking trails meander through the islands. Jekyll Island alone boasts 20 miles of level, paved trails, perfect for jogging or bicycling.

Real Estate: An interesting aspect of real estate in the Golden Isles is the variety from which you can choose. In Brunswick you can select from a wide spectrum from beautiful old mansions in the Old Town district, quiet homes on residential streets or contemporary housing in new subdivisions. The islands themselves offer everything from cottages and beachfront condominiums, to custom homes in wooded settings to the exclusive. The more expensive homes are in gated golf developments with homes on the fairways. From modestly priced homes in Brunswick to the super-expensive exclusiveness of Sea Island, the price range couldn't be broader.

Medical Care: Southeast Georgia Regional Medical Center in Brunswick is a 340-bed hospital serving the Golden Isles area. The facility has a full range of services to offer area residents, including a 24-hour physician-staffed emergency department, general surgical services and specialized units treat patients requiring medical surgical or coronary intensive care.

When Grandkids Visit: St. Simons Island has a wonderful concrete fishing pier jutting into the bay. No license is needed to fish or crab. You rent crab nets, lower them into the water with some bacon or chicken wings for bait, and in a few minutes pull it up, hopefully with a cargo of crabs ready to be steamed for dinner. Another bit of excitement is Summer Waves, a water park on nearby Jekyll Island. One of its rides is Pirates Passage, a totally enclosed speed flume that jets riders in total darkness over three breathtaking humps. You'll probably want to go have a drink while the grandkids do this one.

Addresses and Connections

Chamber of Commerce: Brunswick and Golden Isles Visitors Bureau, 4 Glynn Avenue, Brunswick, GA 31520. (912) 265-0620.
Internet: http://www.bgislesvisitorsb.com
Newspapers: (Brunswick) *Brunswick News,* 3011 Altama Ave., Brunswick, GA 31525. (912) 265-8320.
(St. Simons Island) *Coastal Illustrated,* 3600 Frederica Rd., St. Simons Island, GA 31522. (912) 638-3793.

(Jekyll Island) *Golden Islander,* 5000 Altama Ave., Brunswick, GA 31525.
  (912) 267-7878.
Airport: Glynco Aviation, commuter flights to Atlanta.
Bus/Train: Greyhound service in Brunswick; Amtrak in Jesup, about 40
  miles northwest of Brunswick.

Brunswick/Golden Isles

	Jan.	April	July	Oct.	Rain	Snow
Daily Highs	62	76	89	77	49 in.	.02 in.
Daily Lows	43	58	74	61		

Savannah

Georgia was the last of England's 13 colonies to be settled, and
Savannah was the first British settlement in the state of Georgia. It all
started in 1733, when England was anxious to secure her claim to the
territory against Spanish encroachment from Florida. General James
Edward Oglethorpe selected a spot to settle on the Savannah River, ten
miles from the Atlantic, on the edge of Yamacraw Bluff. Savannah's
historic city hall now sits on the same bluff overlooking the Savannah
River where Oglethorpe landed. Besides a military outpost, Oglethorpe
hoped to create a planned city—a center of agriculture, manufacturing
and export. He was eminently successful.

Unlike some new settlements in the South, James Oglethorpe's
colonists didn't consist of wealthy investors, eager to establish
lucrative plantations. He recruited 114 working class people—carpenters, farmers, sawyers, wheelwrights—just the kind of people
needed to jump-start a colony. Instead of allowing a traditional,
haphazard village layout to develop, Oglethorpe designed a system
of street grids, broken by a series of public squares. From the
beginning, Savannah was designed to be beautiful as well as
defensible. This was the country's first planned city, a masterpiece
of urban design.

Of the original 24 squares in the master plan, 22 still exist. Today,
these squares—tastefully landscaped with live oak, azaleas, fountains and statues—give Savannah that charming flavor that sets the
city apart as a unique as well as beautiful city.

My first visit to Savannah was several decades ago, when the
historic city center was in the first stages of renovation; at that point

Savannah had a long way to go. The city looked somewhat seedy and in danger of succumbing to rampant decay. Then, about 15 years ago we passed through the city on a research trip; things had improved dramatically, but we remained unimpressed. I suppose this was because we had just left beautiful Charleston, and we were anticipating similar neighborhoods—that is, exotic, frilly mansions with Jamaica-style galleries and towering columns, each structure an individual creation, as different as possible from the next. When we didn't find what we were expecting, we assumed that General Sherman had struck again. Wrong assumption! When I wrote about Savannah, I should have remembered my Civil War history. Irate letters from Savannah lovers pointed out that Sherman did *not* harm Savannah, and that indeed Savannah has more antebellum homes than Charleston!

Puzzled at how we could have missed all of this, we returned for another visit. We were delighted to discover that my analysis of Savannah was totally wrong. Apparently, we had missed the forest by concentrating on the trees. It turns out that early architectural styles in Savannah were quite different from that of Charleston's Battery District. Instead of Charleston's ostentatious one-of-a-kind showpieces, built as winter residences for inland planters, Savannah's antebellum mansions were owned by merchants, shippers and townspeople. They preferred the dignified, formal expression of Italianate, English Regency and Gothic Revival. They were designed to harmonize with each other, precisely arranged around park-like landscaped squares, instead of on narrow streets that tend to wander. Homes here are so well-preserved and fit so perfectly in the scheme of things they look as if they were constructed yesterday. When appreciated in this context, I must admit that Savannah is every bit as beautiful as Charleston, if not more so (there's more of it). As one reader wrote in her letter, "France's magazine *LeMonde* named Savannah the most beautiful city in America." To that, I might add that *Condé Nast Traveler* magazine nominated Savannah as one of the "Top Ten U.S. Cities."

Why didn't General Sherman destroy Savannah? Certainly he *threatened* to destroy the city. He wrote the defending General Hardee that if Savannah didn't surrender by December 17, "I shall feel justified in resorting to the harshest measures, and shall make little effort to restrain my army, burning to avenge the national wrong they attach to Savannah..."

General Hardee declined the offer to surrender, almost defying Sherman's burning veterans to destroy the city. Before he was forced to withdraw, he conceived a brilliant plan. He ordered 30,000 bales of valuable cotton to be stored in every home in Savannah—in garrets, cellars and storehouses. If the city burned, the Union Army would destroy a fortune in badly needed cotton. Some people claim that Sherman didn't destroy the town because of gallantry, or because the city was just too beautiful, or because he had a mistress in Savannah. But I'm convinced that the bulldozer-hearted soldier grudgingly accepted the civilian surrender of Savannah for fiscal reasons rather than appreciation of fine architecture, gallantry or a favorite mistress. Thank goodness he did.

With loving care and determined community action, Savannah's downtown historic district (the largest of its kind in the country) has been not only restored, but made exceptionally livable. It changed from an area of above-average crime to a safe place to be. In fact, *Walking Magazine* recently nominated downtown Savannah as one of "The Ten Top Walking Cities in the U.S." You can stroll the historic district, the cobblestone riverfront area or City Market.

Four blocks in the heart of Savannah's historic district have been renovated to capture the authentic atmosphere and character of the old marketplace. Restaurants, open air cafés, jazz clubs, theme shops, crafts and gift shops blend to create a pleasant place to pause during a walk, have lunch and enjoy the scene. The market features artists working in their lofts and exhibits of their works for sale. Savannah's determination to protect and improve its historic sites presents a model for historic preservation efforts.

For a flavor of Savannah, read John Berendt's book *Midnight In The Garden of Good and Evil,* which is set in the heart of the historic district. Tourism in Savannah increased more than 13 percent in 1996, partly by folks who wanted to see the places described in the novel. A motion picture version of the book is underway at the time of writing, with filming on location in Savannah.

In another movie set in Savannah, Forrest Gump is portrayed sitting on a bench in Chippewa Square—in front of the General Oglethorpe monument. The bench was a movie prop, but tourists complain because the bench isn't placed there permanently. They want to know why there's no statue of Forrest Gump there, alongside the statue of General Oglethorpe—to the absolute horror of those who treasure the authenticity of the historic district.

Savannah has 150,000 inhabitants, which makes it too large for some tastes. But Savannah is surrounded by some very livable communities, probably more suitable for retirement than the city's historic center (as well as more affordable). The greater Savannah area comprises a 50-mile radius of Chatham County and has a total population of nearly 520,000.

One of the Savannah's fastest-growing residential areas is on the fringes of the south side, only six miles from the historic district. A collection of attractive neighborhoods offer quality single-family housing as well as a number of apartment complexes, town houses and shopping centers. To zip downtown is a matter of minutes.

Garden City, the largest suburb, is on Savannah's northeast side, with 7,900 residents living in quiet neighborhoods. People here have a tradition of volunteerism. By working together, they've enabled Garden City to operate without property taxes since it incorporated as a city back in 1939. Pooler is smaller, with a population of 4,700, and it shares the hometown atmosphere of Garden City. One advantage is that Pooler sits on the intersection of two interstates, making it convenient to get into Savannah or to travel any direction.

Savannah's Islands. Eighteen miles east of downtown Savannah, Tybee Island is the prototype of a summer beach community. People from Savannah and tourists from all over come here to enjoy sunning and shell collecting on the island's two miles of white-sand beaches on the Atlantic. However, the 3,000 year-round residents enjoy the vacation atmosphere all year long. Accommodations are divided into short-term rentals of condos and apartments and permanent-resident housing, which tends to be older and not fancy. Other island communities on the way to Tybee Island are Wilmington, Whitemarsh and Talahi. Like most Georgian islands, they are not crowded and have several nice-looking developments.

The ultimate in upscale living hereabouts can be found at Skidaway Island, the Isle of Hope, Southbridge and a few other developments. Many of these are gated communities, very posh, and usually offer private golf course membership as a part of ownership fees.

Recreation and Culture: Savannah has four public golf courses and numerous private and semi-private layouts. Tennis is popular here, with about nine public community centers offering a total of 63 tennis courts. In addition to ocean charters and fishing in the creeks, bays and inlets of the islands, there are six fishing piers or bridges where you don't have to get your feet wet to bring in the catch of the day.

There's always something doing in the cultural and entertainment scene here. In the heart of the historic district, the Savannah Civic Center hosts more than 700 events each year, including concerts by the Savannah Symphony, plays and sporting events. This is also the home of the Johnny Mercer Theatre, named for the Oscar-winning lyricist and Savannah native. The City Lights Theater Company moves to historic Washington Square each spring to present "Shakespeare on the Square."

The waterfront is the backdrop for a number of festivals and special events, including such spring/summer delights as the annual Savannah Seafood Festival and the Spring Fling Artists' Market, and other celebrations year-round. Jazz, the definitive music of Savannah, reigns all year, and the new Jazz Society Center in City Market as well as the Coastal Jazz Association add to the city's stature in music circles.

Real Estate: In the Savannah area the range of real estate varies from the very expensive properties on Skidaway Island, where building lots may run into the six-figure prices, to livable neighborhoods in nearby towns where acceptable places can be purchased for less than $70,000. According to local property experts, the average cost of an upscale, single-family dwelling—with 2,200 square feet, four bedrooms, two and a half baths, and a two-car garage in a middle-management neighborhood is about $95,000.

Medical Care: People throughout the 40 counties around Savannah, from Georgia to South Carolina, look to Savannah's excellent medical facilities to fulfill major medical needs. Hospitals here number a comfortable six, with well over a thousand beds among them, and more than 600 physicians representing every possible specialty. Newcomers should feel confident about Savannah's medical care.

When Grandkids Visit: You'll find many things to do, such as going to museums, taking horse-carriage rides through the historic district, visiting the University of Georgia Aquarium or fishing from a pier—you name it, Savannah has it. A special treat for some children will be the Savannah Science Museum. The facility features interactive exhibits that encourage kids to experience hands-on scientific experiments. The museum also has a planetarium exposition every month.

Addresses and Connections

Chamber of Commerce: 222 W. Ogenthorpe Ave., Savannah, GA 9701-9704 phone 912-234-7790
Newspaper: *Savannah News Press*, 111 W. Bay St., Savannah, GA 31401-1108. (912) 233-3671.
Internet: http://savga.com/ourcity.htm
http://www.catalog.com/cgibin/var/savannah/welcome.htm
Airport: Savannah International.
Bus/Train: City buses; Greyhound; Amtrak.

Savannah

	Jan.	April	July	Oct.	Rain	Snow
Daily Highs	60	78	91	78	49 in.	.04 in.
Daily Lows	38	54	72	56		

The Plantation Trace

The Hollywood stereotype of the "Old South"—enormous plantation homes surrounded by fields of cotton and forest in the background—can easily be fulfilled here in Georgia's Plantation Trace. Many of these plantations are still operating and play host to famous dignitaries and celebrities. Because of a warm year-round climate and many outdoor recreational offerings, southwest Georgia has been a place for retirement for over a century.

Long before the plantations and retirees, the Plantation Trace region supported abundant wild game, thick pine forests and vast wetlands. One of North America's largest Indian populations flourished here, evidenced by seven large ceremonial mounds that date back seven centuries or more. Early colonists found themselves in a no-man's land with various Indian tribes not only disputing land ownership between themselves, but uniting against the intrusion of white men. Settlement by white families was a slow process.

Eli Whitney's invention of the cotton gin ushered in a new era in what was to become Plantation Trace, making it practical to grow cotton anywhere in Georgia instead of only along the Colonial Coast. The region's sandy loam soil was perfect for cultivation of Sea Island cotton, a special variety of long staple cotton, and the Plantation Trace flourished. The historic districts of towns and cities here display dramatic evidence of the wealth created by cotton. Beautiful mansions and public buildings grace these cities, turning them into living galleries of antebellum glory.

Valdosta

Valdosta (pop. 40,000) sits at the eastern-most section of the Plantation Trace, only 18 miles from the Florida state line. The town lives up to its nickname, "The Azalea City," every spring, when almost every yard and garden is ablaze with a spectrum of colors blooming from almost every variety of this beautiful shrub.

Every year hundreds of thousands of vacationers on their way to Florida zip right through Valdosta, never suspecting that a delightful little city sits undiscovered just off the Interstate 75 exit ramp. Some may overnight in a motel, or maybe get in some shopping at the manufacturers' outlet stores before steering their cars back onto the interstate to resume the high-speed parade to the saltwater beaches a couple of hours down the cement pavement.

Perhaps because Moody Air Force Base is connected with Valdosta, tourists imagine a typical military "gate town" with a major commerce in honky tonks, pawn shops and fast-food mills. I confess to entertaining a vague image like that myself, before actually visiting Valdosta. What I discovered was one of the better retirement areas in this part of the country, one of the pleasant surprises of the research trip.

Steeped in history and Victorian architecture, as well as modern subdivisions, Valdosta stands out as southern Georgia's dominant city. Featuring immaculately maintained neighborhoods, shaded by enormous trees and landscaping that emphasizes flowering plants, Valdosta's residential sections are exceptionally inviting. Yet, the overall quality of these neighborhoods transcends mere flower beds and magnolia trees.

In Valdosta, the phrase "quality living" is not a shopworn cliché; it's an apt description. One retiree affirmed that this well-groomed, upscale ambience influenced his decision to choose Valdosta as a place to settle, saying, "You can tell Valdostans respect their town by the way they treat it. It's a joy to live among people like that."

The downtown area, too, shows that Valdosta residents care. An ambitious renovation of an already nice-looking town center is going to make this one of the showplaces of the South. To finance this project, a special sales tax measure passed with an overwhelming margin, a refreshing vote of confidence in Valdosta and its future.

As I visited neighborhoods, noticing beautiful, superior brick homes on half-acre lots, a theme kept reoccurring: this is a place where a couple cashing in equity in over-priced sections of the country could "move up" and live in a fabulous neighborhood, in a style never dreamed of—and probably bank some of their profits from the sale of their house.

"The Azalea City" is a university town. Valdosta State University's grounds and campus are in keeping with the elegant look of the surrounding neighborhoods. This is Georgia's newest university, located on two campuses (168 acres) less than a mile apart. The school's 10,000 students add a cultural excitement and flavor to the town, as the University involves local residents in its educational and entertainment programs.

Transportation is another strong point here. Strategically located on Interstate 75 and near east-west Interstate 10, Valdosta is just 18 miles from the Florida state line, and an easy drive to Florida beaches. The city is also served by rail, inter-city bus service (Greyhound), and has an airport with five daily commercial flights to Atlanta. Why Atlanta? Because in this part of the world, no matter where you are flying, the first leg of your flight goes to Atlanta, the South's all-important air transport hub. Frequent air travelers have a saying: "When you die, you don't know if you're going to Heaven or to Hell. But you *do* know you'll be going through Atlanta to get there."

An important consideration for those retiring from other parts of the nation is Valdosta's cosmopolitan retiree community; they come from everywhere! Large numbers of Air Force officers spent training time at Moody Air Force Base. Naturally, when retirement draws near, when military families begin discussing favorite towns, they remember this area with fondness.

One of Valdosta's more memorable citizens was a dentist, a man named John Henry Holiday. In the late 1800s, when the dentist contracted tuberculosis—a common disease at that time—he moved from Valdosta to Arizona to regain his health. There, he abandoned a tedious career of pulling sore teeth for a more glamorous profession:

gambler, gunfighter and sidekick of Marshal Wyatt Earp. In Tombstone, folks affectionately called the ex-dentist "Doc" Holiday and smiled nervously when he looked unhappy, or when his trigger finger itched.

Other Nearby Retirement Possibilities. The nearby town of Lake Park is a pleasant example of lakeside living in southern Georgia. An interesting mixture of small, inexpensive homes and large, extravagant places democratically sit side by side, circling the lake. Moss-draped live oaks and cypress trees shade boat docks and yards that look over the blue water. When a real estate broker quoted home prices, I was astounded at the affordability of Lake Park. (Of course, being from California, *any* real estate looks affordable.) Commercial facilities include a full-fledged medical facility, three shopping malls, several restaurants and a library.

One of the reasons we like to recommend Valdosta is the sincere friendliness of the residents and the determined efforts to bring retirees into the community. The city doesn't hesitate to spend money to conduct a recruitment campaign. When we spoke with Joyce and Ed Eckert, from Long Island, New York, they said, "Valdosta is truly a southern secret. People are genuinely friendly. Down here when people say 'hello,' they really mean it. Not like a 'northern hello'—annoyed and wishing you were out of their way."

Recreation and Culture: The surrounding countryside's woodlands and numerous lakes, particularly the federally-owned Grand Bay Wildlife Area, which provides 5,900 acres of hunting preserve, make hunters and fishermen happy. With a wildlife management stamp firmly affixed to their state hunting licenses, sportsmen decimate ducks and geese as they make their way south each fall. But it isn't all hunting and fishing at Grand Bay. An archery range draws bow-hunters, and there are facilities for camping, nature hikes and bird watching. A "canoe trail" leads you through Blackgum Swamp—an array of wetlands that mimics the Okefenokee—with signs that mark the way and explain the natural wonders of this area. For those who don't happen to bring a canoe with them, there's a 2,000-foot boardwalk and an observation tower. The best bass fishing is usually from January through June. Speckled perch are caught in late winter and early spring. Several private hunting preserves stock quail and pheasant and each hunter's bounty is cleaned, dressed and packed by the staff.

Valdosta has four golf courses and a "golf learning center." The newest golf course is at Stone Creek Golf Community where spacious home sites are situated around this 18-hole championship wooded course. A discount plan for weekday greens fees is offered to seniors.

Valdosta State University, in keeping with its community involvement, has a unique program called "Learning in Retirement." Almost like a club, this program is member-led and university-sponsored. Members take part in courses on a non-credit basis, and the classes offered reflect the interests and desires of the membership. It's a place to learn, have fun and meet new friends. Classes offered in early 1997 included interests such as drawing with brush and watercolors, TaiChi, line dancing, intro to computers, armchair investing and dog obedience. (Our dog has already trained us to obey, so we wouldn't need a class like that.)

A private organization, funded in part by grants from the Georgia Council for the Arts and the Lowndes/Valdosta Arts Commission, established the Cultural Arts Center, where there's a constant stream of classes and workshops, ranging from calligraphy, watercoloring and writing. In addition to operating a gallery that features emerging and recognized artists, the Center sponsors workshops, classes, exhibitions and a lecture/demonstration series. The Theatre Guild presents several productions each season, usually a musical, two shows for children and comedy/drama productions.

Real Estate: A glance at cost-of-living charts indicates that Valdosta is just a little under the national average. This is understandable, because of a recession-proof economy based on military and university payrolls that remain constant the year-round. Home prices, for example, are just 7 percent below the national average. However, this is another instance where statistics can mislead. Even though the average Valdosta home sells for $96,000, that tells you nothing about the elegance and quality you get for that money. According to real estate people, a medium-priced home is about $62,000 and an expensive one $116,000. Because of a high turnover of Air Force families who are transferred in and out for training, there's a wealth of apartment complexes scattered about town—more than a hundred.

Stone Creek, a new, upscale development is laid out around a public golf course, with homes just off the greens. Stone Creek offers some impressive homes starting from $160,000. By the way, this is the last golf course on the tourists' trail before they reach Florida.

Medical Care: Three hospitals with more than 359 beds, some 125 doctors and 34 dentists provide excellent health care services to the immediate area. Numerous health related firms and several nursing homes provide auxiliary care as needed. South Georgia Medical Center, the largest hospital, is a not-for-profit, 288-bed, short-term, acute-care regional hospital serving southern Georgia and northern Florida. The center serves approximately 250,000 residents. Smith Hospital is a 71-bed acute-care hospital in nearby Hahira, with 24-hour emergency services.

When Grandkids Visit: One of Georgia's most spectacular examples of luxurious southern Victorian homes was slated for the wrecking ball a few years ago. But the Valdosta Garden Club raised funds, rescued and restored the Crescent House. It's open to visitors on weekday afternoons, and well worth an hour of your time. Features include a large mirrored fireplace, gold-leaf-tiled ballroom, gardens, a chapel and an octagon-shaped school house. If the grandkids aren't into historic stuff, take 'em to Liberty Farms Animal Park, a petting zoo. A winding nature trail takes them to discoveries, such as deer, kangaroo, wallabies, monkeys and more.

Addresses and Connections

Chamber of Commerce: P.O. Box 790, Valdosta, GA 31603-0790. (912) 247-8100. (Be sure to write or call the chamber and request a copy of their retirement guide.)

Internet: http://www.datasys.net/remax/valdosta.htm
http://www.com/hpi/gamun/ga000429.html

Newspaper: *Valdosta Daily Times*, 201 N. Troupe St., Valdosta, GA 31601. (912) 247-1880.

Airport: Valdosta Regional Airport, commuter flights to Atlanta.

Bus/Train: Greyhound.

Valdosta

	Jan.	April	July	Oct.	Rain	Snow
Daily Highs	70	80	94	83	49 in.	.1 in.
Daily Lows	45	54	71	59		

Athens

If you've read much of my writing, you'll know how biased I am in favor of university towns. The presence of a major university transforms a small city from an ordinary place into an exciting blend of academia, cultural events and lofty entertainment, all leading to a quality lifestyle. Athens has a population of 90,000, with about 26,000 students, and is an excellent example of how the presence of a university makes a difference in your surroundings. When you combine a large numbers of students, professors and support staff with a large population of retired couples, something happens. There's a demand for a higher level of services, nicer shopping facilities and quality restaurants. Because students are chronically short of money and because retirees don't like to be extravagant, prices naturally remain at reasonable levels.

Athens and the University of Georgia started off together. Back in the early 1800s, the university's founders selected a remote location in northeast Georgia where students would be isolated from the temptations of urban life. Since the school was expected to be an important center of learning, the town was named for its Greek counterpart, the ancient capital of Greece. As fine homes and large mansions began to appear around the new campus, the role of Athens as the cultural center of Georgia became increasingly evident. For almost 200 years, the town and the university have grown and matured together. Athen's architecture, business and social atmosphere reflect the bonding between school and community.

Downtown Athens looks exactly as a university town's downtown should look. College Avenue is the main drag, arched over by large trees, with shrubbery at the curbside, old-fashioned lampposts with globes and sidewalk tables and chairs in front of cafés. A mixed crowd of students, residents and tourists stroll the streets browsing stores and restaurants, or simply sitting on wrought-iron benches, observing the passing world with the unhurried casualness only students and retirees can afford to have. If you observe the scene, you just know it's a college town.

Because the commercial district is the central focus of students and residents alike, it has mercifully been sheltered from the curse of strip malls. Folks from towns near and far journey to downtown Athens to browse bookstores and specialty stops for articles not normally found in small Georgia cities. They love to dine in downtown Athens' exotic restaurants that specialize in everything from traditional southern-style cooking to wood-fired pizza, from Mexican enchiladas and Indian tandoori to exotic Japanese cuisine.

The university atmosphere extends to the residential districts. Lovely neighborhoods are packed with tree-shaded mansions and antebellum houses. Victorians and modern brick homes compete with impressive Greek Revival homes with their massive columns, magnolia-shaded gardens and the gracious unhurried way of life enjoyed by the planter class of the "Old South."

Typical of college towns, most residential districts have secondary commercial centers, with small shops, restaurants and services, within easy walking or bicycle distance from home. Residents don't need to go downtown for light shopping and dining. However, several comfortable-to-elegant neighborhoods are within walking distance to downtown and to the university.

Also typical of a university town is the variety of quality neighborhoods. One area we liked is located close to downtown and the university. It's called Five Points, a quiet area of homes built from the 1930s to the 1950s. They vary from modest frame homes to elaborate brick dwellings. Farther away from town, we noted some truly luxurious areas, with large homes tucked away midst wooded hills and forest.

Athens is located approximately 70 miles east-northeast of Atlanta, Georgia, and is at the heart of a three-county metropolitan area of 126,000 people. Athens offers the feel of a hometown, with the amenities of a small metropolis. Like most other southern locations, Athens has a moderate four-season climate with cool winters, colorful falls, and hot, humid summers.

Recreation and Culture: The Athens area has two private golf course developments—the Village at Jennings Mill and Kingston Greens, a golfing community about 20 minutes north of downtown Athens. Several other golf courses are open to the public. Of course, the University of Georgia can be relied upon as a source of year-round athletic events, everything from football and basketball to intramural sports.

In keeping with the academic environment in Athens, the University of Georgia offers free tuition to residents over age 65 for undergraduate and graduate programs in several areas as well as for many continuing education classes. Some of the continuing-education classes have fees. Retirees here join the students to enjoy presentations of theater, lectures, concerts and films at the university. The local community college, Athens Area Technical Institute, has vocational and technical classes.

Real Estate: Five Points is a quiet neighborhood near downtown and the university with frame and brick homes built in the '30s–'50s; prices range from about $60,000 to $100,000 and up for older homes and $150,000 for new homes. In Clarke County, the Village at Jennings Mill has large contemporary homes from $109,000 on an 18-hole private golf course. Kingston Greens, a golfing community in Madison County, about 20 minutes north of downtown Athens, has new three-bedroom homes on large wooded lots from the low $100,000s. South of Athens in Oconee County, Stonebridge has three- and four-bedroom homes for $175,000 to $230,000.

Because of the large student population, visiting scholars and temporary faculty, Athens supports a lot of apartments, condos and rental houses.

Medical Care: Medical care in Athens is superb. St. Mary's Hospital and Athens Regional Medical Center are the two major hospitals, and between them they have about 5,600 beds and more than 150 physicians in all medical specialties. Both facilities provide 24-hour emergency care. Of interest to military retirees, the Navy Corps Supply School offers medical and dental facilities to veterans.

When Grandkids Visit: For a peek into what aristocratic life in Athens was like in the mid-1800s, visit the Taylor-Grady house. A Greek Revival mansion, the house was built around 1842 by General Robert Taylor. The home has been restored to the original splendor it possessed when the cotton planter and merchant lived there. During the Civil War the mansion was taken over by Henry W. Grady, editor of the *Atlanta Constitution,* an influential orator who worked for reconciliation between the North and South after the Civil War.

Addresses and Connections

Chamber of Commerce: 220 College Avenue #7, Athens, GA 30601. (706) 549-6800.

Newspaper: *Athens Daily News* and *Athens Banner-Herald,* 1 Press Place, Athens, GA 30601. (706) 367-4076.

Internet: http://olympus.athens.net/hartman/athens.htm

Airport: Daily commuter flights to Charlotte, NC. Limousine service to Atlanta Airport.

Bus/Train: City buses and university buses; Greyhound; Amtrak in Gainesville (39 miles).

Athens

	Jan.	April	July	Oct.	Rain	Snow
Daily Highs	52	74	89	74	50 in.	2.5 in.
Daily Lows	33	50	69	51		

GEORGIA TAXES
Georgia Department of Revenue
2082 East Exchange Place, Suite 120, Tucker, GA 30084
Ph. (404) 414-3500
Georgia's tax bills rank 11th among the least expensive in the nation

Income Tax

Single:		**Married Filing Jointly**	
Not over $750	1.0%	Not over $1,000	1.0%
$750 - $2,250	2.0%	$1,000 - $3,000	2.0%
$2,250 - 3,750	3.0%	$3,000 - $5,000	3.0%
$3,750 - $5,250	4.0%	$5,000 - $7,000	4.0%
$5,250 - $7,000	5.0%	$7,000 - $10,000	5.0%
Over $7,000	6.0%	Over $10,000	6.0%

Separate schedule with slightly higher rates for married people filing separately.
General Exemptions: $1,500 single, $2,000 dependent, $3,000 married filing jointly
Additional for elderly: None
Private Pension Exclusion: $11,000 for persons age 62 or older
Social Security/Railroad Retirement Benefits: Full exclusion
Expense Deduction: Federal amount
Federal Income Tax Deduction: None
Other: Counties and municipalities may impose a 1% tax on Georgia net taxable income, but not if the jurisdiction levies a sales tax and not in cities which lie in counties with an income tax.

Sales Taxes

State 4.0%; **County** 1.0%; **City** None; **Special district:** 1.0%
Combined Rate in Selected Towns: **Atlanta** 6.0%, **Savannah** 6.0%, **Columbus** 6.0%
General Coverage: Food is taxed, prescription drugs are exempt

Property Taxes

Average assessment on a $90,000 home with homestead exemption, about $990 a year.

Real and personal property is subject to local tax. Intangible personal property is subject to state taxation. In relation to personal income, property tax collections are in the middle third among the 50 states.

Homestead Credit: General exemptions: $2,000 assessed value
65 or older: $4,000 assessed value if net income below $10,000. Disabled veterans and surviving spouses over 62 and residing in an independent or
county school district: $38,000 assessed value; $10,000 assessed value if gross income below $10,000

Deferral Program: Homeowners 62 or older with household gross income below $15,000 may defer taxes on the first $50,000 of assessed value ($125,000 market value)

Estate/Inheritance Taxes

Georgia does not impose an estate tax nor an inheritance tax. It imposes only a pick-up tax, which is a portion of the federal estate tax and does not increase the total tax owed.

Kentucky / Tennessee

Kentucky

Even though some may think Kentucky isn't part of the South because of location, you can be assured that culturally, Kentucky is as much a part of the South as Tennessee or Arkansas. The southern drawls here are almost indistinguishable from those of Tennessee and some other regions in the South. This makes sense when you realize that Kentucky's original settlers came from the Carolinas, Tennessee and Virginia. Cotton, tobacco and other plantation-style crops, grown in the western half of the state, made Kentucky very much a part of the southern plantation tradition. In the mountain regions, people clung to their Appalachian customs, folklore and world views. Subsistence farming was more common there.

An interesting custom of the early settlers throughout the Kentucky-Tennessee mountain regions was the way they took advantage of every occasion to break the monotony and isolation of frontier life. The construction of a new log home, for example, provided a welcome opportunity for a neighborhood gathering in the form of a house-raising. Upon completion of the new structure, its rafters vibrated from the sounds of fiddle and banjo

> **Kentucky**
> The Bluegrass State
> Admitted to statehood: June 1, 1792
> **State Capital:** Frankfort
> **Population (1995):** 3,860,219; rank, 24th
> **Population Density:** 96.3 per sq. mile: urban 48.5%
> **Geography:** 37th state in size, with 40,411 square miles, including 679 square miles of water surface. Highest elevation: Black Mountain, 4,159 feet. Lowest elevation: 257 feet, Mississippi River. Average elevation: 750 feet.
> **State Flower:** Goldenrod
> **State Bird:** Cardinal
> **State Tree:** Kentucky coffee tree
> **State Song:** *My Old Kentucky Home*

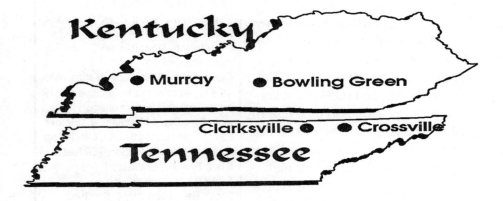

tunes and the shuffling feet of young dancers. Times have changed in Kentucky, but convivial and same-sex-bonding activities continue to have a strong presence in smaller towns throughout the state. Don't ever hesitate to take time to mix and mingle with the local people; like their pioneer ancestors, they are known for their tradition-bound hospitality.

The Mississippi River marks Kentucky's western border and the deep valleys and rugged gorges of the Appalachians line the opposite side of the state. In between you'll find a wide selection of countrysides from which to choose: everything from gently rolling farm country to magnificent panoramas of the Blue Ridge Mountains; from quiet, rural crossroad communities to sophisticated cities and university towns.

Kentucky epitomizes America's hardy frontier and pioneer heritage. This was the country of Daniel Boone, the Hatfields and McCoys and good ol' mountain music. Today it's much more than that. With up-to-date services, neighborly people and modern shopping everywhere, Kentucky is a great choice for retirement.

Modern-day transportation, in the form of paved highways crisscrossing the state, has opened the backcountry to the world. Robust economic development since the end of World War II boosted most rural areas out of Al Capp's "Dogpatch" past. No longer are large parts of the state isolated and populated with illiterate mountaineers and moonshiners. Kentucky today is too civilized for that. This opening of the state also created retirement opportunities that didn't exist previously.

But the entire state certainly hasn't become a carbon copy of middle America. Many charming areas back in the hills are almost as rustic and unspoiled as ever. And since many Kentucky counties have opted for prohibition, you can bet some of those piney wood hills contain moonshiners, as well.

Kentucky, like neighboring Tennessee, is particularly attractive for midwestern and northern retirees who want to retire close to their prior homes, in inexpensive surroundings, in areas of low crime. The relatively mild, four-season weather easily satisfies requirements for those who insist on colorful autumns, invigorating winters and glorious springs.

Bowling Green

Southern Kentucky is the location of one of our favorite places for retirement. The delightful little city of Bowling Green embodies the retirement advantages of a small southern city and college town. Bowling Green is about an hour's drive north of Nashville, and two hours southwest of Louisville. For those who want southern retirement, but still want to be close to their old hometown, Bowling Green's location is ideal. A day's drive will take you to just about anywhere people retire from in the North. In fact, 75 percent of the U.S. population is within a day's drive of Bowling Green. That's one reason why Bowling Green is becoming a popular retirement location for fugitives from crowded northern cities. Between the interstate, a commuter airport and Greyhound buses, friends and family have no problem visiting, and you may get to see your grandchildren more often than if you moved to Florida or Arizona.

Bowling Green was originally called "The Barrens," after the Barren River that runs through town. But in 1797 the town took a more descriptive name: Bowling Green. The second name derived from a habit of court officials and visiting attorneys; they would amuse themselves between trials by bowling on the lawn beside the old courthouse. The town's surrounding countryside is as green as its name, lush with rolling meadows, punctuated by long, white fences that enclose thoroughbred horses munching away at the Kentucky bluegrass. Bowling Green looks exactly as one imagines Kentucky should look.

Due to its location, Bowling Green serves as a regional hub for retail shopping and medical services. Because this the only place between Louisville and Nashville where alcohol is served, Bowling Green's higher-quality restaurants attract folks from miles around for celebrating that special occasion. According to a recent survey, Bowling Green has more restaurants per capita than any other U.S. city except San Francisco.

A big plus in Bowling Green's inventory of pluses is the presence of Western Kentucky University. Recognized as one of the most beautiful college campuses in the nation, the university is situated on a hilltop overlooking the city. The 200-acre campus and surrounding residential area is known as College Heights and commands an impressive view of the Barren River Valley. The school adds 15,000 students to Bowling Green's population and a tremendous amount of vitality and intellectual warmth to the environment.

Participation in university affairs is made easy by Kentucky's policy of senior citizen scholarships that pay the full cost of tuition. This is true for both full-time and part-time students and applies toward either graduate or undergraduate courses. Numerous continuing education programs are also offered—everything from "History of American Presidents" to motorcycle training.

Western Kentucky University is also involved in retirement programs, in an interesting way. A retirement attraction program is an offshoot of the university's Small Business Development Center. Dr. Steve House, the program's director, says, "The program is aimed primarily at northerners, in cities such as Chicago and Cleveland, to let them know that south-central Kentucky is a good place to retire. We stress things such as the mild climate, four distinct seasons and recreation opportunities." To show how much Bowling Green welcomes retirees, there are a couple of billboards carrying the message on Interstate 65.

Although Bowling Green is a fine example of a larger Kentucky town, it's not big enough to suffer from big-city problems. Crime rates here are exceptionally low, pollution is almost nonexistent and the cost-of-living is always below the national average. Housing and utility costs are exceptionally low, with homes selling for 17 percent below average and utilities at an astounding 27 percent less than national averages.

Every downtown has its own personality and character, and Bowling Green is no exception. As one downtown businessman said, "Our historic buildings tell who we are and where we came from. They say what is special about Bowling Green—a beautiful, classic environment." With the university within walking distance, academics and residents mix in the downtown city center.

At the moment, things are moving downtown, with more than $25 million in new construction underway. Fortunately the community will try to blend the contemporary buildings with the existing historic structures, which now are home to banks, offices, shops and restaurants. The central focus of Bowling Green's downtown is an old-fashioned park. Benches arranged along sidewalk paths invite lounging and watching the world go by. The mall is complete with a fountain, sculptures and mature trees. Small commercial buildings dating from the last century, with arched windows and elaborate brickwork, face the park.

In the early 1990s, real estate developers calculated that the Bowling Green real estate market was ready for some "high end" housing. It turns out they were correct; upscale, gated communities became hot properties. Nobody seemed surprised when a home in the gated community of Evergreen sold for $675,000—the highest home sale in the county's real estate history. At least five luxury developments are selling lots and homes at top dollar prices, most in the $150,000 to $350,000 range, one with a golf course and convention center on the grounds. However, at least one developer is of the opinion that the higher-end homes have been overbuilt, and the time will come when they will be bargains.

Recreation and Culture: The city of Bowling Green has three municipal courses—one 18-hole and two 9-hole courses. Two other public courses, an 18-hole and a 9-hole layout, are not far from the city. The surrounding county contains six golf courses, 59 tennis courts, 27 public parks and two country clubs. As is the case anywhere in Kentucky or Tennessee, excellent hunting and fishing are always nearby.

The university maintains a symphony orchestra and two theater groups, and hosts frequent visits from touring artists and entertainers. The Capitol Arts Alliance Center in downtown Bowling Green has a long tradition of providing entertainment to the public. It started as a vaudeville house, then became a movie theater, and now has been expanded and turned into a clearinghouse for the arts. Besides an 840-seat performance hall, the Capitol Arts Center also offers the Ervin G. Houchens Gallery, which places emphasis on exhibits that feature local and regional artists.

Real Estate: Building costs for a high-quality home in a nice neighborhood run about $50 per square foot. Homes just a few years old are going for bargain prices—about 20 percent below the national average—for example, a brick, three-bedroom house with a large lot and detached garage typically sells for $80,000.

Medical Care: Greenview Medical Center, an up-to-date hospital with 600 beds, is currently undergoing a $2 million expansion program to increase the number of treatment and exam rooms. Next is the construction of a new $7.8 million medical center and urgent care facility.

When Grandkids Visit: The grandkids should enjoy the Corvette Museum. More than 50 of these babies are on display in a 68,000-square-foot museum. They have an original 1953 model Corvette and displays of all the models produced since. A favorite is the yellow Corvette that beat out Paul Newman for the GT-SCCA National Championship. Also, the 165-seat Chevrolet Theater has an interesting film on the history of the sports car and the Chevrolet assembly plant is nearby, where all Corvettes are made. Two public tours daily take you inside where you can see the step-by-step production of America's sexiest car.

Addresses and Connections

Chamber of Commerce: P.O. Box 51, Bowling, KY 40108. (502) 781-3200.
Newspaper: *Courier-Journal,* 1344 Adams St., Bowling Green, KY 42101. (502) 843-3717.
Airport: Bowling Green-Warren County Airport.
Bus/Train: Greyhound.

Bowling Green

	Jan.	April	July	Oct.	Rain	Snow
Daily Highs	41	68	88	69	48 in.	3 in.
Daily Lows	24	46	67	46		

Murray

The city of Murray is situated on former tribal land of the Chickasaw Indians that the United States purchased in 1818 when General Andrew Jackson negotiated a treaty with the tribe. For 150 years, much of this land remained undeveloped; it had limited timber, agricultural and industrial resources. In 1963 the government changed things somewhat by creating twin lakes that enclosed a 170,000-acre peninsula called the Land Between the Lakes. The two lakes, Kentucky Lake and Lake Barkley, enclose a wonderland of scenic wildlife and recreational areas. There are over 200 miles of hiking and biking trails, with paths and roads leading to beautiful, secluded bays along the 300 miles of undeveloped shoreline. The Land Between the Lakes is one of the major reasons folks like to retire in Murray, only 15 miles away.

Murray's population is about 90,000, and it's a city that consistently gains recognition from retirement writers as a good place to live. Murray is also an excellent example of how good things can happen to an economy when retirees move in. For years the town's economy remained stagnant, with the population actually falling slightly. Then, a few years ago, Murray received a rash of national publicity when a popular retirement guide designated Murray as the country's "top rated" retirement location—an award it's received several times since. The publicity generated an enormous amount of interest among folks planning their after-work careers. Before long 250 couples had made the move to Murray.

As you might expect, the influx of retirees had a snowball effect on the area's economy. The real estate market zoomed out of the doldrums and before long had exhausted its inventory. Building construction increased to keep pace. At last report, new housing developments were still being built. The economy is healthy; Murray now boasts significant tourism as well as a large industrial base and commerce, agribusiness, finance and transportation industries. Murray's unemployment rate is 26 percent below the rest of Kentucky. In short, retiree "in-migration" has proven to be an economic bonanza. Another positive side effect was: these extra retirees were enough of a catalyst to push the city into enlarging the senior citizens center and adding more services. The staff at the local center, by the way, is dedicated and enthusiastic about plans for the facility's future.

What were the bad effects? Apparently none. According to the FBI's last report, Murray is very high in personal safety. (The statistics seem to indicate that most Murray criminals have opted for retirement.) The cost-of-living may have risen slightly, but since it started at an already low level, the increase is hardly significant. It's still several percentage points below the national average. Naturally, home prices have gone up. But again, they started at a depressed level, so they're also well below the national average. People moving into Kentucky from high-cost areas of the country say they feel like bandits as they sign the escrow papers.

One retired couple from California said there were so many ex-Californians in Murray that they formed a "California Club" composed of other California expatriates who opted for Kentucky retirement. A colleague of mine, another Californian, decided to retire in Murray. When I asked why, he and his wife explained that his children lived in St. Louis and Nashville, and by living in Kentucky, they were within a few hours drive of either place. They also liked fishing in the nearby lake. What were the drawbacks? They had to admit that the snow and ice in the winter took some getting used to, but since they were originally from Canada, that was simply a readjustment. The lack of good restaurants (this being a dry county) was the only other thing they missed from their California experience. They partially solved this problem by joining a country club that had a gourmet chef (and a liquor license—alcohol is permitted in private clubs.)

My friends were particularly pleased with the cultural activities sponsored by Murray State University. Summer dramatic perform- ances are presented in a city park, and concerts and lectures at the school keep them from boredom. The university makes a special effort to reach out to senior citizens and involve them in its curriculum, and many of the school's facilities are enjoyed by the general public. The Special Collections Library contains a large selection of materials on the history and culture of western Kentucky and Tennessee. Live theater, dance theater, and a visual arts gallery are also used by the public.

What does Murray, Kentucky, have going for it that makes it the "best place" in the country to retire? Well, we've already covered most points: low crime and inexpensive real estate, nearby outdoor recreation and a university. But many, if not most towns throughout the South can boast similar advantages. Since I don't believe there is one "best place," I will only admit that Murray is one of the best places to retire in Kentucky. But is it any better than Bowling Green, which offers much of the same attractions? That's something everyone has to judge personally.

Recreation and Culture: Kentucky Lake, Lake Barkley and Land Between the Lakes are only 15 miles from Murray. Connected by a free-flowing canal, the two lakes form one of the largest man-made bodies of water in North America. The Lakes Area, with 2,380 miles of shoreline, is famous for taking anglers to the limit. Fishermen boast of catching their limit of slab crappie, bass, stripers, catfish and bluegill. Kentucky Lake has long been a mecca for inland sailors. The lake's broad expanses, sometimes two miles wide, offer a challenge to even the most proficient sailor.

Murray has two public golf courses, one of which has been designated by the American Society of Golf Architects as one of the best designed 18-hole courses in America. Murray Country Club and Oaks Country Club are private country clubs with golf courses.

The Murray-Calloway County Community Theatre presents performances, and Playhouse in the Park, one of the oldest community theaters in the state, is the scene of live theater and delightful Gourmet Dessert Cabarets. Each year, the Playhouse attracts more than 10,000 people from all over the region to its shows. Playhouse in the Park is one of the oldest community theaters in the state. Productions include serious drama, lighthearted comedy, mystery and lavish musicals.

One of the community's major assets is Murray State University, a regional institution with 8,500 students, offering quality academic programs. MSU offers its students six colleges of study and a variety of master's degree programs. As a resident of the area you have access, not only to the academic offerings, but also to the cultural activities such as plays, musical presentations, art exhibits, lectures, concerts and guest speakers.

The university theater presents a variety of mainstage and experimental productions each year and joins the music department to produce Broadway musicals and opera in alternating years. Selections such as *Anything Goes* and *Charlotte's Web* fill the calendar from September through April. Most productions are presented in the Robert E. Johnson Theater.

Real Estate: Housing costs in Murray average about 15 points below national norms. The average sales price is around $75,000.

New homes are usually over $110,000. Much of the available housing was built since the mid-1980s, when the retiree boom started. A short distance away from Murray are ten or so small, crossroad towns that look like they could be comfortable places to live in.

Medical Care: Murray-Calloway County Hospital is a not-for-profit institution. A 216-bed hospital with 90 physicians on staff, Murray-Calloway is expanding its outpatient services center to the tune of over $4 million. The hospital operates a "Health Express" mobile screening unit that travels the region providing free and low-cost health screenings.

When Grandkids Visit: This is the time to visit the National Scouting Museum, for everything you might want to know about the history of the Boy Scouts from 1910 to the present. The museum is located on the university's campus and features exhibits such as the Amazing Adventure Course, live story telling, the Scoutaround Theater and hands-on Boy Scout exhibits. The museum also features 53 original Norman Rockwell paintings. If the grandchildren are over age seven they can have fun in the adjoining Gateway Park, an outdoor ropes and obstacle course.

Addresses and Connections

Chamber of Commerce: P.O. Box 190, Murray, KY 42071. (800) 651-1603, (502) 759-2199.

Internet: http://www.wkynet.com/MurrayNet/default.html

Newspaper: *Murray Ledger & Times,* 1001 Whitnell Ave., Murray, KY 42071-2976 (502) 753-1916.

Airport: Barkley Regional Airport (Paducah, 50 miles).

Bus/Train: City and county bus; Greyhound; Amtrak in Fulton (40 miles).

Murray

	Jan.	April	July	Oct.	Rain	Snow
Daily Highs	44	71	89	72	49 in.	8 in.
Daily Lows	26	48	68	47		

KENTUCKY TAXES
Kentucky Revenue Cabinet
P. O. Box 1274, Frankfort, KY 40601— Ph. (502) 564-4580
Kentucky's tax bills rank 35th among the least expensive in the nation

Income Tax

Up to $3,000	2.0%	$5,000 - $8,000	5.0%
$3,000 - $4,000	3.0%	$8,000 and over	6.0%
$4,000 - $5,000	4.0%		

General exemptions: $20 tax credit per exemption
Additional for disabled: $40 blindness
Additional for elderly: $40 for persons aged 65 or older.
Private Pension Exclusion: None
Social Security/Railroad Retirement Benefits: Full exclusion.
Standard Deduction: $650 single, $650 married filing jointly
Medical and Dental Expense Deduction: Federal amount
Federal Income Tax Deduction: None
Other: Tax credits prevent any tax liability for income under $5,000 (single) or $5,400 (married filing jointly). Credits are gradually phased out as income rises. Eighty-four cities and 26 counties impose earnings taxes at rates ranging up to 2.95%.

Sales Taxes

State 6.0%
General Coverage: Food, residential utilities, and prescription drugs are exempt

Property Taxes

Average assessment on a $100,000 home about $980.
Real and personal property are subject to local and state taxation. Intangibles are subject to state taxation. In relation to personal income, property tax collections are in the lowest third among the 50 states.
Homestead Credit: Age 65 or older or totally disabled: $21,800 assessed value

Estate/Inheritance Taxes

Kentucky imposes an inheritance tax that ranges from 2% to 16%. The tax rate depends both on the value of the beneficiary's share and the relationship of the beneficiary to the decedent. A surviving spouse receives a full exemption. Other beneficiaries receive partial exemptions depending upon their relationship to the decedent (e.g., infant children or mentally disabled children receive a $20,000 exemption, other children receive a $5,000 exemption).
Kentucky also imposes a pick-up tax, which is a portion of the federal estate tax and does not increase the total tax owed.

Tennessee

Tennessee is somewhat of a mirror image of Kentucky to the north and of Arkansas to the west. Westward, near the Mississippi River, plains of the fertile bottomlands alternate with dense hardwood forests. King Cotton once ruled this domain, a land steeped in the traditions of the Old South. Flat-to-rolling land covers much of western Tennessee: rich agricultural fields hedged with rows of trees and neat and prosperous-looking farmhouses, barns and silos. Most smaller towns here look pretty much like any in Middle America. The two largest cities are Memphis and Nashville.

As you move eastward you come upon Tennessee's heartland, a region of gently rolling hills and bluegrass meadows. Continuing east, the landscape grows more scenic with every mile. The land slopes gradually upward, until the foothills, growing ever more rugged, reach their highest peaks in eastern Tennessee, and finally become the tree-shrouded Appalachian Mountains near the state's border with the Carolinas.

> **Tennessee**
> The Volunteer State
> Admitted to statehood: June 1, 1796
> **State Capital:** Nashville
> **Population (1995):** 5,256,051; rank, 17th
> **Population Density:** 125.8 per sq. mile: urban 67.7%
> **Geography:** 36th state in size, with 42,145 square miles, including 926 square miles of water surface. Highest elevation: Clingmans Dome, 6,643 feet. Lowest elevation: 178, Mississippi River. Average elevation: 900 feet.
> **State Flower:** Iris
> **State Bird:** Mockingbird
> **State Tree:** Tulip poplar
> **State Song:** *Tennessee Waltz*

Every retiree we interviewed in this region emphasized the four-season climate as a major plus. "I like to know what time of year it is," said one lady who had lived in California for some years before retirement. "Here, I get the feeling of seasons. Summer is nice and hot, fall is beautiful and colorful, winter is short and merciful, and then comes spring!" she sighed in ecstasy.

Make no mistake; winter does bring chilly winds, creeks do ice over and your furnace will get a workout. Still, it doesn't begin to compare with winters farther north. And summers are humid, but not unbearable, with 90-degree highs normal. Enough rain falls in the summer to keep things looking green and fresh, streams flowing and fishing good to excellent the year round.

Clarksville

Located on Tennessee's northern border, touching the Kentucky state line, Clarksville is a popular retirement place with folks from northern Illinois, Michigan and Ohio. They not only like the town, but they appreciate Clarksville's convenient location. It's a day's drive from Chicago, Cleveland or Detroit. The interstate highway can whisk them up north for visits just as easily as it brings family and friends south to Clarksville. Also, the big city of Nashville is only a 45-minute drive and the Florida panhandle is convenient for a weekend of beach fun.

Clarksville is our favorite mid-southern hills location because it somehow manages to combine an atmosphere of small-city living with urban conveniences. An estimated 76,000 population places it into the realm of a city, yet it somehow manages to maintain the flavor of a small town. This is a place where friends are constantly waving and honking greetings to each other as they drive around town. Yet shopping malls, medical facilities and services are as complete as you would expect to find in a much larger city.

Three special conditions make Clarksville different from other mid-southern cities. The first is a large army post with 23,000 soldiers and their families. The second is an excellent university with almost 8,000 students. The third is the large number of out-of-state folks who decide to retire here.

Fort Campbell straddles the Tennessee-Kentucky state line adjacent to Clarksville. The base covers 105,000 acres, mostly in Tennessee, but since the post office is in Kentucky, that state claims Fort Campbell as its own. Military retirees enjoy post-exchange privileges and medical benefits. The fort, almost a city in itself, has a population of 38,000, with a post-exchange as large as a shopping center, plus seven on-post schools for military dependents. Military families remember their tours of duty here and often return when retiring, for the post-exchange, medical and other privileges due retirees.

The Cumberland River flows lazily through Clarksville, pleasure boats cruising where huge paddle-wheelers once churned the waters. The river's banks are lined with homes with back porches hanging out over the water or with boat docks sitting in the water. A half-hour's drive from Clarksville's pleasant residential neighborhoods can take you to thick forests or rich farms and bluegrass meadows where horse breeding is a major industry. This is where the famous Tennessee Walking Horse originated.

The early-day prosperity of the tobacco plantations shows clearly in prestigious antebellum mansions gracing Clarksville. Set back from the street among magnificent oaks and magnolia trees, surrounded by acres of lawn, these beautiful homes are among the best preserved in the South. This custom of large lawns originated with wealthy, slave-owning plantation owners, who didn't have to cut the grass themselves. The tradition carries over into today's housing styles; big lots are in. Even humble, two-bedroom homes sit on enormous lots with awesome expanses of lawn—awesome because of the amount of energy spent in keeping the grass mowed. Yet, Clarksville folks will tell you with straight faces, "I really enjoy yard work. Cutting grass is relaxing." (Yes, of course. That's why rich people are always so tense; they hire a gardener to cut the grass and the gardener gets to relax.)

Clarksville isn't all southern mansions on large estates. You'll find homes in comfortable, safe neighborhoods for every income bracket. Besides conventional homes, there are modern subdivisions, golf course developments, apartment complexes and cluster developments and condominiums in and near the city of Clarksville.

Dover: The little town of Dover is 30 miles west of Clarksville, an archetypical small Tennessee town. Dover is just five miles from the Land Between the Lakes recreation area. This 170,000-acre wilderness area stretches over a 40-mile wide peninsula between Kentucky Lake and Lake Barkley. Almost 90 percent of land is unspoiled forest, with just a few scattered farms and facilities for boat launching, hunting and fishing. Some retirees who planned on living in Clarksville changed their minds and chose Dover instead, just to be closer to Land Between the Lakes. Besides Dover's exceptionally low housing costs, typical in rural Tennessee, folks love the peaceful living and the proximity to hunting and fishing. It's a down-home kind of town, and very small, so it might take some getting used to.

Recreation and Culture: For those who love hooking fish and killing ducks, the Clarksville area is great place to retire. You have all the conveniences of a city, plus great hunting and fishing nearby. Sports enthusiasts from all over the country come here to spend vacations at Land Between the Lakes recreational area; people who live in Clarksville can drive 35 miles to the lakes, anytime they please.

Tennessee's benign climate makes golf in the Clarksville area virtually a year-round sport. There are four public courses, including one nine-hole course and three 18-hole layouts. Several private country clubs have excellent golf facilities.

Clarksville is home to Austin Peau State University, which offers many programs oriented toward adult continuing education. The school provides year-round entertainment and cultural events for the community, including an active theater department that produces five shows a season, ranging from comedy to serious theater, and even musicals. A jazz festival is held in March, and a spring opera in May. Guest artist recitals are offered throughout the year, with free admission.

At least one little-theater group involves many people who have fun and produce plays at the same time on a volunteer basis. Fort Campbell also reaches out to Clarksville with its entertainment services office, which produces seven theatrical productions a year, open to the public.

For big city life, nearby Nashville offers fine restaurants, historical museums and theaters. It seems as if every country and western star from Minnie Pearl to Conway Twitty has a museum dedicated to them. And of course, when friends come to visit, you're obligated to take them to the Grand Ol' Opry.

Real Estate: Our previous research showed Clarksville to be one of the bargain-housing places of the nation. Median sales prices are still about 19 percent below the national average. But conditions change here, depending upon what happens at Fort Campbell. When world conditions are peaceful, Fort Campbell operates with a full staff and demand for housing is up. But when military problems arise somewhere in the world, troops here are the first to go. When this happens, vacancies become easy to find and FOR SALE signs sprout on lawns.

Medical Care: Clarksville Memorial Hospital is a modern 216-bed facility, jointly owned by local physicians. There are 110 active doctors on staff, and another 113 in practice around the area.

When Grandkids Visit: A few miles west of Dover, the Cumberland River joins with the Tennessee River at the site of Fort Donelson National Military Park. This was where General Grant turned the tide of the Civil War by bringing the fighting into southern territory for the first time. The fortifications are still visible, and battle sites well marked. When General Grant's forces finally captured this strategic site on the Cumberland River, Kentucky and most of Tennessee were lost to the Union army. It's an emotional experience to stand on ground where so many thousand young men died in such a short battle.

Addresses and Connections

Chamber of Commerce: P.O. Box 883, Clarksville, TN 37041-0883. (615) 647-2331.
Internet: http://www.buyersusa.com/nqc/cities/tn/chamber/0250.htm
Newspaper: *Leaf-Chronicle,* P.O. Box 829, Clarkesville, TN 37041. (615) 552-1808.
Airport: Nashville International Airport (45 minute drive). Limo service to airport.
Bus/Train: City bus; Greyhound.

Clarksville/Dover

	Jan.	April	July	Oct.	Rain	Snow
Daily Highs	46	71	90	72	48 in.	11 in.
Daily Lows	28	48	69	48		

Crossville

While the Great Smoky Mountains are renowned for scenic lakes, forests and beautiful fall colors, they are also known for their extreme overcrowding and long lines of traffic during the tourist season. The Cumberland Plateau, just about an hour west of the

Smokies, is one of the South's best-kept secrets. It boasts colors and scenery just as beautiful as the Smokies, but with lightweight traffic and no overcrowding to spoil the enjoyment.

The town of Crossville is situated on the Cumberland Plateau, centrally located between Nashville to the west, Knoxville to the east, and Chattanooga to the south. It probably received its name because of its location at the crossroads of several main roads—today they are called Interstate 40, U.S. Highway 127 and U.S. Highway 70. Crossville, with a population of 7,000, sits in the center of Cumberland County, a 679-square-mile elevated plateau in the foothills of the Blue Ridge Mountains. The county's population is about 39,000. Much of the land is in rolling valleys and verdant mountains with forests and lakes, streams and waterfalls. Immediately around Crossville, the rich farm land and occasional crossroad villages have a definite rural Tennessee look.

Downtown Crossville follows the main road through town and has a comfortable look about it. The city is working on refurbishing the town center and is converting an old movie theater into a meeting and community hall. On the edges of town, a great deal of new construction is underway and recently, a new manufacturing plant set up shop, a new Super WalMart settled in on the highway and a Lowes store is building a 130,000-square-foot facility.

While doing our research in Crossville, we noticed that the downtown didn't have that "really old" look that similar Tennessee towns often had. Only a few buildings looked as if they dated from the early part of the last century. In fact, much of the downtown construction seemed to be built in the style of the 1930s. Farms surrounding the town also lacked the pre-Civil War homes so common in much of the Tennessee countryside.

When we inquired about the relatively recent look about Crossville, a young lady who worked in a local business disagreed that the buildings were not old. She said firmly, "No sir, Crossville is a very old town. Almost nothing in the downtown is new." When we asked, "How old?" She replied, "Well, I understand that many buildings here date back to the days of the Franklin D. Roosevelt Administration." We had to agree that was indeed a long time ago.

It turns out that until depression days, Crossville was pretty much woods and empty countryside. Despite rich soil and abundant rainfall, the region had been isolated and ignored by the world. As late as 1924 there was not even one graveled road in Cumberland County. Each community had its own church, store, post office, and school, so people did not have to venture far from the community center for everything they needed.

FDR's New Deal administration, searching for worthwhile projects to bootstrap the country out of the depression, seized upon a plan to develop the Crossville region as a model agricultural center. Government workers cleared forests and homesteaders were given loans and seed money to get started. The depression-fighting plan evidently worked, because this is a very prosperous area today. Cheap electricity from Tennessee Valley Authority's projects lured industry into the area, adding jobs and even more prosperity.

A recent change is that restaurants can now serve mixed drinks. Crossville previously had been a "dry" town—the restaurants at Fairfield Glade, Lake Tansi Village and some private clubs previously had been the only places where liquor was served. Residents routinely made the trek to Knoxville for booze—a 70-mile drive each way. However, it was pointed out to us that there were plenty of bootleggers in town, and it was easy to buy what you needed without having to drive to Knoxville. This weird custom of a community supporting prohibition and bootleggers at the same time never fails to puzzle me.

Fairfield Glade: When retirement writers speak of Crossville, chances are they have one of the special country-club developments in mind. There are several. Fairfield Glade is the oldest and the largest in the area, possibly the largest in the entire state. It's about 15 miles from Crossville and has been under development for 25 years. Its year-round population is between 4,500 and 5,000, but thousands more enjoy the facilities on a vacation and part-time retirement basis. The corporation that put the package together has lots of experience—they have similar operations throughout the retirement areas of the nation.

Over the years, Fairfield Glade has matured gracefully. It has changed from a glitzy country-club promotion into a series of stable, pleasant neighborhoods scattered throughout the 12,000 acres. Eleven lakes and four championship golf courses with all the country-club adjuncts—such as tennis, swimming pools and restaurants—uphold the original country-club tradition. It's a private development, however; only members and guests can play golf.

Homes surrounding this lake-golf-course complex are well built, attractively priced and architecturally pleasing. Acres of green and wooded space separate the various tracts. A bus service takes residents into Crossville.

Holiday Hills: Formerly called Thunder Hollow, this posh development is closer to Crossville, just a few miles from the downtown section. It spreads over 1,200 acres of prime land around a lake and a golf course. Apparently this one started as a time-share resort, but retirement homes have become the style. The tennis and clubhouse facilities are excellent.

Homes are priced comparably to those in Fairfield Glade, and its natural setting is just as beautiful. An interesting feature is the Cumberland County Playhouse, located just outside Holiday Hills' main gate. Dramas, musicals and ballets draw visitors from all over the nation.

The Orchards: Nearby is another retirement development, a no-frills place called the Orchards. In recognition of retirees' propensity for recreational vehicle travel, they built carports high enough to accommodate RVs. The Orchards attracts retirees from Indiana, Ohio and Illinois, but the hottest place of origin is Michigan, particularly from the Detroit area, which is an especially popular place to be from.

Lake Tansi Village: This 5,000-acre hideaway encloses the magnificent 550-acre Lake Tansi, offering 14 miles of shoreline for myriad sports and relaxation. The village has an excellent marina providing berths for 90 boats, and vacationers can enjoy fishing, boating, sailing, and waterskiing. An 18-hole golf course is nestled around the beautiful lake, and youngsters will enjoy the village's community center and clean playgrounds.

Deer Creek: Yet another golf club residential community is Deer Creek Golf Club and Crossville Golf Community. It contains a well-stocked 35-acre lake for fishing, a swimming pool, lighted tennis courts, an 18-hole golf course and residential homesites on wooded lots bordering either the lush golf greens or the sparkling lake.

Recreation and Culture: The Crossville area is becoming known as the golf capital of Tennessee. An astounding number of top-flight golf courses are available for play here. The total is 162 holes on nine courses, and six of the nine golf courses are public. There were over 360,000 rounds of golf played in 1995 in Cumberland County, representing over half a million players.

The Cumberland County Playhouse, a nationally recognized professional theater, features productions from Broadway as well as original scores by local producer Jim Crabtree. It underwent a 25,000-square-foot expansion in 1992, when shop and rehearsal studios, a flexible 220-seat second stage, classrooms and audience service areas were added. The outdoor "Theater-in-the-Woods" offers a third stage for special events. But the big news is the new Roan State College, which will be in Crossville.

Real Estate: Property is quite affordable in Crossville and its environs. In 1997 the median price for a three-bedroom home was around $84,000 with many selling for $65,000 or even less. Homes in town are usually on large lots with plenty of mature shade trees. On the town's outskirts, larger lots are the rule, with small farms commonly used as retirement homes. Recent building surges are dominated by two classes: ranch-styles of 1,200 to 1,700 square feet in the mid- to upper $60,000 range and more traditional styles with 1,600 to 1,700 square feet in the $80,000 to $90,000 price range. All recent neighborhood developments are within minutes of town and mix well with existing residential construction.

In Fairfield Glade, the closer to the golf course, the more expensive the homes; some are really luxurious. Prices range from the mid-$100,000s, those with lake views from the $180,000s. We saw one for $229,000 that was a veritable mansion.

Some of the really older homes in Fairfield Glade sell from $50,000, but those were built for summer resort occupancy years ago and do not have the class of some of the newer ones. Around $60,000 to $70,000 is the normal range for nice three-bedroom homes on attractively landscaped lots. Condos are also available, most of them with lake views starting from $35,000 on up to $100,000.

Medical Care: Cumberland Medical Center is a private not-for-profit regional facility with 186 medical/surgical beds and a 16-bed sub-acute-care unit. The hospital features an emergency room with 24-hour physician coverage, same day surgery suites, outpatient services, cardiac rehabilitation, home health services and more. The medical center has just added an additional facility, which will offer state-of-the-art technology and expertise in the oncology field, to complement the wide array of healthcare services available now through Cumberland Medical Center.

When Grandkids Visit: The Cumberland Homestead Tower and Museum tells the story of the Cumberland Homesteads, a community that was built as part of President Franklin D. Roosevelt's New Deal during the 1930s to combat the Great Depression. Visitors can climb the winding staircase in the tower to enjoy a gorgeous view of the southern end of Cumberland County.

If you don't feel like climbing a bunch of stairs, take 'em to Crossville's 300-acre Meadow Park Lake, which is said to be one of the best fishing lakes in the state, a place where you can enjoy peace and tranquillity while fishing. No buildings are visible from its shores, giving one a chance to simply commune with nature—just in case the fish are not cooperative.

Addresses and Connections

Chamber of Commerce: 108 South Main, Crossville, TN 38557. (615) 484-8444.
Internet: http://crossville.midtenn.net/Chamber
http://www.crossville-chronicle.com
Newspaper: *Crossville Chronicle,* P.O. Box 449, Crossville, TN 38557. (615) 484-7510.
Airport: Knoxville Macgsee-Tyson Airport (60 miles).
Bus/Train: Greyhound.

Crossville/Fairfield Glade

	Jan.	April	July	Oct.	Rain	Snow
Daily Highs	47	71	87	70	52 in.	12 in.
Daily Lows	29	48	68	48		

TENNESSEE TAXES

Tennessee Department of Revenue, Taxpayer Services Division
Andrew Jackson State Office Building, Nashville, TN 37242
Ph. (615) 741-2594

Tennessee's tax bills rank 3rd among the least expensive in the nation

Income Tax

Tennessee levies a tax only on dividends from stocks and interest from bonds and other obligations at a rate of 6%. There are exceptions for certain commercial instruments, for certain instruments of indebtedness issued by Tennessee banks and thrifts, federal obligations, and certain other such income.

Personal Exemptions or Credits: $1,250 single, $2,500 married filing jointly, full exemption for property held by blind persons and elderly age 65 or older whose gross income is $9,000 or less.

Sales Taxes

State 6.0%, **County** 1.0% - 2.75%, **City:** 0.25% - 0.75%
Combined Rate in Selected Towns: Chattanooga: 7.75%, **Knoxville:** 8.25%, **Nashville:** 8.25%
General Coverage: Food is taxed, prescription drugs are exempt

Property Taxes

Average assessment on a $100,000 home about $1,940 annually.

All real and personal property is subject to taxation. Some intangibles are subject to taxation. In relation to personal income, property tax collections are in the lowest third among the 50 states.

Eligibility: Elderly and disabled homeowners and certain disabled veterans and their surviving spouses

Income Ceiling: $10,000 except for qualified veterans

Maximum Benefit: Refund of taxes paid on the first $15,000 market value for elderly and disabled persons. Refund of taxes paid on the first $120,000 market value for qualified veterans

Deferral Program: Local option to defer tax for homeowners age 65 or older on first $60,000 of market value for households with gross income below $12,000, or defer increased taxes over 1979 levels if market value is below $50,000

Estate/Inheritance Taxes

Tennessee imposes an inheritance tax that ranges from 5.5% to 16.0%. The tax rate depends both on the value of the beneficiary's share and the relationship of the beneficiary to the decedent. A marital deduction equal to one-half the value of the taxable transfer is allowed. Other classes of beneficiaries receive partial exemptions (e.g., children receive a $10,000 exemption). Tennessee also imposes a pick-up tax, which is a portion of the federal estate tax and does not increase the total tax owed.

Natchitoches

Alexandria
(England Oaks)

Toledo Bend

Leesville/
DeRidder

Baton
Rouge

Lafayette

New
Orleans

Houma

Louisiana

Louisiana

Nowhere in the United States can you find such a rich diversity of people, customs and worldviews as in Louisiana. These differences aren't imaginary. You can travel 50 miles in almost any direction and you'll hear distinct accents, jargon, music and possibly different languages. Even the cuisine will be different. With eight ethnic groups tracing their ancestors back in Louisiana's history, it isn't surprising that many people are bilingual, sometimes with English as their secondary tongue. Visiting Louisiana is almost like visiting a foreign country.

To truly understand Louisiana, you need a background in the state's history. The region was first explored by the French in 1682. Twenty years later, French colonists arrived and replaced Indian villages with their own settlements. Before long the French were joined by the Spanish, who came to trade and decided to settle. The British tried to get a foothold here with less success. Then traders and merchants from the American Colonies became regular visitors via flatboats from Pennsylvania. They drifted down the Ohio and Mississippi rivers to the Gulf of Mexico, sold their goods and trekked back home via the Natchez Trace.

Louisiana
The Pelican State
Admitted to statehood:
April 30, 1812
State Capital: Baton Rouge
Population (1995): 4,342,334; rank, 21st
Population Density: 99.0 per sq. mile: urban 75%
Geography: 31st state in size, with 49,650 square miles, including 6,084 square miles of water surface. Highest elevation: Driscoll Mountain, 535 feet. Lowest elevation: New Orleans, minus 8 feet. Average elevation: 100 feet.
State Flower: Magnolia bloom
State Bird: Brown pelican
State Tree: Bald cypress
State Song: *You Are My Sunshine*

Hundreds of German families were recruited in 1719 by the Company of the West (which held the French royal charter for the development of Louisiana). These European pioneers settled up river from New Orleans along a section of the Mississippi River that is still called the *Cote des Allemands,* "German Coast."

Next, a wave of exiled French-speaking Acadians (Cajuns) from Nova Scotia arrived to bolster the French personality of the region. West African slaves were imported to work the plantations, further adding exotic customs, cuisine and languages to the mixture. More French influence was added by French aristocrats escaping the bloodbath of the French Revolution and those fleeing slave revolts in the West Indies. After the Revolution, many of Lafayette's French and Italian troops decided to stay instead of returning to Europe.

In the mid-1800s, legions of Irish and Italians made Louisiana their New World destination when famine and depression drove them from their countries. These immigrants found ready employment in dangerous jobs—constructing waterways and bridges and clearing swamps. Slaves were too valuable to risk on such projects. A slave cost $2,000; an Irishman worked for a dollar day.

Spanish influence never died out, even though France held Louisiana in its grip for most of its early years. You might be surprised to learn that many famous structures in New Orleans' "French Quarter" were actually built by the Spanish, during the time Spain ruled Louisiana. Many old Louisiana families have Spanish surnames, and Spanish is still spoken in some communities, particularly in St. Bernard Parish, below New Orleans.

Prior to the Civil War, Louisiana was the most liberal-thinking state in the South regarding slavery. This was particularly so in New Orleans, where free blacks had many educational and professional opportunities. They became skillful carpenters, masons, blacksmiths and artisans. Many became successful businessmen, even teachers and doctors. Free blacks amassed some of Louisiana's largest land holdings and made major contributions to the culture. Things changed, however, after the Civil War, when the notorious Black Code laws forbade people of color certain occupations.

Other immigrant nationalities represented in Louisiana are Yugoslavians, who specialize in oyster harvesting on the Gulf Coast, and Hungarians, who became cultivators of strawberries and other crops in the Albany area. You'll notice that most of Louisiana's many local festivals are celebrations of particular ethnic contributions to the "cultural gumbo" of this unique state.

Suffice it to say that Louisiana has an eclectic collection of nationalities and cultures. Of course, France quite naturally left the strongest heritage on Louisiana, as evidenced by the widespread use of "Cajun French." Other artifacts of French influence are the concept of *parish* instead of "county" and Louisiana's legal procedures, which bear a stronger resemblance to the Napoleonic Code than British common law.

The foregoing history explains how Louisiana acquired such an interesting collection of cultures, peoples and customs. But most outsiders know little about the state other than through an occasional visit to New Orleans. They tend to think Louisiana is all Mardi Gras, bayous and filet gumbo.

The state's cultural geography can be subdivided into five general regions, each based on historical background. One division runs across the top quarter of Louisiana, an area that the state tourism board likes to refer to as "Sportsman's Paradise." The culture here is a sort of melting pot of all Louisiana cultures, with an accent almost indistinguishable from that of adjacent Arkansas.

The next cultural division is a strip of land cutting across the center of Louisiana. This is often referred to as the "Crossroads Country" because ten or so important roads converge on Alexandria, the region's largest city, crossing like spokes on a wheel. People here proudly trace their origins to the original French and Spanish colonists, before the arrival of the Acadian refugees. There are also a few Creole communities, mixtures of French, Spanish, Mulatto and Indian—also dating from pre-Cajun times. We'll discuss some crossroad towns later on in this section.

In the southwestern quadrant, reaching down the bayou country to the Gulf of Mexico, is the world-famous land of the Cajuns—or "Acadiana." This country conjures images of bayous, crawfish and folk music. You'll read about several places which are well worth a visit, even if you don't decide to relocate there.

The fourth region is called "Plantation Country," along the Mississippi plain. This area hasn't been covered in this edition of *Choose the South.* Although the countryside is beautiful, it's too thinly populated to make any recommendations. The region is worth a visit, however, if only to see some of the imposing architecture and picturesque plantation country.

The last region is "Greater New Orleans." This city has taken all the cultural elements introduced by immigrants, mixed them thoroughly, and produced a yet another cultural blend. New Orleans residents have distinctive accents, unique cuisine and a faster pace of life. Although I wrote about New Orleans in earlier retirement books, we chose not to cover it in this book because of the city's reputation for high crime rates. However, you'll find many delightful retirement choices in safe suburban areas a short distance from the metropolitan limits of New Orleans. We understand that the state is considering plans for retiree welcoming committees in this region. We'll probably report on suburban New Orleans in the next edition of *Choose the South*.

One thing Louisiana misses out on is Gulf Coast beach property. Except for a short stretch of sand in the western part of the state—humorously referred to as the Cajun Riviera—most of coastal Louisiana is swamp, mud flats and bayous. People in Texas claim they can tell Louisianians by the high-water marks on their legs. Beaches start when you get to Texas, and Texans feel smug about that. Of course, Louisianians enjoy making snide remarks about Texans, so they're even.

Since our earlier retirement research in Louisiana, the economic picture changed dramatically. A few years ago, the state had fallen on hard times. The petroleum industry had all but collapsed. High-paid workers were leaving the state to find work elsewhere. They sold their nice homes for pennies on the dollar just to cover the mortgage. Housing developments were left uncompleted; real estate prices couldn't possibly go lower. Louisiana's treasury suffered too, since oil revenue is the backbone of the state's financial structure.

Today, the situation has reversed. Oil money is flowing into the state treasury once again, and good jobs are luring workers back to Louisiana. The housing market has recovered nicely, although compared to where most folks come from, it's still cheap here.

Finally, we arrive at the icing on Louisiana's relocation cake: taxes. An enormous amount of money goes into the state's treasure chests from taxes on each barrel of petroleum pumped from Louisiana's fields. Consequently, collection of taxes from individuals and businesses isn't as critical as in states where most revenue comes from property taxes. The bottom line is: there is no Louisiana state property tax. However, while the state doesn't assess property taxes, cities and parishes can, and do.

So, here's the kicker: each homeowner is entitled to a $75,000 tax deduction on his home before the city or parish starts figuring the tax bill. And in most towns listed in this book, a $75,000 home is a pretty nice place—a home that might cost $200,000 in some parts of the country. Therefore, that pretty nice place looks even prettier when you consider that you pay no taxes on it. Most couples we interviewed in our Louisiana research had a zero tax bill. That's right, zero. One couple—who dwell in what some might consider a mansion, one that would deserve a $6,000 yearly tax bill in many states—pay less than $300 a year in property taxes!

When interviewing folks who've retired in Louisiana from outside the state, we always find them enthusiastic about their new homes. This reinforces our overall favorable impression of Louisiana as a retirement possibility. But there's another ingredient that colors our perception of Louisiana—the state's recent experiment with innovative retirement attraction programs. At the moment, at least two pilot programs are under way, and others are in the mill. One retirement booster program is called PAL (People Who Appreciate Louisiana). Several communities described in this book participate in the PAL program.

The idea of newcomer welcoming committees has been discussed earlier, but it bears reiteration. Small towns and cities derive tremendous economic benefit when retired couples from out of the state add their financial assets and enthusiastic energies to the community. Newcomers spend their money locally, don't strain the school system or law enforcement and they make the most energetic volunteers. Twenty couples create the same effect as a new factory hiring 60 low-wage workers. And that's only part of the picture. Therefore, official recognition of the value of out-of-state retirees makes it much easier to recommend some of these places as relocation possibilities.

Natchitoches

Strangers always have problems pronouncing *Natchitoches*. We usually try to pronounce it as it's spelled, which brings polite smiles to the faces of natives, if not outright guffaws. It's pronounced *NAK-a-tish*.

This is an Indian word meaning Place of the Paw Paw, or Chinquapin nut.

History buffs will find plenty to marvel over in this fascinating little city of 17,000 inhabitants. Natchitoches has one of the most picturesque and authentic downtown sections of any place we've yet seen in this region, reminiscent of the French Quarter in New Orleans. The town has the proud distinction of being the oldest settlement in the entire Louisiana Purchase Territory. French explorers first made contact with the Natchitoches Indians in 1700, and 14 years later established the village of Natchitoches as a trading outpost on the Red River. The site was selected because it was as far as boats could travel upriver. (At that point the Red River was blocked by a massive log jam that may have been in place for centuries.) Before long, the village became a town, then a bustling river port and an important crossroad. Natchitoches early on saw the rise of vast cotton empires along the river banks. Wealthy planters not only built imposing plantation houses, but they also maintained elegant showplaces in town.

Sometime during the 1830s, the U.S. government decided to clear the log jam so river barges could travel upstream to what is now Shreveport. Theoretically, this would make Natchitoches even more prosperous. After several years of hard work the task was completed. But to the dismay of Natchitoches residents, the Red River changed its course, leaving the once-thriving river town high and dry, several miles from the new river course. The town's potential as a bustling port town became history. The river bed became a spring-fed creek. Although this disaster isolated Natchitoches, it safeguarded its historic buildings from the curse of progress and urban renewal. It also preserved the deeply ingrained traditions of its residents.

Fortunately, Natchitoches came up with a great idea. Why not dam the old channel and create a lake? Today a 26-mile ox-bow lake, called Cane River Lake, runs through upscale Natchitoches residential areas and is the showpiece of the downtown National Landmark District. Cane River Lake looks very much like a river, but aesthetically is much better than a river. It doesn't have a current, doesn't carry flotsam and debris from upstream, and it provides a place for peaceful boating and good fishing in its clear, spring-fed waters. The lake-river doesn't flood or become silty in rainy weather. Best of all, it lends an air of Old-South dignity to Natchitoches, with huge oak and magnolia trees arching over the lake's bank and weeping willows trailing branches into the still water.

Natchitoches' rich historical background encompasses French, Spanish, Native American, African and Anglo-Saxon influences. Contemporary residents take pride in this colorful palette of tradition, and carefully maintain their ties with the past by preserving the older part of the city. This is what makes Natchitoches special. The historic downtown fronts on Cane River Lake, surrounded on three sides by a wonderful collection of historic old homes, some dating from before the American Revolution.

A tour of restored plantation houses surrounding Natchitoches is obligatory. Besides magnificent showplaces like Magnolia and Beau Fort, there's the drama of Melrose Plantation. Melrose was founded by Marie Therese Coin-Coin, a freed slave, on a land grant given her by her former owner. Determined to make a success of the plantation, she did so well that she was able to purchase the freedom of her children.

To get an idea of what the town looks like today, rent the movie *Steel Magnolias* from your local video store. The picture was produced on location here, using homes in the downtown area as stages and local people as extras. The actors—including Sally Fields, Olympia Dukakis, Dolly Parton and Shirley McLaine—acquired the local accents (Dolly didn't have to work too hard) and they did a great job of portraying Natchitoches. Just about every home in town has a copy of the video.

Large antebellum "town homes" of cotton planters sit next to ornate Victorian homes and substantial houses dating from the early 1800s. Some have been converted to bed-and-breakfasts. (In all, Natchitoches has 21 bed-and-breakfasts.) These historic buildings are more than museum pieces; they are homes of residents who enjoy being within a short walk of the fascinating downtown. One former Vermont resident said, "Originally, we wanted to buy an historic home in Charleston, but we couldn't find anything we could afford. Someone suggested that we visit Natchitoches. Now we're the proud owners of a bed-and-breakfast!"

At first we suspected that Natchitoches's commercial district might be a clever remodeling project. The brick streets, wrought-iron balconies and storefronts—all in the style of the 1850s—looked too authentic to be real. But several stores display photographs taken of downtown businesses more than a century ago. They clearly show that, indeed, this is how Natchitoches looked in its prime. In addition to numerous good-to-fantastic restaurants—tastefully decorated to reflect the historic theme—several interesting stores invite serious browsing. You'll find a huge, old-fashioned general/hardware store that will keep you busy for some time.

Recreation and Culture: Natchitoches has ten public parks, two golf courses and many tennis courts. A country club provides social life and golf privileges for those addicted to this lifestyle. For other outdoor recreation, residents enjoy canoeing and fishing in any of the parish's freshwater rivers or slow-moving bayous. Nearby Kisatache National Forest has 129,174 acres of lush woods full of wildlife and trails.

Natchitoches has acquired the status of an artists' colony, and one of the featured niches on the main street is Heritage Gallery, sponsored by the Natchitoches Art Guild. Rotating displays of more than a hundred works are arranged within the gallery, with member artists submitting new exhibits every month. The Guild is open to artists and would-be artists to display their works and promotes the professional development of member artists. The Guild holds workshops and seminars to cultivate the talents of residents.

Natchitoches's claim to being a good retirement choice is further enhanced by the presence of Northwestern State University. In addition to its symphony, dinner theater, ballet and other entertainment, the school offers many interesting continuing education programs for mature adults. The university sports department also provides football, baseball, softball, basketball, track and field events for public enjoyment.

Real Estate: Natchitoches's housing prices seem low when compared to the national average. But for this region, prices in Natchitoches are probably $10,000 above average, but this is understandable when the setting is considered. Historic homes, however, sell for half of what similar places would fetch in Charleston or Savannah. In the area immediately surrounding the historic downtown, beautiful old homes can be bought for as little as $100,000; large, stately ones probably cost double that amount. Several modern neighborhoods, like Pecan Park, have beautiful brick homes starting at $80,000, ranging upward depending on location. Properties backed up to Cane River naturally cost more, many well over $200,000. A limited number of condos are priced between $90,000 to $100,000.

Medical Care: Natchitoches Parish Hospital is a complete acute-care hospital serving residents of Natchitoches Parish. Services include outpatient physical and respiratory therapy, geriatric services, a senior care unit and a skilled nursing home for long-term care. The addition of a cardiac unit is under consideration. Larger hospitals for more extensive care are located in Shreveport and Alexandria.

When Grandkids Visit: The time for them to visit is the first Saturday in December, when throngs of local citizens and visitors take delight in participating in what has been billed as the "Mardi Gras" of north Louisiana. (Yes, I know—Mardi Gras isn't at Christmas, but it's their celebration.) Each year, Natchitoches plays host to over 150,000 people who pour into the city for a gala display of Christmas lights and fireworks show. The daylong festivities kick off in the morning with a "fun run," parades, food, entertainment and arts and crafts displays. The main event begins at dusk as two sets of fireworks go off simultaneously over the river and conclude with the official turning on of the Christmas lights. Each evening throughout the month of December, over 170,000 bulbs shine softly over the downtown historic district.

Addresses and Connections

Chamber of Commerce: 700 Front Street, Nachitoches, LA 71457. (318) 352-8072.
Newspaper: *Natchitoches Times,* P.O. Box 448, Natchitoches, LA 71458. (318) 352-3618.
Internet: http://www.cp-tel.net/natchitoches
Airport: Alexandria International, 55 miles.
Bus/Train: Greyhound.

Natchitoches

	Jan.	April	July	Oct.	Rain	Snow
Daily Highs	56	78	92	79	58 in.	.7 in.
Daily Lows	36	55	73	55		

Acadiana (Cajun Country)

Louisiana's most famous ethnic people are the *Cajuns,* those French-Canadians who were evicted from the Canadian province of Acadia (today's Nova Scotia) back in 1755. The English authorities in Acadia—with the typical British tact and understanding that was in vogue at that time—insisted that the Acadians not only swear allegiance to the Crown, but that they renounce their Roman Catholic faith and join the Church of England or get out. The mass exodus that followed was recounted in Henry Wadsworth Longfellow's "Evangeline." (Somehow I always assumed the Acadians fled Canada rather than submit to English cooking. The Brits boil everything they can't fry.)

The exiles went through terribly difficult times. Some families were shipped to the West Indies, some to the New England colonies, others went back to France. Many wandered, homeless for 20 years, before finding a welcome in the French-speaking environs of Louisiana. They established small farms along the Mississippi River, Bayou Teche, Bayou Lafourche and other streams and bayous in the territory's southwestern section. The word *Cajun* comes from a modification of the original French pronunciation of Acadian (A-ca-jan), describing their French-Canadian origins.

At one time, Cajuns were noted for their closed society. As a defense mechanism, they jealously maintained their French language and their private way of living, excluding outsiders from their lives, referring them to as *les Americaines*. But World War II and the Korean and Vietnam wars brought Cajuns into contact with the outside world. Television, radio and movies added to the momentum of change. Acadiana society is open today, with retirees from out of state trying retirement in Cajun Country. Traditional Cajun hospitality now extends to all.

Occasionally, Cajun French, the archaic French spoken by original settlers more than two centuries ago, can be heard today. Cajun music—played on the fiddle, accordion and triangle—is still featured at dances. However, it's mostly older people who regularly speak French; the younger generation understands the language and still can converse if need be, but seems to prefer English.

This is particularly interesting country for those who love hunting and fishing. For over two centuries, people living in these isolated and heavily wooded areas have hunted, not only for sport but also to put meat on the table. Extensive networks of bayous, rivers and streams provide fresh fish to supplement the diet, making hunting and fishing an integral part of every Cajun family's life. From almost any rural home, it is rarely more than a few minutes by foot or pickup to a "camp" (what Cajuns call their favorite hunting or fishing places). Roast duck, venison and wild boar perk up many Cajun menus.

Although we've traveled in Cajun Country and love the people—with their quaint accents and spry sense of humor—we used to question whether out-of-state people could feel at home in such a different culture. During our last trip through Louisiana, we did some in-depth interviews and are now confident about recommending that people investigate Cajun country for retirement possibilities. Certainly, it's an option we personally favor (but since we have friends there, we could be biased). Our experience is that Cajuns are exceptionally friendly.

We witnessed an endearing example of Cajun hospitality: Last spring, during a trip through Louisiana, we were invited to lunch at a Cajun couple's home. The meal was just being placed on the table when a stranger knocked on the kitchen door. Our friends were puzzled. They'd never seen this man before. It turns out he was a telephone repairman whose truck was stuck in the mud just down the road. Our host explained, "Can't help you right now. We're just sittin' down to eat. Why don't you have lunch with us? Got plenty of food. After we eat, we'll take my tractor and pull you out of that mud." Newcomers moving into this neighborhood won't be strangers for long.

From the perspective of someone who loves good food, a big plus to living in Cajun country is the Cajun cuisine. A first cousin to New Orleans' Creole cuisine, Cajun cooking is way ahead in terms of the creativity of its dishes and the artistic inspiration of its seasonings. Favorite Cajun dishes include jambalaya, gumbo, *cochon du lait* (suckling pig), *boudin* (a blood, pork and rice sausage), soft-shell crab, stuffed crab, crawfish *touffe*, crawfish bisque, crawfish pie, and shrimp fixed every possible way that a Cajun chef can imagine. That's just for starters.

Upscale restaurants all over the world are jumping on the Cajun cooking bandwagon. They've discovered that simply tacking the term *Cajun* to a menu item works miracles. Should the chef make a mistake and burn something, it's advertised as "Cajun Blackened Broccoli," or whatever. One Cajun, angry at worldwide plagiarism of cherished recipes, declared: "My Mama never blackened anything in her life and put it on the table. If my Mama ever blackened somethin' it was a pure mistake, and she wasn't ashamed to *call* it a mistake. But she'd feed it to the *dogs!*"

Lafayette and Vicinity

Cajun country lies within a broad triangle in southeast Louisiana. Imagine the Gulf Coast as the base of the triangle and Marksville, in east-central Louisiana, as the triangle's apex. The region encompasses 22 parishes and dozens of picturesque and livable towns, including the region's largest city, Lafayette, with a population of about 95,000. Lafayette is often called the "Cajun Capital City," and it offers a full range of activities and services, anything seniors need for quality retirement.

The oil and gas industry is a big factor in the economy here, and with the resurgence of Louisiana oil on the world market, Lafayette is once again riding a wave of prosperity. This is also the home of the University of Southwestern Louisiana.

For those who feel that Lafayette is too much like a city, they'll find several delightful choices away from town. Southwest of Lafayette, the charming little city of Abbeville (pop. 12,000) is known for its two quaint town squares. Abbeville claims to be the "most Cajun place on earth." Also, there's New Iberia (pop. 32,000) to the east, set among breathtaking plantations and gardens of Shadows-on-the-Teche. Another major center of Cajun culture is Opelousas (pop. 18,500), the third oldest city in Louisiana, famous as the site of Jim Bowie's residence and well-known for having produced many fine Creole and Cajun chefs. The nearby towns of Marksville, Bunkie, Simmesport, Bordelonville and others are wonderfully steeped in history, yet lie quietly and unpretentiously as places for peaceful living.

Recreation and Culture: Lafayette and the surrounding Cajun heartland offers horse racing, boat tours of the Atchafalaya Basin Swamp golf and tennis facilities. Nearby Abbeville is known for excellent duck and goose hunting and hosts a duck festival every Labor Day. Golf courses, while not numerous, are scattered throughout Cajun country so that you can play if you don't mind a 30-minute or so drive. City Park Golf Course in Lafayette is an 18-hole facility open to the public.

In addition to a branch of Louisiana State University, Lafayette has a local community college, affectionately known as "Gumbo U," that provides excellent adult education programs for cultural backup. Festivals are big here, with one taking place nearly every weekend. There's a crawfish festival in Breaux Bridge, a French music festival in Abbeville, a rice festival in Crowley, even a Boudin Festival. (Boudin is a special Cajun sausage.) Lafayette is host to the South's second largest Mardi Gras, complete with parades, balls, masking and more.

The Acadiana Symphony Orchestra is headquartered in Lafayette, and is one of the most outstanding in the state.

Real Estate: Housing of all kinds in all price ranges is available for retirees, including several specialized housing developments, such as Azalea Estates and Courtyard at South College with independent and assisted living arrangements. New developments are in progress away from the center of the city, with some impressive "plantation manor" homes on half-acre lots.

In addition to friendly people and nice places for relocation across Acadiana, the region offers a buyer-oriented real estate market and almost nonexistent property taxes. Home prices in the best of neighborhoods are said to be at a ten-year low. We've seen some impressive homes for $150,000, as well as comfortable places selling for well under $60,000.

Medical Care: As the heart of medical care in Acadiana, Lafayette has six hospitals with 1,134 beds. The region also has numerous surgery centers, rehabilitation clinics and nursing homes, as well as the nation's largest rural ambulance company, offering ground/air paramedic services. Opelousas General Hospital serves as a referral medical center and offers a comprehensive community health care facility with a wide range of medical specialties and state-of-the-art technology.

When Grandkids Visit: Encourage them to come in late spring, during the last of April and first part of May. That's when the crawfish festivals turn staid town squares into uproarious celebrations with people dancing the *fais do-do* to zydeco music. Of course, the featured guests are tons of succulent boiled crawfish, sweet, spicy and delicious. The most famous festival is in Breaux Bridge. If you miss that one, try the crab festival in Bayou Lacombe in late June.

Addresses and Connections

Chamber of Commerce: (Lafayette) 804 E. St. Mary Blvd., Lafayette, LA
    75053. (318) 233-2705.
(Opelousas) 121 W. Vine St., Opelousas, LA 70570. (318) 942-2683.
Newspapers: (Lafayette) *Daily Advertiser,* 221 Jefferson St., Lafayette,
    LA 70501-7009. (318) 235-8511.
(Opelousas) *Carencro News, Daily World,* 49 S. Service Rd., Opelousas,
    LA 70570. (318) 896-0032.
Airport: Lafayette Regional Airport.
Bus/Train: Local bus service; Greyhound; Amtrak in Lafayette.

Cajun Country

	Jan.	April	July	Oct.	Rain	Snow
Daily Highs	62	79	91	79	54 in.	.5 in.
Daily Lows	42	58	73	59		

Houma

French Acadians first settled around Houma in 1765, when 250 exiles arrived from the Caribbean island of Santo Domingo. They were so delighted to finally have a homeland, the settlers christened the region *terre bonne,* which means "good earth." With fertile land and abundant fish and wildlife, their isolated geographic location ensured a minimum amount of governmental intervention. They lived in seclusion for generations and some continue their family traditions of living off the land today.

The city of Houma is located in southeastern Louisiana, 56 miles from New Orleans, anchoring the eastern portion of the Cajun triangle. Retirement writers have given Houma favorable publicity as one of the better places for retirement, so we first visited here several years ago to see what it was all about. We found it a very pleasant place; I recommended it as a retirement location in one of my previous books.

Water access played a major role in Houma's development. The town was founded on the banks of Bayou Terrebonne where seven bayous converge, including the famous Bayou Lafourche. The Intracoastal Waterway and Houma Navigational Canal also come through here, providing ready access to the Gulf where saltwater fishing is very popular. Because of this network of waterways, Houma is sometimes compared with Venice, Italy. Fifty-five bridges of all types span these bayous and canals. Some of the more notable bridges include swinging, lifting and bascule bridges as well as a pontoon bridge. Antebellum homes along the bayous lend grace and southern ambience.

Houma is only an hour's drive from fabulous old New Orleans, less than two hours from the state capital of Baton Rouge and a little more than two hours from Lafayette and the famed Evangeline Country. This is an excellent location for the retiree who wishes to experience the unique sights and sounds, the *joie de vivre* so well known in the Cajun Country and the "work hard and play hard" attitude of the people whose ancestors settled the bayou country so many years ago.

Small cities such as Houma (pop. 37,500) generally report unusually low incidence of crime. When we visited Houma a few years ago, it was ranked 10th in the nation in safety from FBI statistics. Occasionally it drops a few places, but that doesn't mean much. In a smaller city like Houma, a few isolated problems or a visiting burglar can magnify crime statistics, making it appear as if a crime wave had struck.

Its residential streets and homes are comfortable looking: neatly mowed lawns, children roller skating on sidewalks and neighbors talking over backyard fences. If that's what you are looking for, you might investigate any number of towns like this, within striking distance of New Orleans, but far enough away not to be struck back.

Several tribes and groups of Native Americans are located in Louisiana. They maintain strong tribal identities and cling to traditions. A state-recognized tribal community, the Houma, live primarily in Terrebonne and Lafourche Parishes around the towns of Montagne and Dulac. The Houma are among the strongest francophone communities in Louisiana and proudly retain many ancient customs. Palmetto weaving, wood carving, and herbalism are important tribal traditions.

Recreation and Culture: The waters hereabouts teem with shrimp, crawfish, crabs and oysters. If fishing is your sport, the area around Houma boasts saltwater, freshwater and brackish-water fishing. You can fish inland, shoreline and offshore; rigs and reefs; day or night. You'll find many other opportunities for outdoor recreation, including hunting, boating, camping and other sporting activities. Houma has one golf course and 30 tennis courts.

Proud of their Cajun background, the people of Houma express their heritage and joy of life through their festivals and fairs—events like the Agricultural Fair and Rodeo, the Downtown on the Bayou

Festival and the Lagniappe Community Fair and Rodeo. Mardi Gras is celebrated in Houma as enthusiastically as in New Orleans, but the celebration is more family-oriented and has a special small-town flavor.

Historic sites, museums and specialized nature tours display the rich cultural heritage of the area. Playgoers will enjoy one of the five productions presented each year by Le Petit Theatre de Terrebonne.

Real Estate: Back in the 1980s, real estate bargains were unbelievable in the Houma area. The bottom had dropped out of the oil market; high-paying jobs evaporated. As oil workers left the area for better horizons, they put their homes on the market as distress sales. But today, oil has made a comeback, and so have real estate prices. This is not to say that prices are out of line, just back to where they would be in similar places in the state. Today, $80,000 will buy a very nice home, $160,000 will buy an extravagant place.

Medical Care: Chabert Medical Center is a 201-bed hospital and Terrebone General Medical Center has 261 beds. Both are full-service institutions and are nationally recognized in their fields. Chaubert also serves as a medical teaching facility for nurses, psychologists, therapists and several other types of professionals.

Oil is still king, but in recent years diversification to the medical field has made Houma a world-class medical community. Like the oil industry, the medical industry has created a need for support services requiring considerable numbers of technicians, teachers and specialists.

When Grandkids Visit: Terrebonne Parish is more than half water, so you can be sure that there is no shortage of things to see and do along the many bayous and waterways. Take a boat trip into the bayous and mysterious moss-draped cypress swamps. The grandkids will probably catch a glimpse of alligators slithering off the banks into the murky water. The area is loaded with wildlife such as ducks, pelicans, herons, raccoons, nutria, and deer. One guided tour visits an Indian fishing village as well as a Cajun village.

Addresses and Connections

Chamber of Commerce: 1700 St. Charles St., Houma, LA 70361. (504) 876-5600.

Internet: http://www.virtualhouma.com
http://www.houma.com

Newspapers: *The Courier* (daily), 3030 Barrow Street, Houma, LA 70361. (504) 879-1557.

The Bayou Catholic (weekly), 1801 Louisiana Highway 331, Houma, LA 70361. (504) 868-7720.

Airport: Houma-Terrebonne Airport for connecting flights. New Orleans airports (55 miles).

Bus/Train: Local bus service; Greyhound.

Houma

	Jan.	April	July	Oct.	Rain	Snow
Daily Highs	62	79	92	79	57 in.	.2 in.
Daily Lows	42	59	72	60		

Toledo Bend Lake

Toledo Bend, a 186,000-acre man-made reservoir made by damming the Sabine River, is the fifth largest man-made lake in the country. The body of water stretches north-south for 70 miles, with 1,100 miles of irregular shoreline. Inlets and bays make great places for lakeshore homes and boat docks, though some sections have dead trees and stumps sticking out of the water. Apparently local fishermen prefer these areas because that's where the fish are. However, the Sabine Recreation Authority has three cutting barges working full time clearing stumps and trees in addition to improving existing boat lanes. Eventually most of the lake will be pristine.

Toledo Bend country is in the first stages of development and is anticipating growth in the near future. In the meantime, the lake affords sports fun and excitement for tourists as well as low-keyed and quiet lakeside living for residents. We visited one couple who started building a few years before retirement and just recently finished and settled into their new house. They had a stunning view of the lake and were especially proud of their elaborate boat dock at the water's edge. A trot-line extended about 50 feet from the dock, providing the couple with more catfish than they could possibly eat. They said, "We bought our lot four years ago. First we built the boat dock and a fishing camp. We spent vacations here. When retirement came around, we knew exactly what to do. We started building our house as soon as we could."

Living in an isolated and rustic area like Toledo Bend has certain drawbacks. It's still sparsely populated, so depending on where you live, you must depend on nearby towns of Shreveport, Many, Leesville or DeRidder for your medical services and major shopping. However, the way the area is developing, it may only be a matter of time until WalMart, Walgreens and Wendy's make their appearance. Residents hope not.

The real surprise in recreational facilities is the new public golf course at Cypress Bend. The $3-million-dollar, 18-hole championship layout fronts on the lake and was funded as a joint project by the federal and state governments. Plans are on the drawing board for adding a multi-million-dollar resort, complete with a 100-room hotel, condominiums and a convention center. If this comes to pass, you can be sure there'll be a proliferation of jobs and new residents to swell the population.

The area surrounding Toledo Bend is home to many species of birds—pelicans, egrets, cranes, bald eagles, ducks and a host of migratory birds. Other wildlife in the area include whitetailed deer, fox, armadillo, opossum, raccoon, coyote, beaver and wild hog.

Wild flowers carpet the roadside in spring; the azaleas, dogwoods, wild plum, Indian paintbrush, crimson clover, buttercups and bluebonnets bloom in a kaleidoscope of colors. Vast National Forest lands have an abundance of hardwood trees that seasonally change colors from tender greens in the spring to autumn hues of crimson, gold and orange in the fall. Contrasted with the pine greenery, the autumn colors make a spectacular display. A 10,000-acre wilderness area within this forest is open to the public for recreational use.

Recreation and Culture: The lake is said to have a fish population of 300 pounds per square acre. Local residents swear that the lake is so full of bass, crappie and catfish, the fish regularly engage in fistfights to see who gets to be next on your hook. In order to promote "catch and release" protocol, fiberglass replicas of lunker bass are awarded those sportsmen who catch and release the big guys. (We've seen these fiberglass replicas; they look very natural, but local fishermen complain that they're difficult to clean, and you have to cook them a long time to make 'em tender.)

A garden club known as the Wildflowers, with 83 members, is the nucleus of a social group that holds residents together. Since this area is one of the state's pilot Certified Retirement Communities, we assume that there will be programs not only to welcome retirees, but to create social groups for residents in the process. Since the communities here are small and unincorporated, you'll not find amenities such as continuing education, adult centers and the like immediately around the lake. The closest community college is in the town of Many.

Real Estate: Residential and business construction in the Toledo Bend area is on the increase. In the past five years there's been a 40 percent increase in population, over 900 new homes constructed and almost 600 mobile homes brought in to house new residents. Real estate offerings vary from rustic fish-camps by the water's edge to gorgeous lake-view homes where lots start at $40,000. Building costs here can be higher than in the larger towns, simply because workers and materials must be brought in from neighboring cities. This should change as the volume of building accelerates.

When Grandkids Visit: They'll enjoy exploring the lake on your pontoon boat, dropping lines overboard to lure fish. If you don't have a boat yet, you can rent canoes and paddle into areas of the lake that are impossible to reach by any other mode of transportation. Frequent white sandbars and primitive campsites are abundant along the miles of lake, rivers and inlets.

Addresses and Connections

Chamber of Commerce: Janell Ross, 15091 Texas Highway, Many, LA 71449. (318) 256-3523.
Internet: http://www.sra.dst.tx.us/rec/areas/lakes/tb.htm
Newspaper: *Around the Bend,* Hwy. 6, Many, LA, 71449 (313) 256-3495.
Airport: Shreveport.
Bus/Train: Greyhound.

Toledo Bend Region

	Jan.	April	July	Oct.	Rain	Snow
Daily Highs	56	77	94	79	44 in.	.7 in.
Daily Lows	36	55	73	54		

Leesville and DeRidder

When World War II exploded, the government hurriedly constructed a large army post in an almost deserted part of western Louisiana. They called it Fort Polk. Generals Eisenhower, Patton and

Clark used the region to train several million soldiers. The first draftees pushed through Fort Polk for training retained bad memories of those rustic early days, so it's understandable that the installation acquired a poor reputation among the military. But over the years the government gradually improved conditions. They constructed quality off-post quarters in Leesville and DeRidder and added amenities to the post itself, such as a championship golf course, park-like landscaping and quality housing. Those who did tours of duty at Fort Polk in later years look back with fond memories of Leesville and DeRidder. One retiree from Klamath Falls, Oregon, said, "The first time I came to Fort Polk, the Army dragged me here kicking and screaming. But six years ago, I decided to retire in DeRidder!"

Leesville: In line with recent Pentagon policy, Leesville's Fort Polk has been downsized. Local residents were delighted that the fort wasn't shut down entirely, something which would have been disastrous for the economy. However, as part of the cutbacks, the government ordered all enlisted men to live on base. This created a buyer's market for quality housing in Leesville and nearby DeRidder. These favorable real estate prices, along with the presence of retirement welcoming committees in both Leesville and DeRidder, prompted our research for relocation opportunities here. Retirement committee volunteers are available to take visitors on a tour of their area and share their pride in the community.

When we first happened upon Leesville several years ago, we were surprised to see such an attractive town popping up out of nowhere. To get here required 50 miles of driving through isolated forest and occasional farms. A small city of about 12,000 residents, Leesville's homes were well designed, mostly of brick construction and set on generous plots of tree-shaded land.

The historic downtown center, off the highway going through Leesville, is undergoing a dramatic renovation. An old theater has been beautifully restored as a special events place for banquets, proms, parties and dignitary meetings. Electric lines are now underground and attractive lighting has replaced old light poles. Because of community efforts, Leesville won first place in the district's Cleanest City contest.

The older residential section, immediately around the town center, is stocked with pre-war traditional white frame homes, mostly suitable for low-cost housing. There's a potential for restoration here as well.

They would be suitable for people who like being within walking distance of downtown.

DeRidder.: Leesville's neighbor sits down the highway 20 miles. DeRidder is slightly the smaller of the towns, with an estimated population of around 10,000. DeRidder has a section of old, elegant homes, a legacy of the bounty the town realized through timber harvests in the early part of the century. These elaborate showplaces attest to the wealth of the timber barons and merchants. Several modern neighborhoods have more upscale housing, and some are showplaces in their own right. Like Leesville, DeRidder is a home-buyer's market because of the downsizing at Fort Polk.

The city is in the process of revitalizing its historic downtown section. The downtown is starting to look as if it might make a comeback, with several businesses flourishing. The historic railroad depot has been converted into a museum with a unique collection of antique dolls, bringing tourists to the downtown.

One of the absolute jewels of DeRidder's downtown renovation project is its new library, which is fast becoming the heartbeat of the community. This is one of the first places newcomers should check in. An exciting part of the library is a program called the "Cyberspace Launch Pad," an innovative approach to community involvement in computers and the Internet. Thanks to a generous grant from the state, a sophisticated computer network offers free computer connections to all county residents. The emphasis is on communications via the Internet. For retirees, this means staying in touch by e-mail with children and grandchildren—anywhere in the world. Since the younger generations are already familiar with computers and are usually connected to the Internet, e-mail is no problem. Those seniors who don't have computers can use the library's equipment, and are issued their own e-mail accounts. Those who don't know computers are given lessons and hands-on training. An example of the library's innovative approach is the "Cyber-Grandparent Program." This project links grandparents and grandchildren by e-mail and Web pages so they can work together to perform school projects. The cyber-grandparents help their grandkids with homework as they maintain close relationships.

Leesville's library is also a gem. An ultra-modern facility just two years old, it also has public access to the Internet, CD-ROM reference, genealogical materials and more.

Recreation and Culture: The golf course at Fort Polk is the local pride and joy, and its beautiful 18-hole layout is always open to the general public. Travel agents arrange popular golf-tour packages, offering a combination of golfing at Fort Polk and Cypress Bend course at Toledo Bend. Leesville also has a municipal golf course, the only one between Shreveport and Lake Charles, also featuring lighted tennis courts, a swimming pool and other amenities. DeRidder has a golf course at a private country club. Emerald Hills, a few miles north of Leesville, has an 18-hole golf course that's said to be one of the best in a three-state area.

With all the lakes, rivers and forests nearby, outdoors people have plenty of opportunities for fishing and hunting or just enjoying a hike or boat ride. The 84,000 acres of Kisatchie National Forest in Vernon Parish has hunting grounds for upland game birds and waterfowl, as well as deer and turkey.

Both towns are surrounded by marvelous waterways, popular with boaters and canoeists. All are stocked for excellent fishing. Some of the waterways are: Sabine River, Whiskey Chitto, Alligator Lake, Toro Bayou and Kisatchie Bayou, just for starters. Birders find the area rich in opportunities, since half of the birds of North America have been spotted in southwest Louisiana (not at the same time, of course).

In Leesville, the Vernon Arts Council takes an active part in promoting the arts in the area. The Kisatchie Playhouse and Showboat Dinner Theater is located at Fort Polk and gives performances for the general public throughout the year.

The Beauregard Community Concerts Association raises enough money to fund five or more concerts annually. Funding comes from membership dues and from individual and business donations in the community.

In both towns, many celebrations, festivals and fairs are held throughout the year, a popular one being DeRidder's Grant Fall Harvest Festival. It's held the first three Saturdays following Thanksgiving and draws visitors from all over to watch authentic old-time syrup making with a mule-drawn cane press. Another treat is scrumptious homemade biscuits, cooked in wood stoves, served with fresh cane syrup, sausage and gravy. Leesville is host to the West Louisiana Forestry Festival, an annual five-day event that dedicates one day to senior citizens.

Leesville/Fort Polk is blessed with a branch of Northwestern State University for adult education. The school offers courses in several professional fields in addition to leisure learning classes. Seniors may take one course per semester tuition free, with an application fee of $15.

Real Estate: The towns of Leesville and DeRidder were blessed with the government's creation of subdivisions of quality homes for enlisted men and officers' families. Since most of it has been in place for some time, the trees and shrubbery have had a chance to add a sense of stability and homeyness to the neighborhoods. Nice-looking brick homes on shaded lots are bargains, from $60,000 to $70,000. Houses in more elegant neighborhoods cost as much as $95,000—still bargains in our book. On the outskirts of Leesville, Kurthwood Village is an elegant development with impressive homes in the $150,000 to $200,000 range.

DeRidder also has several upscale neighborhoods, with prices about the same in both towns. Bargains are to be found in either community due to the present buyers' market.

Louisiana's unique property tax system is highly praised by residents who relocate here from other states. Because real estate prices are low, the generous $75,000 tax exclusion is higher than the value of the average home. In this case the homeowner pays little or nothing in the way of property taxes. George and Mary Thompson, from New Jersey said, "The home we built is worth $75,000 here, but back in New Jersey it would be worth double or triple that. In New Jersey we would be paying $3,600 a year in property taxes. Here we pay nothing."

Medical Care: Leesville's medical needs are met by the Byrd Regional Hospital, a 70-bed facility with a full range of services. The medical staff has specialists in family practice, internal medicine, general surgery, cardiology and more. The hospital was completely rebuilt recently and is continually adding on and acquiring new equipment. The top floor of the building is devoted to seniors' health needs.

For military retirees in either town, Fort Polk hospital has a modern 165-bed hospital with a full complement of service to the military retiree community.

In DeRidder, there's Beauregard Memorial Hospital, a not-for-profit facility. As a 102-bed acute-care hospital, Beauregard Memorial combines the latest medical technology with a full range of services. Complete cardiac care and most other specialties are provided for the community, including a 24-hour emergency department.

When Grandkids Visit: Take them to Hodges Gardens, Louisiana's renowned 4,700-acre "Garden in the Forest." Set in rolling hills and towering pines, Hodges Gardens is unique in Louisiana for its rock formations, waterfalls and multi-level gardens. There's also a 250-acre pleasure-boating and fishing lake.

Addresses and Connections

Chamber of Commerce: (Leesville) U.S. Highway 171 N., Leesville, LA 71496. (318) 238-0340, (800) 349-6287.
(DeRidder) 111 N. Washington Ave., DeRidder, LA 70634. (318) 463-5533.
Internet: (Leesville) http://www.leesville.com
(DeRidder) http://www.beaulib.dtx.net
Newspapers: *Leesville Daily Leader,* 206 E. Texas St., Leesville, LA 71446. (318) 239-3444.
Beauregard Daily News, 903 W. 1st St., DeRidder, LA 70634-3701 (318) 462-0616.
Airport: Alexandria (45 minutes from Leesville), Lake Charles (45 minutes from DeRidder).
Bus/Train: Greyhound.

Baton Rouge

Baton Rouge received its name when French explorer Pierre Le Moyne (Sieur d'Iberville) organized the first permanent European settlement there back in 1682. The site he selected for the village had a tall bloodstained cypress tree on the riverbank that marked the hunting territory of two Indian tribes. The villagers christened the area *Baton Rouge,* "red stick."

The region around Baton Rouge is among the prettiest and most historic in the state. Gracious old plantation homes with huge porticoes, wrought-iron balconies and lead-sheathed roofs sit half-hidden by enormous trees, looking pretty much as they did 200 years ago. The surrounding countryside is dotted with delightful little towns, some dating from the 1700s. Their streets meander about the town (evidence of early settlement, before the age of planning commissions), past shuttered houses, ancient trees and mature camelia bushes.

As a retirement candidate, Baton Rouge has a lot going for it, even though it's one of the largest cities discussed in this book (pop. 225,000). Being a college town removes Baton Rouge from the category of ordinary cities of similar size. Cosmopolitan is one word to describe this city where some of the world's most advanced industrial facilities sit side by side with antebellum mansions. Cutting-edge technology has secured a firm foothold here, yet Baton Rouge manages to retain the charm and romance of the Old South. For those with technological skills, or those being prematurely removed from the workplace, Baton Rouge may be a place to investigate for part-time employment or consulting opportunities.

Baton Rouge is not really a part of Cajun country, and it's a little too far north to be called Greater New Orleans. Centrally located, the city is just 70 miles by interstate to New Orleans for those extra special nights on the town or for the hilarity of Mardi Gras. You can reach the beaches at Pass Christian in two hours by car. For riverboat gambling you don't have to go far—Baton Rouge has two riverboat casinos—The Belle of Baton Rouge and Casino Rouge.

Baton Rouge is Louisiana's state capital, a handsome city with neat, prosperous-looking neighborhoods, attractive subdivisions and one of the prettiest university campuses in the country. The city fulfills the image of a state capital as well as a university town. Its distinctive blend of French, Creole, and Old South traditions makes Baton Rouge as much a part of Louisiana as the great river on which it thrives.

Although not the most inexpensive place to live in Louisiana, living costs are always several points below the national average, so Baton Rouge remains an affordable retirement option. But it's the quality of the setting that makes the area attractive for relocation.

Most university towns have plenty to offer retirees. Baton Rouge, with its prestigious Louisiana State University, is no exception. The school is a source of intellectual enrichment and it brings the community a wealth of entertainment and cultural offerings. But just as important, the school attracts scholars, professors and university employees from all over the country. They bring a wide range of viewpoints and social mores, mingling them together in the academic community. The stereotypic conservative atmosphere of many southern cities is tempered by these newcomers and their varied worldviews. Students, faculty, support personnel and families of these outside people nourish fresh views and lifestyles throughout the community.

Baton Rouge offers a variety of safe, clean neighborhoods each with a distinct style of living and architecture. Single-story homes often have high, broad roofs with gables peeking out from upstairs rooms in what normally would be an attic—an interesting home design, based on centuries-old French and Acadian styles. Often they feature Acadian wrap-around porches—very practical for shading the windows from the sun's rays.

Baton Rouge is proud of its historic past and takes vigorous steps to preserve and restore its two registered historic districts: Spanish Town and Beauregard Town. An appealing mix of homes can be found in neighborhoods east of the university campus, everything from small bungalows to large estates on tree-shaded lakes.

If small-town living appeals to you more than city life, Baton Rouge offers several great choices within an short drive from the city center. The peace and quiet of country living can be enjoyed in the neighboring communities of Baker, Denham Springs and Zachary. Several new upscale residential developments have appeared over the past few years. The rolling farmlands and pine-covered hills, just north of Baton Rouge, are called the Felicianas, also known locally as "Hill Country." The Felicianas are famous for historic homes and gardens of the plantation era. Perhaps the best known is St. Francisville, where John James Audubon painted in the early 1800s.

Recreation and Culture: The university touches the community culturally as well as educationally. The school's theater, music and fine arts departments present outstanding programs for the community's enjoyment. Every year a 10-block stretch of downtown is closed to traffic while potters toil over their wheels and artists work at their easels. Musicians and mimes entertain the crowds while craftspeople of all kinds sell their wares. Two ballet groups bring stars from major companies to work with local students on this event. The Baton Rouge Opera is in its eighth season—and two light opera companies, a symphony orchestra and a professional theater company round out the cultural offerings.

Real Estate: You'll find a wide choice of housing ranging from basic to opulent. Homes of substantial brick construction seem to be the preferred style here. Because it's a good-size city, Baton Rouge offers a wide range of neighborhoods and prices. Most people will probably prefer living either near the university or in one of the many outlying developments.

Medical Care: Baton Rouge serves as central Louisiana's medical center. It has seven hospitals with first-class medical facilities and excellent physicians. The hospitals have a total of over 3,000 beds. Residents can choose from more than a thousand doctors and 300 dentists in the Baton Rouge area.

When Grandkids Visit: Take them to the Greater Baton Rouge Zoo in nearby Baker. This 140-acre park has more than 900 wild birds and exotic animals from all over the world, roaming in natural habitats. There's also a "Kidzoo" with petting animals such as sheep, goats, pigs and miniature horses.

Addresses and Connections

Chamber of Commerce: P.O. Box 3217, Baton Rouge, LA 70821-3217. (504) 381-7125.
Newspaper: *Baton Rouge Daily News,* 8252 W. El Cajon Dr., Baton Rouge, LA, 70815-8036. (504) 926-8882.
Internet: http://www.brchamber.org
Airport: Baton Rouge Metropolitan Airport.
Bus/Train: City bus service; Greyhound.

Baton Rouge

	Jan.	April	July	Oct.	Rain	Snow
Daily Highs	61	80	91	80	55 in.	.1 in.
Daily Lows	41	58	73	55		

Alexandria / England Oaks

Between 1988 and 1995 the U.S. government closed down 536 military bases, handing over a total of six million acres to state and local control. This was the largest transfer of land since the Oklahoma Land Rush. From what we hear, this is just 30 percent of the closures; there are more to come. The big question is: what are we going to do with these multi-billion dollar properties?

Of course, all military bases aren't exactly prime real estate. Many were constructed in deserts, swamps or inaccessible back country. They'll probably sit and gather sagebrush and cactus until the next war. But many bases are ideally located for residential and industrial development. The government spent untold billions constructing homes for officers and enlisted men, building PX facilities resembling

WalMarts, top-quality golf courses, swimming pools and other amenities that made the bases like self-contained cities.

However, many localities feel highly threatened by these abandoned housing units. If sold to the public, these homes could glut the market, causing real estate values to plunge through the floor. Bad enough, the military pulled many thousands of consumers from the region, without adding more chaos. Yet, it's a shame to let all of these expensive amenities go to waste.

One solution to this dilemma: convert base housing to senior housing and bring in over-55 seniors (and their money) from outside the community to rejuvenate the local economy. As pointed out earlier in this book, the net effect of a retired couple relocating in your community is the same as three new jobs. The incoming retirees occupy homes that would otherwise be empty and will be boosting the economy to boot.

Let's look at an example of this kind of conversion. When England Air Force Base—on the outskirts of Alexandria, Louisiana—was decommissioned, the city turned the air field into its major commercial airport, re-naming it Alexandria International. Warehouses and repair facilities were leased to manufacturers and other buildings converted to offices. The base hospital became a satellite facility for the state's health care system, and the school reopened as the area's first magnet elementary school.

This left a large collection of housing, mostly two- and three-bedroom homes in pretty good shape, and ready for occupancy. Since the redevelopment authority didn't want to damage the local real estate and rental markets, they restricted the base housing to two categories of tenants: retirees and employees of businesses located on the former air base.

The England Authority set aside 184 homes for redevelopment as a senior living community. They named the complex England Oaks because of the many live oak trees that shade the housing. After careful consideration, the authority awarded the senior housing conversion to California Lutheran Homes, a non-profit organization with considerable experience in retiree housing. Unlike developments planned for other former military base locations, England Oaks facilities will be leased, rather than sold. This is a pleasant, secure neighborhood of homes shaded by oaks and pecan trees, with a golf course, hiking and bike trails, a gated community that gives you a feeling of security.

England Oaks development is aimed at a distinct niche of retirement service that needs to be filled. This niche is independent living facilities for middle-income seniors who are capable of living alone, but who desire greater security and the availability of special services and a maintenance-free lifestyle. Independent living combines the advantages of conventional homes with group social and recreational activities, yet does not sacrifice comfort, space and privacy.

The two- and three-bedroom homes (formerly non-commissioned officers' housing) have been remodeled with a view to attract active seniors as well as those who might need limited help, but whose health is such that assisted living is somewhere down the road. Homes are equipped with emergency response systems, safety features for elderly, even telephones with large, easy-to-read pushbuttons and a voice that echoes back the number so that a person with poor eyesight can know he or she has made the right connection.

Because all exterior and yard maintenance is the responsibility of England Oaks, newcomers don't have to and will never have to maintain the yard. The lawnmower can be left behind. Merle Martin (retired US Army) said, "Seems I have a bad ticker, so the doctor advised me not to cut the grass any more. But I plan to whack golf balls two or three days a week, and let somebody else do the lawns." Some residents do have gardens, and a community garden is under construction—for those who don't want to give up gardening entirely.

Because the site was a military base, it especially appeals to those used to military housing, and many of its first tenants are retired military. However, England Oaks is open to all, and despite its sponsorship, is non-sectarian, with many faiths represented.

Perhaps one reason an arrangement like this appeals to retired military is that they're familiar with this type of independent living complexes, places like Air Force Village in San Antonio and elsewhere. The new concept here is that instead of large, non-refundable deposits of thousands of dollars, England Oaks only requires a $300 refundable deposit and $595 to $695 per month on a year's lease.

Recreation and Culture: The biggest recreational asset for England Oaks is the nine-hole golf course just across the boulevard from the development. Bike paths run throughout the area, and walking paths are traffic free inside the gated compound.

Social life in England Oaks is centered around the development's club house, where regular meetings, pot lucks and social hours are held. The city of Alexandria has many cultural offerings and is in the process of revitalizing the downtown with a new convention center, museum and other amenities.

England Oaks residents have numerous opportunities for continuing education. Two universities have opened satellite campuses at England Airpark. England Oaks is presently working with both of these schools to develop several non-credit courses for residents.

Festivals in Alexandria celebrate everything from dogwoods to corn to Indian heritage. Every spring, the city's cochon de lait festival (suckling pig roast) ushers in the warm weather. Other attractions include the art museum, local theater groups and the zoological park. Weekenders hike on the Wild Azalea National Trail, 31 miles of pine woods and hardwood bottom land in Kisatchie National Forest. For a popular day trip, try nearby Natchitoches, site of the movie *Steel Magnolias* and home of world-famous meat pies.

Medical Care: Major medical services are supplied by Rapides Regional Medical Center in nearby Alexandria. This facility has a staff representing more than 30 specialties plus the state's largest hospital-base home health/hospice care.

When Grandkids Visit: Within England Oaks, grandkids have their own play palace—a playground built like a castle with swings, slides, and lots of hiding places. Since traffic into the gated community is exceptionally light, the oak-lined streets and sidewalks are safe for biking, roller blading. A must-do is visit the Alexandria Zoo, with its new multi-million-dollar "Louisiana Habitat" exhibit.

Addresses and Connections

Chamber of Commerce: Area chamber: 802 3rd Street, Alexandria, LA 71301. (318) 442-6671.

England Oaks, 1008 B Norman Drive, Alexandria, LA 71303. (318) 445-0520 (800) 786-OAKS.

Newspaper: *Alexandria Daily Town Talk,* 1201 3rd Street, Alexandria, LA 71301. (318) 486-6397.

Airport: Alexandria International Airport, almost next door.

Bus/Train: Greyhound intercity buses, city buses and on-demand special services, plus a casino bus to nearby Avoylles Casino.

ALEXANDRIA

	Jan.	April	July	Oct.	Rain	Snow
Daily Highs	56	78.7	93.3	79	42 in.	.7 in.
Daily Lows	36	55.6	73.5	55		

LOUISIANA TAXES
Louisiana Department of Revenue and Taxation
P. O. Box 201, Baton Rouge, LA 70821— Ph. (504) 925-7532
Louisiana's tax bills rank 7th among the least expensive in the nation

Income Tax

First $10,000   2.0%   Next $40,000   4.0%
Over $50,000   6.0%

General exemptions: $4,500 single, married filing separately $9,000, married filing jointly, head of household $1,000 each dependent, or blindness, or 65 years old or older
Additional for disabled: $100 tax credit, blindness, deaf, loss of limb, mentally incapacitated
Additional for elderly: Ten percent of federal tax credit up to $25l
Private Pension Exclusion: $6,000 for persons age 65 or older
Social Security/Railroad Retirement Benefits: Full exclusion
Standard Deduction: Combined with personal exemptions
Medical and Dental Expense Deduction: Federal amount
Federal Income Tax Deduction: Partial to full exclusion

Sales Taxes

State: 4.0%; **Parish (county):** 0.0% - 5.0%; City 1.0% - 2.5% (many small municipalities have 0.0%)
Combined Rate in Selected Towns: Baton Rouge: 8.0%, Shreveport: 8.0%, **New Orleans:** 9.0%
General Coverage: Food is taxed, prescription drugs are exempt from state tax but generally subject to local taxes

Property Taxes

No state property tax. Local taxes subject to a $75,000 exemption.
Intangibles are subject to state taxation. In relation to personal income, property tax collections are in the lowest third among the 50 states.
General exemptions: $7,500 assessed value ($75,000 market value); doesn't apply to municipal taxes except on Orleans parish.

Estate/Inheritance Taxes

Louisiana imposes an inheritance tax that ranges from 2% to 10%. The tax rate depends both on the value of the beneficiary's share and the relationship of the beneficiary to the decedent. A surviving spouse receives a full exemption. Other beneficiaries receive partial exemptions depending upon their relationship to the decedent (e.g., children receive a $25,000 exemption). Louisiana also imposes a pick-up tax, which is a portion of the federal estate tax and does not increase the total tax owed.

● Holly Springs

● Oxford

● Tupelo

Columbus ●

Madison ● ● Clinton

● Natchez

Hattiesburg ●

Mississippi
Beach

Mississippi

Mississippi

For most folks from outside the South, Mississippi comes as a pleasant surprise. I have to admit, my preconceived image of Mississippi was of endless fields of cotton and occasional poverty-stricken small towns where "outsiders" might not be welcome. These stereotypes faded on my first research trip and dissolved entirely upon subsequent visits. I found a delightful landscape of great diversity, from picturesque Appalachian foothills in the northeast, to sandy beaches on the sunny Gulf of Mexico. In between are affluent towns and cities graced with lovely pre-Civil War mansions on landscaped grounds, as well as contemporary houses, ranch-style homes in golf course communities and developments situated on fishing lakes or surrounded by forested hills. The quality of life in Mississippi retirement is unsurpassed anywhere.

> **Mississippi**
> The Magnolia State
> Admitted to statehood:
> December 10, 1817
> **State Capital:** Jackson
> **Population (1995):** 2,697,243; rank, 31st
> **Population Density:** per sq. mile: 56.9, urban 30.7%
> **Geography:** 32nd state in size, with 48,286 square miles, including 1,372 square miles of water surface. Highest elevation: Woodall Mountain, 806 feet.
> **Lowest elevation:** Sea level, Gulf of Mexico. Average elevation: 300 feet.
> **State Flower:** Magnolia
> **State Bird:** Mockingbird
> **State Tree:** Magnolia
> **State Song:** *Go Mississippi*

Best of all, I found friendly, welcoming people, folks I knew my wife and I could become best friends with in short order. I interviewed a wide range of retired couples who moved to Mississippi from places like California, New Jersey, Minnesota and Florida. All attested to the genuine hospitality and friendliness of their new neighbors. Typical comments were: "We've only been here a year, but we have more friends now than we ever had in 30 years of living in our old neighborhood."

Mississippi's cities jealously preserve their "Old South" heritage of lovely homes to compliment modern subdivisions and tasteful commercial centers. Classic university campuses and medical centers are just as prominent as graceful residential districts and upscale restaurants and shopping. In short, the state of Mississippi has everything most retirees might need for a successful and pleasant retirement. I suppose you could find cotton fields if you look hard enough, but offhand, I don't recall seeing any.

Newcomers Welcome! Even though this has always been a great place for retirement, a recent development makes Mississippi a prime place for relocation. There's a well-funded and professionally managed state campaign to get the news out about retirement here. It's called *Hometown Mississippi Retirement.* The state allocates more than a half-million dollars a year for this program, spending more than any other state on retirement attraction. The money isn't spent on a mere propaganda barrage to lure warm bodies to the state. Their message isn't just "Come to Mississippi" and leave the results up to chance. They follow through with a well-considered program to welcome individuals into each community.

Participating towns form committees of volunteers—mostly retirees who have relocated from out-of-state. They call themselves "retirement connectors," or "retirement ambassadors." These connectors greet newcomers, show them around their new hometown and make sure they find everything they need to blend into their new surroundings. This makes retirement decisions painless and makes new friends inevitable. Often the newcomers become retirement connectors themselves.

The Hometown Mississippi Retirement program can't be used by just any community. The town first must be certified as a desirable place for retirement, taking the welfare and comfort of the retiree into consideration. This is done through another program called *Mississippi's Certified Retirement Cities.* Only towns that surpass certain standards can be certified or recommended. The first requirement is that the community and city leaders prove they actually *want* retirees. As evidence of this support, they must form a series of committees devoted to retiree attraction, including the all-important welcoming committee.

A qualified community must have an attractive appearance, a hospital within a 30-minute drive and readily available, quality housing. The community must also have low crime rates and a continuing education program aimed at bringing adults together at the local university or community college. Even then, towns can be rejected by the state director for any number of subjective reasons. Fortunately, political pressure has been kept out of the process; in fact, Mississippi's governor was disappointed when his hometown was disqualified until the community could bring itself up to standards. (Eventually it qualified, but only after considerable effort on the part of the residents.)

The director of Mississippi's retirement program is Barbara McDonald, a dynamic and enthusiastic Mississippi booster. She says, "We realize that many people throughout the country have never thought of Mississippi as a retirement haven. But we're committed, from the grass roots level to the governor, to providing retirees with *hometowns,* not just *homes.* Our Certified City volunteers dedicate themselves to making and maintaining personal contact with those who inquire about retirement here. So, when the prospects come to visit, they already have friends in place to welcome them. Our motto is: 'Once you visit, you'll want to stay!'"

To further enhance Mississippi's status as a retiree-friendly place, the legislature voted to exempt retiree income from state income tax. Along with low property taxes and favorable living costs, this provides more dollars to be spent on recreation, travel or investments. For those over 65 or disabled, there is a $60,000 property tax exemption from the assessed value of their home.

The Certified Cities are not the only nice places to retire in Mississippi, but they are the only places I can consistently recommend, places I'm confident you'll find a quality place to live with friendly neighbors who genuinely want you to join them in their hometown.

Certified Retirement Cities can be found throughout the state. Corinth, Columbus, Oxford and Aberdeen are all in north Mississippi. Lush woodlands, honeysuckle and rolling hills surround these towns in a scenic background. Writers and artists come from around the world to pay homage to William Faulkner and Tennessee Williams, natives of this part of Mississippi.

Central Mississippi offers the towns of Starkville, Meridian, Clinton and Madison. Some of the best hunting land in the state and the state's capital city highlight this region. Many cultural and recreational advantages accrue to residents here.

South Mississippi is the most diverse region of the state, featuring unique places like Natchez, Hattiesburg, Picayune and Mississippi Beach. All of these towns have distinctive appearances and support diverse lifestyles. You'll find everything from stately antebellum homes and peaceful rural living to deep-sea fishing and casino gambling. Mississippi has just a short stretch of Gulf Coast seashore, but the 30 miles or so of sandy beaches make up in quality for what they've missed in quantity. The portion west of Ocean Springs to Bay St. Louis is one of Mississippi's major tourism retirement destinations.

All of Mississippi's Certified Retirement Cities provide a quality retirement environment for its residents. Every city offers a wealth of cultural and recreation opportunities as well as quality health care facilities. But the most impressive aspect of these towns is that, somehow, they all feel like home.

Another Mississippi stereotype that is fading is that of racial disharmony. I made a special point of interviewing African-Americans who retired to the South after careers in other parts of the country, as well as some black couples who had never lived in the South. One lady—who retired from a career as a school administrator in Illinois—when asked about how she felt about relocating in the Deep South responded, "Anywhere in the country, you'll find a certain amount of prejudice against professional women, and against professional women of color, possibly even more. But I feel accepted and welcome here. It's no different than back in Illinois, where I lived most of my life." She is a member of the local retiree welcoming committee, a volunteer for the chamber of commerce and involved in many local activities. Another man I interviewed was one of the children we saw on TV in the 1960s, being escorted to school by National Guardsmen. When asked about racial harmony in Mississippi today, he said, "That was then. Tell your readers to come to Mississippi today, and they'll find a different world."

Oxford

Snuggled midst the forested hills of northern Mississippi, Oxford is a picture-book example of a gracious, southern university town.

Handsome antebellum mansions—partially concealed by flowering wisteria, redbud and creeping ivy—hold court under ancient magnolias and magnificent oak trees. Oxford is positively saturated with the history and traditions of the Old South. Quiet, tree-shaded streets, with the silence broken only by the joyous song of a mockingbird or the occasional barking of a dog in the distance, recall memories of an era made obsolete by today's frantic rush toward urbanity.

Yet Oxford shows its modern side with a large shopping mall and all the usual businesses and home developments—mercifully located toward the outskirts of town. The outskirts, by the way, aren't all that far away. With a population of only 11,000, the town doesn't spread out to eternity.

Were I to rank communities as to the "best place for retirement," Oxford would surely rank in the top ten. I confess that as an author, I could be biased by a certain mystical literary connection between Oxford and the outside world. Oxford has fostered and developed writers from its very beginning as a university town, even before William Faulkner made his home base here, and continues to support them today with several best-selling authors choosing to bask in Oxford's nurturing literary climate. It seems as if every third person we met in Oxford has written a book. The docent at Faulkner's Rowan Oak home casually mentioned that her newest hardcover book was now available at Square Books. When we commented on this to our hostess at a luncheon, it turned out that *her* sixth nonfiction book had just been published that month. (Made me want to get an Oxford post office box.)

However picturesque and traditional Oxford may appear, the University of Mississippi's presence takes Oxford into another realm of being. Affectionately known nationwide as "Ole Miss," the school adds 11,000 students to Oxford, doubling the town's population. This unique mixture of students and retirees creates a unique consumer demand: quality shopping, pleasant restaurants and affordable entertainment.

Oxford's charming downtown square is a perfect illustration of how the presence of a university can preserve the character of a town. Commerce generated by students and residents keeps downtown enterprise alive and healthy instead of abandoned to strip malls and shopping centers on the highways, as happens in many small towns across the nation. Downtown Oxford looks the way a downtown should look. A classic 120-year-old courthouse, with massive columns and centuries-old oak trees, dominates the scene, complete with the obligatory statue of a Confederate soldier standing guard.

Among the square's treasures are: a department store dating from 1839, a wonderful art gallery and enough shops and boutiques to make leisurely shopping a pleasure. The town square also supports several good-to-excellent little restaurants. You could easily find yourself dining at a table next to a best-selling author like Richard Ford, Barry Hannah or Larry Brown, who also make Oxford their home. Until recently, John Grisham was Oxford's best-known author-in-residence; he moved to Charlottesville, Virginia.

Across from the Confederate Soldier statue is a well-known Oxford tradition, "Square Books" bookstore, which features a second-floor veranda that looks out over the square, where friends meet to sip capuccino and talk about books. The 25,000-volume collection, on every subject imaginable, makes you aware that the owner operates the store with a respect for books and literature, rather than an eye on quick turnover, best sellers and high profits—which seems to be the trend lately. On the staircase, you'll find stacks of autographed copies of books by local authors. A favorite happening is Square Books' presentations by well-known authors who discuss their works and philosophical approaches in their literary accomplishments.

Oxford is a perfect location for those who enjoy southern hospitality (in a setting where many residents come from the North), those who prefer a small city with an exceptionally low crime rate, and finally, those seeking cosmopolitan, upscale living at affordable prices. Its small-town warmth is apparent as people who've never seen you before say "good morning" as they pass on the downtown square.

One retiree who came here after trying Florida for retirement said, "Everyone in Florida seemed to come from someplace else. I wanted to find a *real* town, a place where I could interact with people *from* that town. That's when I started thinking about Oxford." On another occasion, I was introduced to one of Oxford's city councilmen, also a professor at the University; I remarked on his non-southern accent. He explained that he came here from Illinois to get his PhD in Pharmacology. He found the people of Oxford so friendly, and the town so delightful, that he remained to teach and later became active in local politics.

Another retiree, a lady from Idaho whose husband is a retired attorney, volunteered, "It was wonderful how quickly we made friends without work-connections or children in school. Our friends predicted that we would never be completely accepted. But the opposite was true. I'm presently serving on the arts council and as a volunteer for the Cedar Oaks museum and for other groups, and am chairman of a committee. I'm so busy, I've had to turn down invitations to join groups. One group I belong to buys season tickets to the symphony in Memphis, and once a month we all travel there. Next month we're going to Jackson for a ballet."

Recreation and Culture: Topping the cultural attractions is the university, which is an integral part of the community. Residents of all ages participate in school activities; people over the age of 65 are encouraged to take classes at the University of Mississippi without charge.

The school's calendar brims with activities appropriate to the town's academic orientation. A well-known example is Oxford's springtime "Conference on the Book." A recent event was chaired by Stephen King and John Grisham. Artistic endeavors aren't exclusively literary, however. Sculptors, painters and ceramists are well represented, as are photographers, potters and weavers.

All activities in and around Oxford aren't intellectual. Outdoor fans have plenty of bass and crappie fishing in nearby Sardis lake, and also exciting basketball and football games when the Ole Miss Rebels host nationally ranked powerhouses. A new retirement complex features golf as one its central attractions. Two public courses include one at the university. Another golf course is a private layout on the local country club's grounds.

Real Estate: Oxford offers a wide variety of housing styles, from historic pre-Civil War mansions to ranch-style modern or southern revival homes. Yet prices are surprisingly affordable, not much more than in ordinary towns of the same size. In 1997, the median value of a home in Oxford was around $80,000 for a three-bedroom, two-bath home. Several nice developments are found on the edge of town, some quite plush, with all amenities. Azalea Gardens—an innovative, full-service retirement community—is nearing completion, with 62 apartments, 15 single-family cottages and 18 assisted-living villas.

At one time, Oxford's lovely old mansions, sitting on large city lots, were selling at tract-home prices, but this was too good to last. Prices shot up when home-lovers saw the potential in restoring these gems. Small farms—with homes surrounded by trees, ponds and an occasional lake for bass fishing— are favorites with Oxford area retirees and they can be found just a few minutes away from Oxford city limits. During our last visit, a hundred acres of woodlands was advertised for $25,000. (The ad didn't mention whether utilities were in place.)

Medical Care: The Baptist Memorial Hospital is fast becoming a regional center for health care in northern Mississippi. More than 60 physicians at the hospital represent 30 specialty areas of medicine. The hospital works closely with a variety of home health agencies in the Oxford area that strive to meet the specialized needs of individuals and families.

When Grandkids Visit: William Faulkner's home, Rowan Oak, dates from the 1840s, and is one of the lucky homes that escaped the torching during the Civil War. This fascinating primitive Greek Revival house is where the author wrote most of his works. It's furnished just as it was when he lived there from 1930 to his death in 1962 at the age of 64. A high-point of the tour is the room where Faulkner wrote his Pulitzer Prize-winning novel *A Fable*. As he worked on this book, he outlined the plot on the walls to keep track of the characters and actions. The outline is still there today.

Addresses and Connections

Chamber of Commerce: 299 Jackson Ave., P.O. Box 147, Oxford, MS 38655. (601) 234-4651.
Internet: http://www.decd.state.ms.us/Retire/Cities/oxford.htm
Newspaper: *Oxford Eagle,* 916 Jackson Ave. E, Oxford, MS 38655-3636. (601) 234-4331.
Airport: Tupelo (50 miles southeast), Memphis (80 miles northwest).
Bus/Train: Greyhound; local bus service.

Oxford

	Jan.	April	July	Oct.	Rain	Snow
Daily Highs	51	75	93	76	56 in.	2 in.
Daily Lows	31	50	69	49		

Holly Springs

Surrounded by wooded hillsides and national forest, the historic town of Holly Springs presents yet another living museum of Mississippi antebellum homes. With a population of only 7,500, the town's natural beauty sets the stage for a relaxed way of small-town living. Yet the big city of Memphis is only a 34-mile drive. The city is a source of countless museums, exhibitions and cultural events, not to mention some great shopping.

Before the Civil War, when cotton was king, Holly Springs was one of the largest cities in Mississippi. It was the focus of the region's social and cultural life as well as a beautiful and prosperous center of commerce and trade. The original settlers of Holly Springs came from Virginia and brought to the town their own distinctive style of elegant architecture that expresses the world of southern civility and grace.

As the Civil War raged on, the citizens of this already historic community could only hope and pray that their homes might be spared, and not burned to the ground, as was the Union Army's custom. As fate would have it, an extraordinary event rescued their treasured hometown from the flames.

It seems that General Ulysses S. Grant's wife, Julia, was a guest in a lovely Holly Springs mansion while Union soldiers occupied the area. Early one morning, while Grant was visiting Oxford, the Confederate General VanDorn raided Holly Springs with the objective of capturing General Grant. When his troops surrounded the house, Mrs. Grant made a plea for the protection of herself and her husband's personal papers. True to southern chivalry, the general agreed. He even declined to search the house. As a token of gratitude, General Grant forbid his troops to torch the town as they did in Oxford and other nearby Mississippi cities.

Thanks to this event, many timeless homes of classic proportion greet visitors to today's Holly Springs. The courthouse, the town square and the old train station seem to be suspended in time. Because of the doldrums following the war and lasting into the present century, a zero-growth rate helped Holly Springs avoid modernization. In size and appearance, the town changed little over the decades. Two hundred of its buildings are listed on the National Register of Historic Places, including more than 60 antebellum homes. Occasionally an old home will appear on the real estate market.

Holly Springs isn't *all* large mansions, though. Historic cottages are scattered throughout the city, some outdating the antebellum estates. Every April the streets throng with visitors when the Holly Springs Garden Club hosts the town's antebellum home pilgrimage. Events like pageants, pilgrimages and tours of historic homes are an accepted part of everyday life here.

Along with its historic heritage, Holly Springs preserves its small-town feeling and welcomes outsiders. A couple who moved here from Chicago said, "We found people here very friendly. We were not only made to feel welcome; we discovered that when you join a group, they want to make you an officer." Housing is very affordable, traffic is light and recreation and civic activities are plentiful. Residents still talk about the weather over coffee at the local cafés and take evening strolls around the neighborhood.

Recreation and Culture: Golfers instinctively reach for their woods and irons once they see the beautiful fairways, doglegs and greens at Kirkwood National Golf Club. Recently voted one of the top five new public golf courses in the country, the golf course is just two miles from town. Holly Springs Country Club also offers golf, tennis, swimming and dining.

Three recreation parks are within minutes of Holly Springs for quick access to wooded nature trails, picnic sites, campsites and beaches. The abundance of woods, rivers, streams and lakes provides the best in fishing, hunting and water sports. For gambling, you can catch a shuttle to visit the Mississippi riverboat casinos near Tunica. It takes about an hour to drive there.

A carnival atmosphere of rides, arts and crafts, live music and championship barbecue takes over Holly Springs during the annual Kudzu Festival. For those northerners who don't know about Kudzu, you will get an education. Holiday season features a spectacular display of lights, a parade, a holiday tour of homes, a tree-lighting ceremony and high tea at the art gallery. For the tops in educational opportunities, it's only a 30-minute drive to Oxford, where there's free tuition for those over 65.

Real Estate: The cost-of-living is well below the national average, partly because of affordable housing. Three-bedroom, two-bath homes start in the $65,000 range. A wide selection of housing is available, from older homes within walking distance of the lively downtown, to newer, conventional homes outside of the city limits. Acreage is also affordable.

Medical Care: Holly Springs Memorial Hospital takes care of most health care needs. It's a small facility, with 40 beds and 10 physicians. Memphis, with its excellent range of high-tech hospitals, is 30 minutes or less via Interstate 78.

When Grandkids Visit: It's only a hop, skip and a wiggle to Elvis Presley's Graceland in Memphis. The grandkids should get a kick out of what kind of music you listened to in the 1950s. You'll see Elvis's collection of motorcycles and gold records, his pool room and other mementos. You say you weren't an Elvis fan? Okay, then drop the grandkids off at Graceland while you tour the Coors Brewery. They give out free samples.

Addresses and Connections

Chamber of Commerce: 154 Memphis St., Holly Springs, MS 38635. (601) 252-2943.
Internet: http://www.decd.state.ms.us/Retire/Cities/hsprings.htm
Newspaper: *The Chronicle,* 145 S. Center St., Holly Springs, MS 38635-3040. (601) 252-3193.
Airport: Memphis International Airport (35 minutes).
Bus/Train: Greyhound; Amtrak service in Memphis.

Natchez

Stately Natchez sits on a scenic bluff overlooking the mighty Mississippi River on land that was originally a tribal center of the Natchez Indians. The French constructed a fort here in 1716—after chasing away the Indians—making Natchez the oldest European settlement on the Mississippi River. After 82 years as home of Spanish governors and French plantation owners, the U.S. flag first appeared in 1798 when Natchez was made the seat of the Mississippi territory.

During its history the city has flown six different flags, the penultimate one being the Stars and Bars of the Confederacy.

Very early, the town blossomed as a prosperous cotton-raising and exporting city. It quickly became one of the South's wealthiest cities— possibly the richest in the entire nation. The large number of awesome homes and mansions testify to this. When war between the North and the South threatened, some Natchez plantation owners were staunchly opposed to secession. They fully realized that war would be a financial disaster as well as a tragic spilling of blood. Therefore, when the war descended upon the nation, Natchez support was less than enthusiastic. When the first Yankee gunships drifted down river, ready to bombard Natchez, they were greeted by a huge white flag of surrender fluttering on the bluff. The city of Natchez negotiated a peace that guaranteed the preservation of the magnificent mansions that graced the city.

The plantation owners were correct about financial ruin from the war. Despite cooperating and assisting the Federal troops, most families were left destitute—their possessions looted, homes vandalized, crops destroyed. The only treasures left to Natchez were the stately homes that were spared as agreed. This made the city a unique showcase of aristocratic southern architecture. Approximately 500 antebellum homes grace the quiet streets of modern-day Natchez, some dating back to the era of Spanish and French rule. Throughout the huge historic district, lovely Victorian homes add to the feeling of stepping back in time.

Today, Natchez is a quiet town of 20,000 friendly people with well-cared for neighborhoods and affordable housing. Even if not your choice for retirement, it's well worth a visit to delight in Natchez's antebellum glory. There's something magical about the historic city center. One woman said, "When we were investigating places to retire, we went everywhere, including Hawaii. But when I saw downtown Natchez, I knew I was home. Somehow, I felt as if I had been here before, and it was perfect."

The big industry here is tourism, as you might imagine, with folks coming from all over the world to marvel at the living museum of architecture. This has a spinoff benefit for local residents, in that many more nice restaurants are available than in other towns of this size. Another consequence of tourism is the large number of old homes being operated as bed-and-breakfasts. In a place like Natchez, we much prefer these accommodations to ordinary hotels or motels. We counted over 35 B&Bs, and we probably missed a few.

The wealthy aristocrats had their homes on the high ground, but the rough-and-tumble steamboat crowd, rogues and river pirates strutted their stuff down by the Mississippi River bank, at Natchez Under-the-Hill. This was a district of docks, saloons and bordellos—famous for gambling houses and illicit excitement. Today, at least some of the excitement has returned to Natchez Under-the-Hill in the form of riverboat gambling. In addition to a casino and gambling aboard a ship, several unique restaurants have been embellished to keep alive the wicked, 1800s decor.

In keeping with southern traditions, the social scene in Natchez revolves about "garden clubs." These clubs seem to have little to do with gardening, but more with social activities and organizing civic events. Charities and volunteer work fall under the domain of the garden clubs. We were told to advise newcomers to seek an invitation to join. (Some of the more exclusive garden clubs probably require that your grandmother was a member.) The easiest way to make new friends is to contact the Retiree Partnership, a group specially dedicated to attracting retirees to the area and making them feel at home.

Recreation and Culture: Natchez has three golf courses, all open to the public, although one belongs to a membership country club. One of the town's two tennis facilities is located at the country club. Because Natchez is surrounded by sparsely populated, forested countryside, hunters and fishermen have ample opportunity to pursue their hobbies. A large variety of game is found in the surrounding wilderness: whitetailed deer, turkey, dove, squirrel, quail and rabbit. Local fishermen claim that Natchez State Park offers the best bass fishing in the state. Many bass in the 20-pound class have been hooked and netted in the park's 3,000-acre lake.

Natchez works hard to keep a full calendar of cultural entertainment for tourists and residents alike. Its famous Opera Festival is enjoyed by longtime opera lovers as well as those who've never seen an opera before. Each season residents enjoy an unparalleled variety of musical performances, ranging from serious dramatic opera to Broadway musicals. The Literary Festival held every summer focuses on literature, with lectures and seminars by well-known authors. A recent addition to the cultural scene is a "Learning in Retirement" program, designed for those interested in continuing education.

Many places in the South hold an annual Pilgrimage, in which antebellum homes are opened to the public. But the Pilgrimages that Natchez puts on three times a year are probably the most famous of all.

Real Estate: The South has numerous towns with proud antebellum homes, many of them for sale at what seem to be bargain prices. But in our opinion, no southern town has as many beautiful places for sale at such low asking prices as Natchez. (I once said something like that about Oxford, but at last visit, prices had risen dramatically.) We looked at one home that dated back to the late 1700s, and when we asked about the price, we were told, "Why, I think they're asking $125,000 for that old place. But that's *way* too much!"

Of course, Natchez isn't all historic mansions; you'll find plenty of modern, conventional homes. Newer subdivisions and custom homes are found on the fringes of town. The heavily forested countryside has many acreage-sized lots carved into the woods for small estates, ranch-style homes and clusters of conventional houses. In 1996 the median price of a home was slightly less than $70,000. Some subdivisions had homes selling for a high of $55,000, others for $90,000, while three subdivisions had homes selling for over $200,000. Newcomers certainly have a choice.

Medical Care: Two modern, full-care hospitals and a large group of medical professionals serve the medical needs of Natchez. Between them, the hospitals have 306 beds and employ the latest in medical technology. In addition to the hospital staff, 54 physicians practice in the area.

When Grandkids Visit: First take them on a horse-and-carriage tour through the historic area, then visit the Grand Village of the Natchez Indians, the ceremonial mound center and main settlement of the Natchez Indians. French soldiers destroyed the village in 1730 after the Indians attacked their fort at Natchez. A museum displays artifacts and reconstructs the life of the original inhabitants of Natchez.

Addresses and Connections

Chamber of Commerce: Retiree Partnership, P.O. Box 700, Natchez, MS 39121. (800) 762-8243.
Internet: http://www.decd.state.ms.us/Retire/Cities/natchez.htm
Newspaper: *Natchez Democrat,* 503 N. Canal St., Natchez, MS 39120-2902. (601) 442-7355.

Airport: No commuter service at this time.
Bus/Train: Natchez Transit System travels through downtown and to Under-the-Hill areas. The senior citizens' center has five buses to serve the general public as well as seniors.

Natchez

	Jan.	April	July	Oct.	Rain	Snow
Daily Highs	61	79	91	80	55 in.	.5 in.
Daily Lows	41	58	73	56		

Mississippi's Capital

Jackson is not only the capital of Mississippi, but also it's the state's cultural, financial and population center. Jackson is a beautiful city in its own right—and for many folks, a good retirement choice; however it *is* a large city, and when we find a place as nice as Jackson, we like to look for retirement places just outside of the metropolitan center. In the course of our research, we discovered two delightful small towns, both within a few minutes drive of Jackson's center—a compromise between living in the city of Jackson and living in the "country" yet being close enough to enjoy all the cultural and civilized amenities to be found in the city.

These two communities are Clinton and Madison. Both have a lot to offer retirees, both communities have active welcoming committees and both towns have women mayors. Since we couldn't decide which we liked best (both the towns and the mayors), we decided to include both places. Clinton sits beyond the western limits of Jackson, and Madison is to the northeast. We'll start (in alphabetical order) with Clinton.

Clinton

Clinton began as an Indian trading post back in 1805, when it was known as Mount Salus, meaning "mountain of health." The name was justified by the area's many refreshing, healthful springs. Located at the junction of the Natchez Trace and the road to Vicksburg, the settlement became an important stagecoach stop and the crossroads of the territory. Clinton almost became the capital of the newly-formed state of Mississippi; it missed by one vote. Today it's one of the fastest-growing cities in the state, with a population nearing 25,000.

Because Clinton is just a short commute from Jackson, its suburban quality is unmistakable. Quiet streets and quality neighborhoods make for tranquil living. Choosing a place like Clinton is like finding the best of two worlds: a place with a peaceful, small-town disposition, yet minutes away from the convenience and action of the city. As an example of the kinds of cultural advantages in living close to a city: when we visited Clinton for our research, we were privileged to take in an exposition at the Mississippi Arts Pavilion in Jackson. "The Palaces of St. Petersburg: Russian Imperial Style" was an exhibit never before displayed anywhere outside of Russia.

In keeping with its small-town image, the charming downtown area has been restored, complete with historic brick streets and tasteful shops, and named "Olde Towne." However, Clinton isn't strictly a bedroom community; several manufacturing facilities provide jobs and add to the overall feeling of prosperity. Clinton is also a college town. With the founding of Mississippi College in 1826, Clinton became known as the "Athens of Mississippi." One of the oldest universities in the country, the school prides itself on community involvement in a variety of activities, from collegiate sports to concerts and pageants.

Folks who've retired here swear by the small-town friendliness, yet they appreciate the nearby big-city conveniences. One retiree (Al Nieminen) from Ohio, said "When my company moved us down here, we liked Clinton so well that I turned down promotions in order to stay. When retirement came around, we didn't even think of leaving."

Recreation and Culture: Besides hunting, fishing and boating—all within a short distance from the city limits, Clinton has access to a public golf course in nearby Raymond and several private clubs in Jackson. Walking and biking trails run through town. For indoor recreation, the floating gambling casinos on the Mississippi River at Vicksburg are only 30 miles away, via 70-mile-per-hour Interstate 20.

Because Clinton is just a 10-minute drive from Jackson, residents here enjoy a rich source of cultural entertainment such as symphony concerts and chamber music recitals to be enjoyed year round. There's always something going on at Jackson's Museum of Art and the Jackson Zoo, and there are even street parties with downtown stages for blues, rock, country and gospel. There's a full calendar of events the year round.

In Clinton, the city's Arts Council keeps cultural and fun events going. Among its activities is the Brick Streets Festival, which starts in April with a month-long series of festivities. The brick streets of Clinton's restored "Olde Towne" are enlivened by music, food, and arts and crafts displays, as well as a Shakespeare festival.

District and regional sporting events sponsored by Mississippi College draw athletes and fans from across the southeast. Hinds Community College also serves the community with continuing education.

Real Estate: You have your choice of any kind of neighborhood you might desire. There are older homes along tree-shaded streets or newer houses in upscale developments. Several garden and patio townhomes or condos are popular with those retiring who want smaller, easy-to-care-for places. An average three-bedroom, two-bath home in an above-average neighborhood sells for around $85,000.

Medical Care: Clinton is home to a wide range of medical professionals and facilities, from family practitioners and dentists to optometrists and chiropractors. Because Jackson is just minutes away, Clinton residents have access to some of the finest medical care in the South. Six major medical facilities are located minutes away in the Jackson metropolitan area, with specialists in just about every medical field.

When Grandkids Visit: Ask them to try to visit in April, to coincide with the Civil War reenactment depicting the Battle of Clinton. The action is enhanced by firing cannons, charging horses and all the trimmings. In the original battle, Yankees burned so many homes in Clinton that it bore the nickname "Chimneyville" for many years afterward, so we can surmise that the Confederate troops will lose the reenactment. But, you never know; this is Mississippi, after all.

Addresses and Connections

Chamber of Commerce: P.O. Box 143, Clinton, MS 39060. (601) 924-5912.

Internet: http://www.decd.state.ms.us/Retire/Cities/clinton.htm

Newspaper: *Clinton News,* P.O. Box 66, Clinton, MS 39060. (601) 924-7976.

Airport: Jackson International (18 miles).

Jackson

	Jan.	April	July	Oct.	Rain	Snow
Daily Highs	57	78	93	79	52.8 in.	1.2 in.
Daily Lows	35	53	71	52		

Madison

The second suburb of Jackson that caught our eye is the small city of Madison. Located about the same distance from Jackson as Clinton, where the Natchez Trace skirts to the north of Jackson, Madison is smaller than Clinton, with about 15,000 residents. But it has a totally different flavor. For one thing, Madison is definitely upscale; the homes and developments are tops in quality and price. Its residents have the highest per-capita income in the state. Shopping districts and outlying residential development clearly show this affluence.

Unlike other Mississippi towns and cities discussed in this book, Madison is not long-established, and has a history of gradual development. While the town has roots going back to pre-Civil War days, until about 16 years ago Madison was little more than a farming crossroad community with about 1,000 residents. Since development started from scratch, residents seized the unique opportunity of planning, guiding and shaping the way the town progressed.

One of the first things you'll notice about Madison is the lack of "strip mall" clutter—no blinking signs, flashing lights or bright plastic decor. Strict regulation of signs and business architecture should make Madison a model for other small cities—an example of how downtowns should be kept alive and well. (Unfortunately, it's too late for most towns; their depressed downtowns are filled with closed shops and painted-over display windows. Their shops, markets and businesses were forced to go out of business or join the movement to the highway on the edge of town.) I urge city planners to visit Madison to see how it's done.

Much of the credit for Madison's success goes to Mary Hawkins who has been mayor since she was first elected in 1981 at the age of 26. Mary is extremely controversial with contractors and developers, upon whom she places stringent rules that she enforces with unrelenting vigor. (They're forever dragging her into court, accusing her of being dictatorial, but Mary is forever winning.) On the other hand, she is absolutely adored by voters and residents of Madison for sticking up for their desire to keep Madison from becoming just another bedroom community. (She ran unopposed in the most recent election.) A typical Mary Hawkins battle: The architectural design for a new post office conflicted with the general decor of Madison's downtown center, so the mayor took the U.S. government to task, and after a hard battle forced architects to redesign the post office and to build it in a more desirable locale. Another battle: When a new factory located in town, the mayor refused to connect the water until they agreed to landscape the grounds, remodel the building's facade to match the downtown's architectural theme and to replace the hurricane-and-barb wire fence with a nice-looking (but expensive) wrought-iron fence. "We probably have Mississippi's most beautiful factory building," Mary Hawkins said, with a satisfied grin.

The result is a tasteful, high-quality town center. Stores, banks and office buildings all have been specifically designed or remodeled to harmonize with the overall plan. Quaint antique shops filled with treasures, tasteful restaurants and upscale boutiques occupy space once allocated to self-storage sheds. (The mayor went to court over that one too.) Yes, even gasoline stations must have an antique design that complements Madison's ambiance—or they don't sell gas. The city complex now includes more than 60 carefully planned subdivisions, among the most upscale (and expensive) in Mississippi. As a planned community, Madison places emphasis on safety, comfort and maintaining a quality small-town atmosphere.

As an indication of the community's interest in retiree relocation, Madison recently sent 14 volunteers to the annual Southeast Retirement Symposium. With this enthusiasm, you can be sure of being welcomed.

Recreation and Culture: For baseball fans, a short drive to Jackson takes them to see games by the Generals, the AA ball club for the Houston Astros. For avid golfers, in addition to golf layouts in Jackson, Madison has three golf clubs that offer tennis and fine dining in addition to golf. One course was designed by Jack Nicklaus.

Jackson's symphony, opera, ballet, theater companies and the Mississippi Museum of Art, with its international exhibitions, are well worth the 15-minute drive; however, the arts have a home in Madison as well. The Madison Square Center for the Arts is listed on the National Historic Register and is home to the Madison Civic Ballet. Residents with a creative side can also take classes in dance, theater, art and music there. We attended a delightful potluck at the Center and were entertained by a children's ballet performance.

Madison is also a favorite spot for antique shoppers. Those in search of something special from a bygone era will fall in love with the pieces of antebellum and Victorian grandeur found in Madison's shops. Twice a year, 30,000 crazed antique-shoppers descend upon the Madison area for the Canton Flea Market, which features 1,200 vendors of arts and crafts, antiques and collectibles.

Madison's Strawberry Patch Park is the site of many good times for the Madison community. The park has a lake for fishing and a trail for walking, with exercise stations. A picnic on the park grounds celebrates Easter, and the Fourth of July is celebrated with games, a fishing rodeo and fireworks. The Simmons Arboretum, a 10-acre nature area, showcases Mississippi's diversity of plant life.

For continuing education, Hinds Community College in nearby Raymond sponsors an Institute for Creative Learning in Retirement program. Like other community colleges in Mississippi, these programs are designed and operated by retirees, for retirees. Class topics are selected from suggestions of class members and often taught by retirees.

Real Estate: The inevitable result of restrictive zoning and building codes is high-quality homes, but a dearth of low-cost housing. You won't find mobile home parks or inexpensive tract homes here. Apartment rentals are all but nonexistent, and we saw no condominiums. The average price of houses sold here is $115,000; that's about $25,000 to $50,000 higher than in most Mississippi communities. But if you can afford higher prices, you definitely get your money's worth. Madison has at least one lovely golf course development, complete with a country-club type center for residents. All developments are required to have landscaped entrances and sidewalks. St. Catherine's Village, a $50 million complete life-care center, is an impressive complex for seniors who prefer not to care for a house and yard.

Medical Care: Since the excellent medical facilities in Jackson are just minutes away, Madison needs little more than local physicians to oversee health care. Six major hospitals are located in Jackson. One of them, St. Dominic-Jackson Hospital, is known for the technically advanced Mississippi Heart Institute. The University of Mississippi Medical Center in Jackson serves as a diagnostic and treatment center for the entire state, and is internationally recognized for pioneering in organ transplantation and cardiovascular treatment.

When Grandkids Visit: The 33,000-acre Ross Barnett Reservoir, just east of Madison, is a great place for hooking some crappie or bluegills, having a picnic or waterskiing. You can fish from a boat, a pier or from the shore. There's bound to be a mess of fish with your grandkid's name written all over it.

Addresses and Connections

Chamber of Commerce: P.O. Box 544, Madison, MS 39130-0544. (601) 856-7116.
Internet: http://www.decd.state.ms.us/Retire/Cities/madison.htm
Newspapers: *Clarion-Ledger*, 331 E. Pearl Street, Jackson, MS 39217. (601) 961-7000.
Madison County Journal (weekly), 105 N. Central Ave., Ridgeland, MS 39157. (601) 853-4222.
Airport: Jackson Airport (20 minutes).
Bus/Train: No local bus or train service.

Tupelo

When Hernando DeSoto's expedition entered northeast Mississippi in the 1500s, present-day Tupelo was the site of a large Chickasaw Indian village. The Chickasaws weren't particularly hospitable to newcomers in those days—and these strangers were not only from out-of-state, but they also came from another country! Brandishing tomahawks and spears and shouting war-whoops, the Chickasaw "Chamber of Commerce" chased DeSoto and his companions out of the village, past the city limits and clear into the next county. This would never happen today; Tupelo residents *love* to welcome folks who relocate here!

No longer a village, Tupelo has become a prosperous town of 34,000 inhabitants, where warm smiles and hometown hospitality are the rule, not the exception. This place has one of Mississippi's most enthusiastic retiree welcoming committees eagerly waiting to bring you into the fold, to make sure you get settled in your new home and are introduced all around. They'll have you working on a community project before you know what happened. A couple from Orlando, Florida, said, "We first came here in 1984 for a wedding and were impressed with how things worked and with how many things Tupelo has that other cities don't have."

One of the bonuses of living here is Tupelo's pride in being a place where both natives and newcomers share in the community's vitality. Tupelo has received national recognition—by the *Wall Street Journal,* National Public Radio and other media—for the city's outstanding community development initiatives.

Nestled in the scenic beauty of northeastern Mississippi's rolling countryside, Tupelo sits on the Natchez Trace—about halfway between Natchez and Nashville. Memphis is an hour-and-a-half drive via Interstate 78, and Mississippi's lovely state capital at Jackson is a pleasant three-hour drive along the scenic Natchez Trace. The trace, by the way, is a nature wonderland you'll not want to miss. You'll see wild turkeys, deer and birds, and light motor traffic (no trucks allowed) makes a leisurely drive along the Natchez Trace a pleasure. We've driven this road many times, occasionally pausing for a picnic or a hike along one of the historic pathways that branch off from the Natchez Trace.

Twice named an All-American City, Tupelo enjoys a prosperous base as a manufacturing, retail and distribution center; its furniture industry rivals that of North Carolina. Our impression is that this is an exceptionally pleasant place to live, with welcoming neighbors and plenty of opportunities for community participation. And in case you didn't already know it, residents will proudly inform you that Tupelo was the birthplace of Elvis Presley.

Like most Mississippi communities, this is an affordable place to live. Tupelo's mild winters mean low heating bills and, combined with competitive utility and insurance rates, help lower the cost-of-living.

Recreation and Culture: Five public and private golf courses and mild winters make for golfing pleasure year round; there's also excellent golf at the Tupelo Country Club. The city has tennis courts in abundance, with instructors available to help you learn or sharpen your game. The 1,600-mile-long Tennessee-Tombigbee Waterway is minutes away from Tupelo, providing outdoor fun in the form of fishing, boating, picnicking or camping.

Tupelo has two colleges: a branch of the University of Mississippi and the Itawamba Community College. Those over 65 do not have to pay tuition! In addition to continuing education opportunities at the colleges, the Lee County Library offers year-round lecture series and "brown bag luncheons" with informal presentations for workers on their lunch break, and retirees on their shopping break.

Tupelo's community theater and symphony are the pride of the region. And the new Tupelo Coliseum brings top-name performers to the area. Elvis Presley once gave a benefit performance here to raise money for a 15-acre park. The park today encompasses the house where Elvis was born as well as a museum of Elvis memorabilia. Another cultural attraction is the Tupelo Art Gallery, which brings famous traveling exhibits to town and displays work of well-known local artists. The Old Lyric Theater has been restored and remodeled to provide Tupelo with one of the finest live theater facilities in Mississippi. The theater boasts 376 floor seats and 270 balcony seats.

Real Estate: Tupelo has a wide range of homes in a variety of comfortable neighborhoods. The average sales price of a home in the Tupelo area is approximately $90,000. From stately, older homes to new residential construction, Tupelo provides choices for every budget and lifestyle. Neighborhoods are peaceful and tend to be closely knit, with residents benefiting from well-trained, professional fire and police protection.

Medical Care: North Mississippi Medical Center, a full-service health care facility, is located in Tupelo and is the largest non-metropolitan hospital in the nation, with 650 beds. The hospital offers a broad range of services, including a wellness center that promotes a variety of exercise and fitness opportunities as well as educational programs on diet and preventative care. Nearly 300 physicians serve the county, providing a high patient-to-doctor ratio.

When Grandkids Visit: There's no question about this—you *must* take the grandkids to the Elvis Presley Center and Museum. Yes I know, your grandkids may not be very interested in Elvis Presley; he was way before their time. But *you'll* have fun gazing at Elvis memorabilia, remembering his music, reliving memories of the 1950s. Of course, should Elvis be alive (as some believe), you just might see *Elvis* showing *his* grandkids around the museum! Today, Elvis Presley would be 62 years old, retired, drawing Social Security and looking for a nice place to retire. I can't believe it either.

Addresses and Connections

Chamber of Commerce: 117 North Broadway, Tupelo, MS 38801. (800) 488-0739, (800) 533-0611, (601) 840-2078.

Internet: http://www.decd.state.ms.us/Retire/Cities/tupelo.htm
Newspaper: *Tupelo Daily Journal*, 1655 S. Green St., Tupelo, MS 38801-6557. (601) 842-2611.
Airport: Tupelo Municipal Airport, commuter connections to Memphis.
Bus/Train: Greyhound; no city bus service at the moment.

Tupelo						
	Jan.	April	July	Oct.	Rain	Snow
Daily Highs	49	74	91	75	51 in.	4.5 in.
Daily Lows	31	51	71	50		

Hattiesburg

Hattiesburg, a lovely town of 48,000, is another of the many surprises Mississippi seems to be continually pulling on us. Our first experience with Hattiesburg was a visit during a research trip to the rolling piney woods area of south Mississippi. Fortunately, our visit coincided with a dinner meeting of a group called "the Hattiesburg Retirement Connectors." This is a group of retired volunteers whose main purpose is to make newcomers to Hattiesburg feel at home. Retirement Connection members are familiar with problems involved in relocating; all retired here from somewhere else. We had a great time as folks discussed their motives for choosing Hattiesburg as a retirement destination. The Hattiesburg retirement relocation program is one of most successful in the state. It has welcomed 273 households from 35 states since the program began in 1993. New residents who join the group go on quarterly outings, take adventure trips and receive gifts from area merchants. If you choose to retire here you'll meet people who have relocated from places as far away as New York, California and Florida.

When newcomers visit the city, they understand why Hattiesburg was awarded the United States Conference of Mayors 1992 "Livability Award" for cities under 100,000. Furthermore, as a college town, Hattiesburg reaps the benefits of the academic economy, which gives the town a lively and attractive downtown area.

Unlike some Mississippi cities listed in this book, Hattiesburg doesn't have a collection of antebellum homes. This is because the town's development didn't get underway until some years after the Civil War. But Hattiesburg's 23-block area of lovely, turn-of-the-century homes in the Historic Neighborhood District truly compensates for the lack of pre-Civil War homes. Residents are proud of these perfectly restored Victorian, Queen Anne and Greek Revival style houses.

Hattiesburg calls itself the "Hub City" because of its convenient location. Saltwater fishing and gambling casinos on Mississippi's Gulf Coast playground is only a 70-mile drive through the DeSoto and Brooklyn National Forests. The bright lights of New Orleans, with Bourbon Street fun and French Quarter restaurants, are less than an hour-and-half drive along Interstate 59. You can drive into New Orleans to watch an afternoon Saints football game, have dinner and be home in time for bed. Mobile, Jackson and Meridian are each about an hour and a half from Hattiesburg.

One of the biggest novelties for those moving from the frigid north to the sunny South is mild winter weather. A couple from Rochester, New York, smiled smugly as they said, "We feel like it's springtime all winter long. In January—when you wouldn't even think of going outside in New York—we were in the backyard planting raspberry and blueberry bushes."

Recreation and Culture: Located in Mississippi's piney wood hills country, Hattiesburg is adjacent to vast acreages of national forest land. There are plenty of lakes, streams and wooded areas for hunting, fishing, hiking and camping. Hunting in DeSoto National Forest east of town is open to the public; hunting licenses are free of charge for seniors 65 and older. The woods are a haven for turkey, whitetailed deer, dove and other small game.

Hattiesburg is a golfer's paradise. Ten year-round golf courses are always ready for play, including a championship course that has been described as one of the finest in the South, often hosting PGA events. There's also a swim and racquet club with eight lighted tennis courts.

Do you think of the game of checkers as a spectator sport? If so, you might enjoy watching a game of checkers played on a floor-size checkerboard at the International Checker Hall of Fame in the nearby town of Petal.

The University of Southern Mississippi (USM) and William Carey College enrich the community with theater, concerts, lectures and exhibits. The university offers free auditing of classes for those 65 and older. The art departments of both schools provide classes in ceramics, painting, drawing and sculpture. For sports fans, college athletic events include football, basketball, baseball and soccer.

Of special interest is USM's Institute for Learning in Retirement. Located in a lovely, off-campus house, the program offers a relaxed setting for learning and sharing experiences. This is a great place to make new acquaintances in the community. Having no grades or exams takes the stress out of the continuing educational process.

Although the cultural ambiance of Jackson is within easy driving distance—with opera, museums and such—Hattiesburg residents don't have to leave town to enjoy a rich cultural life. Musical, theatrical, concerts and other events that you'd expect from a big city are enjoyed right here. The Hattiesburg Civic Light Opera produces Broadway musicals; Just Over the Rainbow entertains with dinner-theater productions. A gallery featuring works of Mississippi artists is maintained by the Hattiesburg Arts Council.

Two community events—the Old Time Festival in May and Hubfest in October—are said to draw crowds of over 50,000 in downtown Hattiesburg to enjoy food, fine arts exhibits and music. During the holiday season, folks come from miles around for the Candle Lit Victorian Christmas, which is held in the Hattiesburg Historic Neighborhood District, with tours of homes, carriage rides and caroling.

Real Estate: You'll find a wide variety of homes here to fit any lifestyle, and because Hattiesburg real estate is about 10 percent below national averages, prices are affordable. Within the city limits, average homes in nice neighborhoods sell for about $60,000. Places farther from the center can be found for as little as $50,000, with averages around $85,000. Homes located on golf course developments start at $125,000. We looked at one very stylish development, featuring large wooded lots arranged along the shore of a private lake. Amenities include tennis, boating and trails for hikers—with homes selling for less than many California tract homes.

Medical Care: Hattiesburg is rightly proud of its two state-of-the-art hospitals which serve as the health care center for the southern Mississippi region. The hospitals, Forrest General and Methodist Hospital, with more than 700 beds between them, have specialists representing all fields of medicine. Hattiesburg Clinic is one of the largest multi-specialty group practices in the state, with more than 100 physicians and 650 health care personnel. The superb medical facilities in the area have earned Hattiesburg a high ranking in the nation

When Grandkids Visit: The Hattiesburg Zoo, at Kamper Park, sits on the banks of Gordon's Creek, with landscaped grounds and walking trails. Of the zoo's prize displays are an unusual prairie dog exhibit as well as Siberian tigers and an African Veldt display with monkeys, zebra, ostrich and other African animals. Nearby Paul B. Johnson State Park is a fun place for fishing, camping and hiking.

Addresses and Connections

Chamber of Commerce: P.O. Box 751, Hattiesburg, MS 39403. (800) 238-4288.

Newspaper: *Hattiesburg Daily American*, 825 Main St., Hattiesburg, MS 39403. (601) 582-4321

Internet: http://www.decd.state.ms.us/Retire/Cities/hburg.htm

Airport: Hattiesburg-Laurel, with commuter flights to Memphis.

Bus/Train: Hattiesburg Public Transit; both Amtrak and Greyhound inter-city transport.

Hattiesburg

	Jan.	April	July	Oct.	Rain	Snow
Daily Highs	57	78	92	78	53 in.	.5 in.
Daily Lows	34	52	71	50		

Columbus

This is a comfortable-sized city of 28,000 people. Add 2,000 to the total if you count the military personnel on the air base. Columbus is known for its historic old residences. Its antebellum homes were miraculously spared during the Civil War. Although 238 battles were fought in Mississippi, Columbus wasn't a prime military target and the city was never invaded by Union troops. Today, these grand antebellum and Victorian mansions are the pride of the region, proudly lining the old brick streets and tree-shaded lanes. Each April the town conducts a Pilgrimage Tour of historic homes. Visitors are greeted by gracious hosts dressed in authentic period costumes, who conduct the visitors through their homes and proudly recite its history.

The most famous of Columbus's historic homes is a wonderful yellow and gray Victorian, the birthplace of playwright Tennessee Williams. Some believe it was the setting of his play *Summer in Smoke*, and I can also envision it as the set for *The Glass Menagerie*. Once, when he returned to visit his boyhood home, he commented, "Home is where you hang your childhood, and Mississippi to me is the beauty spot of creation." The Tennessee Williams house is now used as the Mississippi Welcome Center. Another famous home is Twleve Gables, a Greek Revival built in 1838. This is where the ladies of Columbus met in 1866 to honor the fallen soldiers of the Civil War—Union as well as Confederate. That meeting was the origin of our present-day Memorial Day commemoration.

It isn't surprising that many military families decide to relocate in Columbus upon retirement. When service personnel leave the military they naturally remember the more pleasant tours of duty and long to return. Retirees can take advantage of the commissary, post exchange and recreational opportunities on the base. This is the home of Columbus Air Force Base, one of only three pilot training facilities in the United States. Although the base hires 1,500 civilian workers and pumps millions into the local economy, Columbus it isn't just a "military gate" town. More than 50 manufacturers, the two universities and a healthy agricultural sector make for a diversified economy. For those who've reached retirement age, but aren't quite ready for the rocker, part-time work is an option in Columbus. Skills are valued and expertise is welcomed in a variety of fields.

Like all Mississippi cities listed in this book, Columbus has a welcoming committee for newcomers; the city has adopted a "Silver Eagles" program for this purpose. The Silver Eagles are growing in popularity in other parts of the South as an organized social group bringing newcomers and residents together. The group organizes trips, potlucks, dances and other congenial events. An important endeavor is offering visitors personally conducted tours of Columbus, to help retirees make up their minds about relocation here. So, when you visit here, expect to be met by "Silver Eagles."

Volunteers find ample opportunities to get involved in interesting projects in Columbus. Events like the annual pilgrimage and the Possum Town Pigfest Barbecue Competition bring people together for fun and social interaction. Said one person, "We came here to retire, but we found out that Columbus is definitely *not* the place to do that! There's too much to do."

Recreation and Culture: The recreational jewel of Columbus is the scenic Tennessee-Tombigbee Waterway. Part of 16,000 miles of inland waters, it eventually connects with the Gulf of Mexico in far away Mobile. Unlimited water and natural woodlands encourage boating, hiking and fishing as well as hunting and camping. Columbus is ideal for year-round golf play, with eight public and private golf courses within a 30-minute drive. You'll find plenty of tennis and handball at public and private facilities.

Columbus is justifiably proud of its Center for Cultural Arts, which presents professional performing arts throughout the year, and the Arts Council, which involves the community in the activities. There's also a community dinner theater, year-round festivals and ongoing events at the Mississippi University for Women (MUW). The university is headquartered on a beautiful campus with 23 buildings listed on the National Historic Register (this was the first public college for women in America). And of course, as is the custom in Mississippi, the school offers retirees 65 and older the right to attend classes, audit or credit, at no cost. The university has scheduled an "Institute for Learning in Retirement" program, soon to be offered on the MUW campus. Courses will be chosen by retirees, who will not only decide what subjects they want to take, but will also select the instructors.

Real Estate: As with most smaller cities, condos aren't too plentiful, but a new development, Plantation Point, is presently under construction and will include condos as well as lakeside homes. Another complex, Elm Lake, offers an upscale, semi-private golf course development for those who want their homes close to the fairways. Average homes in nice neighborhoods are generally priced from $65,000 to $125,000, and rural acreage sells for between $500 to $1,000 an acre.

Medical Care: More than 85 physicians staff Columbus' 330-bed Baptist Memorial Hospital. The facility provides comprehensive medical care for the region, and is the seventh largest provider of medical/surgical services in the state. Of special interest to retirees is a wellness center for those physically fit and want to stay that way. In addition to exercise classes, which include aerobic conditioning, the center has stationary bicycles, treadmills and weight lifting equipment for all ranges of ambition.

When Grandkids Visit: Sunshine Farms is a unique, hands-on working farm where children and adults alike have a good time and learn as well. The grandkids can watch ducks chase after corn and let goats lick feed from their hands. (Yuck!) The farm has a great variety of animals, including miniature horses, which the children can ride. The livestock aren't kept as exhibits, but as part of a well-run farm.

Addresses and Connections

Chamber of Commerce: P.O. Box 1016, Columbus, MS 39703. (601) 328-4491.
Newspaper: *Commercial Dispatch*, P.O. Box 511, Columbus, MS 39703. (601) 328-2424.
Internet: http://www.decd.state.ms.us/Retire/Cities/hsprings.htm
http://www.discoverypress.com/aarc/cbus.html
Airport: Golden Triangle Regional Airport, with connections to Atlanta, Memphis and Dallas (8 miles).
Bus/Train: Dial-A-Bus local transportation for seniors; Greyhound intercity service.

Columbus

	Jan.	April	July	Oct.	Rain	Snow
Daily Highs	53	77	93	77	56 in.	2.5 in.
Daily Lows	32	50	70	50		

Mississippi's Gulf Coast

People searching for an ideal place to relocate have been coming to Mississippi's Gulf Coast for nearly 300 years, starting back in 1699, when the French first explored and claimed the land as their own. For various reasons, the title to this gorgeous beachfront property was transferred first from France to Spain, then to England, to the West Florida Republic, to the Confederate States of America, until finally the United States of America ended up with it.

Residents of Mississippi Beach—the term residents now use to identify Gulfport-Biloxi—took these frequent government changes in stride; they were too busy opening seafood restaurants and constructing beachfront condos, marinas and miniature golf courses to worry about it. Once the tourist rush began, it never slackened. A recent innovation is the appearance of 11 gambling casinos that energize the coastline with bright lights, slot machines, blackjack and roulette. Retiring on Mississippi's beachfront is like going on permanent vacation. Gambling provides tourists from surrounding states with an additional excuse to congregate here—golfing, sunning on the beaches by day and shouting at the dice by night. In the winter, regular tourists are replaced by snowbird tourists, a large percentage of them Canadians, who don't mind the cooler water and occasional nippy days. Compared to Montreal or Moose Jaw winters, the Gulf Coast's coldest days are tropical paradise.

Some folks here bemoan tourism and gambling, but there's a another side to the coin: without tourist demand, there would never be the great facilities available to year-round residents—items like quality golf courses, great restaurants and world-class shopping. And, they enjoy some side benefits from these glittering gaming palaces. For one thing, residents take advantage of the great dining and top-notch entertainment the casinos offer at giveaway prices—attractions designed to lure tourists into the casinos so they can be properly fleeced. (You don't *have* to gamble, you know.) Another positive side for retirees: gambling casinos need plenty of part-time employees, thus creating work for those who feel the need to be "doing" something besides volunteer work.

Don't let gambling prevent you from considering Mississippi's Gulf Coast. Floating casinos are popping up all over the South. You'll find them on the coast, in Mississippi River towns and Florida ports, and anywhere there's an Indian reservation. You're not easily going to avoid gambling; it's a sign of the times. Those who remember the olden days, when this coast was sedate and tranquil, might feel disappointed at today's energy, but others, with no memories with which to compare, find the excitement and sparkle a delightful experience.

Gambling's effect on the local economy brings a mixed bag of assets and deficits. On the one hand, gambling has created more than $1 billion in direct investment and 15,000 jobs (including part-time work for retirees). The 70 percent increase in tourism has warmed the hearts of many local businesses. On the other hand, that old-fashioned, "Deep South" charm and honeysuckle neighborliness wears thin when trampled by herds of tourist-gamblers, traffic congestion and inevitable increases in crime levels.

As a favored retirement destination, Mississippi Beach somehow manages to combine a summer carnival atmosphere with the sedate values of the Old South. The combined population of Gulfport and Biloxi is around 90,000, and the cities are so closely connected that it's impossible to tell where one ends and another begins.

Mississippi Beach isn't all tourism and glitz—not by any means. When you get away from the casinos, the scene is different: vast stretches of sugary beach, gentle waves lapping at the sand and side roads arched over by majestic oak and magnolia trees. Large, formal estates still survey the scene with southern majesty. Antebellum homes and elegant Victorians still line the beach and grace the older neighborhoods, with ancient live oak trees sheltering them from the sun. One of the highlights of the beach-side boulevard is the mansion where Jefferson Davis chose to live out his days, writing memoirs of his days of glory as president of the Confederacy. You'll find several delightful communities, appropriate for retirement or relocation, spread along miles of white-sand beaches, away from the hubbub of the casinos.

The military has maintained a strong presence here for years. Keesler Air Force Base and the Naval Construction Battalion Center contribute economically to the area. Many military couples choose to retire here because of convenient medical and post-exchange privileges at Keesler Air Force Base. Most of these military retirees, at one time or another, were stationed in the area and developed a fondness for the beaches and the climate.

The Mississippi Gulf Coast is a transportation hub, with Interstate 10 just a few miles off the gulf and Interstate 59 to the east. Amtrak's Sunset Limited, which runs from Jacksonville to Los Angeles, stops in Gulfport and Biloxi. Four major airlines service the regional airport.

The best bets for retirement around here are towns *near* Gulfport-Biloxi. When most people talk of retirement on the Mississippi coast, they really mean the towns of Ocean Springs, Long Beach, Pass Christian and Port St. Louis. With the convenience of good hospitals and other emergency facilities in nearby Gulfport-Biloxi, many retirees look to the reasonably priced housing and pleasant neighborhoods away from the hustle and bustle of the tourist world. A bonus is exceptionally low crime rates in these towns; according to FBI statistics, they are among the lowest in the country.

Places like Ocean Springs and Pass Christian are representative of "hometowns anywhere," with quiet, mature neighborhoods within walking distance from shopping, as well as newer subdivisions of quality homes. The quiet and peaceful atmosphere is one of the first qualities that local residents proudly point out. "Gulfport-Biloxi is too crowded and too honky-tonk," said several retirees in Pass Christian. "Here, we have miles of quiet beach, all to ourselves."

Long Beach: A former farming community to the west of Gulfport, Long Beach (pop. 22,000) at one time proclaimed itself—for lack of any other distinction—"the Radish Capital of the World." Today its quiet residential areas attract retirees who enjoy the comfortable neighborhoods as the town struggles to live down its wild reputation as the world's radish capital.

You'll find an interesting mixture of homes here, varying from extraordinarily inexpensive to amazingly extravagant. One home, facing the beach, carried a price tag of $350,000—which sounded overpriced for the area, until we looked it over. It was a *Gone with the Wind*-type home: three stories, rooms with 12-foot ceilings, four bedrooms, four baths, fireplaces scattered throughout the place and a swimming pool outside. Even the garage had a second story and its own bathroom. Then, the price seemed reasonable, but who could afford the servants? In contrast, we looked at a three-bedroom brick home on an acre for $58,000 and an acceptable three-bedroom frame house for $42,000.

Old homes are treated like valuable jewels, continually polished and restored to yesterday's splendor. The city of Long Beach has strict local ordinances against cutting live oaks or magnolia trees without permission of the planning commission and approval of city officials.

Pass Christian: Pass Christian (pop. 6,500) is the elegant member of the retirement trio. Long a vacation center for wealthy New Orleans residents, Pass Christian is rich in history and past opulence. At one time steamboats regularly made the 55-mile voyage from New Orleans, bringing high-society families to their second homes, and a commuter train service started in 1880. The original families are gone, but their homes remain as do the gracious lifestyles of the last century. Mansions with manicured lawns line the beachfront and invitations for afternoon tea indicate social standing. But all is not tea and crumpets; there is another side to Pass Christian, just as there is to most gracious southern towns. Fishermen, craftspeople, artists and laborers make up the community's backbone, living in houses that are smaller and located on streets away from the beach. Twenty-two percent of the residents here are retired.

The town had its beginnings when a Frenchman from New Orleans named Nicholas Christianne settled here in 1745. The pass refers to the deep channel that passes through the oyster reefs, and the town became referred to as "the pass of Christianne." The French pronunciation was retained, becoming Pass *Chris-ti-AN*. Its seafaring tradition continues to the present day, with shrimping, oystering and fishing the major occupations and also colorful elements of the economic life. The Pass Christian Yacht Club dates back to 1849 and is the second oldest yacht club in the country.

In addition to fishing and boating, golf and tennis are popular. Twenty-two golf courses between Gulfport-Biloxi and Bay St. Louis encourage play. The beach is prominent in local recreational possibilities, with 7 of the 26 miles of Mississippi's beach available for Pass Christian residents' enjoyment.

Bay St. Louis: Called "the Bay" by local residents, Bay St. Louis (pop. 8,500) is even older than neighboring Pass Christian. It was founded in 1699 by the French and was named after the King Louis XIV. Its historic downtown, with palm-lined streets, Victorian mansions and an old Catholic seminary, contrast with modern shopping and commercial centers. Not to be outdone by Long Beach's motto of "the Radish Capital of the World," the Bay adopted its own slogan, "the Praline Capital of the World." Throughout its history, the region has suffered from assaults by pirates, missionaries, tourists and praline slogans.

One of the appealing aspects of living here—or anywhere in Mississippi, for that matter—is low tax rates. The per-capita tax burden in Mississippi is said to be only 57 percent of the national average. This is based on taxes from personal income, retail sales, residential property, gasoline and auto registration. Compare this with taxes in Illinois, 98 percent; Wisconsin, 132 percent and Michigan, 124 percent of the national per-capita average.

Recreation and Culture: There are so many golf courses along the Mississippi beach that some refer to the area as the "Golf Coast." If you like the game, you'll find your heaven here, with 18 courses to choose from. That's why travel agents call this "the Myrtle Beach of Mississippi." Many golf courses around the country won't permit youngsters to play alongside adults—even well-mannered kids with their own clubs. That's not the case in Mississippi Beach, so bring your grandkids with you if you like.

Besides golf, there are other outdoor sports to choose from—everything from jet skiing and sailing in the summer to tennis and fishing in the winter. Happily, because of the Gulf Coast weather, all of the above can be done all year round. The gulf waters are perfect for swimming, although a bit too cool in the winter for some people's taste. Saltwater fishermen travel for many miles to be able to tangle with the sea trout, grouper and bill fish in these waters. Several rivers and two large bays provide great brackish-water and freshwater fishing. Gulf Islands National Seashore, a series of long, narrow islands about 10 miles from shore, are perfect for beach combing, picnicking or camping.

Mississippi Beach celebrates its rich history and unique location with festivals spaced throughout the year. The coast's French Catholic heritage is commemorated through Mardi Gras celebrations and parades. Then there's the Oyster Festival, a Crawfish Festival and the Biloxi Shrimp Festival, all glorifying Mississippi Beach delicacies. The opening of shrimp season is celebrated with live music and food treats as decorated shrimp boats parade in front of a priest for the Blessing of the Shrimp Fleet. Several Blues and Jazz festivals eulogize Mississippi's contribution to music traditions.

Like in all Mississippi cities in the Certified Retirement Program, an Institute for Learning in Retirement (ILR) is in place. Mississippi Gulf Coast Community College offers a program with full campus benefits and use of facilities, including parking, library facilities, that features study groups, class trips and monthly luncheon lectures. Classes usually meet for two hours one day a week. Class topics are selected from members' suggestions. They may include conversational foreign languages, computers, history, art and music appreciation, philosophy, gourmet cooking and others.

Real Estate: The average price of housing used to drop every the winter after students went back to school and tourists went home to their jobs. That's no longer the case. Gambling has brought in many new residents, thus putting year-round pressure on housing markets. The lavish mansions, for which the Gulf Coast is so famous, have risen dramatically in price. A block or so away from the beach, the homes become rather ordinary, mostly single-family bungalows in pleasant, comfortable and mature neighborhoods. Newer subdivisions on the outskirts offer excellent choices, such as new brick homes starting around $85,000. Condos and apartments are also available in the newer sections.

Medical Care: Mississippi Beach is unusually blessed with good health care. Facilities include seven modern hospitals—with a total of more than 1,200 beds—several nursing homes, two urgent care centers, ten physical therapy centers and several home health care providers. For retired military personnel, Keesler Medical Center provides health care and treatment, and the Veterans' Affairs Medical Center has two facilities for eligible veterans. There's a U.S. Naval Retirement Home for qualified vets with wartime service, and the Naval Construction Battalion Center in Gulfport provides limited services to retired Seabees and families.

When Grandkids Visit: An unusual experience might be to take them on a shrimping trip. A reconditioned shrimp boat takes passengers on a demonstration shrimping expedition, showing how shrimp are netted. Along with the shrimp, the nets also bring in any and all sea creatures encountered in its path. The grandkids will see things like squid, stingray, blue crabs, flounder and more. If saltwater waves make you queasy, an alternative trip would be to visit the Ocean Springs museum dedicated to the "Mad Potter of Biloxi." An eccentric artist left a treasure of whimsical ceramic works of art, pieces that can't fail to bring a smile to the faces of young and old. The photo of the artist riding his bicycle, with long handlebar mustaches flowing in the wind, will bring forth a chuckle. Although described as being "one fork short of a full setting," George E. Ohr was actually far ahead of his time in modern art.

Addresses and Connections

Chamber of Commerce: Mississippi Beach Retirement, P.O. Box 569, Gulfport, MS 39502. (601) 863-1815.
Newspaper: *Gulf Coast Free Press*, 15168 Evans St., Gulfport, MS 39503-4302. (601) 863-0057.
Internet: http: //www.decd.state.ms.us/Retire/Cities/msgfcst.htm
Airport: Gulfport/Biloxi Regional Airport.
Bus/Train: Local bus and trolley; Greyhound and Amtrak.

Mississippi Beach

	Jan.	April	July	Oct.	Rain	Snow
Daily Highs	61	77	90.	79	61 in.	—
Daily Lows	43	59	74	60		

MISSISSIPPI TAXES
Mississippi State Tax Commission
P. O. Box 960, Jackson, MS 39205 — Ph. (601) 359-1141
Mississippi's tax bills rank 4th among the least expensive in the nation

Income Tax

First $5,000	3.0%	Over $10,000	5.0%
$5,001 - $10,000	4.0%		

General exemptions: $6,000 single, $9,500 married filing jointly, $1,500 each dependent
Additional for elderly: $1,500 taxpayer or spouse, over age 65
Additional for disabled: $1,500 blind
Private Pension Exclusion: Full exclusion
Social Security/Railroad Retirement Benefits: Full exclusion
Standard Deduction: $2,300 single, $3,400 married filing jointly
Medical and Dental Expense Deduction: May itemize as per federal rules or take standard deduction
Federal Income Tax Deduction: None

Sales Taxes

State 7.0%; County None; City None
General Coverage: Food is taxed, prescription drugs are exempt

Property Taxes

Average assessment on a $90,000 home about $325 annually.
Real and personal property is subject to local taxation. Some intangibles are subject to taxation. In relation to personal income, property tax collections are in the lowest third among the 50 states.
General exemptions: $240 maximum tax credit
Age 65 and over: $6,000 assessed value ($60,000 market value)

Estate/Inheritance Taxes

Mississippi imposes an estate tax ranging from 1% on taxable estates less than $60,000 to a tax of $1,082,840 plus 16% on taxable estates over $10 million. Property up to the value of $600,000 is exempt. Mississippi also imposes a pick-up tax, which is a portion of the federal estate tax and does not increase the total tax owed.

● Jefferson

● Boone

● Asheville

● Hendersonville

● University Triangle

● Sanford

● Pinehurst

North Carolina

North Carolina

During the Civil War, the state of North Carolina endured more economic devastation than any other state. It supplied the most soldiers for the Confederacy and suffered more losses than any other southern state. Recovery came at a painfully slow pace, with tobacco and furniture-making virtually the only money-makers. The doldrums lasted so long that in addition to North Carolina's nickname, "the Tarheel State," it was dubbed "the Rip Van Winkle State."

The economy improved slightly during World War II, partly because large numbers of military personnel were stationed at Ft. Bragg and Camp Lejeun, as they trained and made ready for overseas duty. New industries were also introduced: electrical plants, rubber and plastic manufacturing and light machinery.

> **North Carolina**
> The Tarheel State
> Admitted to statehood:
> November 21, 1789
> **State Capital:** Raleigh
> **Population (1995):** 7,195,138; rank, 11th
> **Population Density: 145.1 per sq. mile: urban 66.3%**
> **Geography:** 29th state in size, with 52,672 square miles, including 3,594 square miles of water surface. Highest elevation: Mt. Mitchel, 6,684 feet. Lowest elevation: Sea level, Atlantic Ocean. Average elevation: 700 feet.
> **State Flower:** Dogwood
> **State Bird:** Cardinal
> **State Tree:** Pine
> **State Song:** *The Old North State*

After the war, things started to perk up for North Carolina. Industries began leaving the North, moving south in search of low-cost, non-union labor. This helped, but did little for the economy other than to increase the number of people working for subsistence wages. The leverage that tipped the economic scale in North Carolina was the state's dedication to education. As the state's top universities turned out highly qualified graduates, native industry as well as potential runaway industries in the north began to look upon the North Carolina as a source of skilled workers.

The establishment of Research Triangle Park in 1958, the nation's largest governmental and industrial research laboratory, marked a turning point in the state's direction. The park brought in droves of laboratory scientists, technicians, business experts and academics of all descriptions. More manufacturers moved factories and laboratories to North Carolina—not for cheap labor, but because they liked the growing pool of qualified employees. They also wanted to be near the all-important research facilities here.

The economy gathered momentum as more well-paying jobs were created and businesses flourished. North Carolina finally shed its Rip Van Winkle image, and today is the South's most highly industrialized state and one of the nation's leaders in technology. These new trends are most beneficial to the economy, especially since tobacco is being threatened as a cash cow.

These modern enterprises are different in quality from those of the conventional Pittsburgh or Chicago "smokestack" industries. Instead of having smog-producing foundries, steel mills and other heavy activities, most of North Carolina's new enterprises are high-tech, with low-environmental impact. Instead of working at low-skill jobs to earn minimum wage, workers tend to earn wages high enough to further contribute to North Carolina's economic well-being. The old picture of subsistence has changed.

Something unforeseen happens when a growing number of downsized, highly talented employees leave the northern industrial regions to move south after being forced "early retirement." These not-yet-over-the-hill personnel continually swell the pool of qualified labor available for full- and part-time jobs. This creates more incentive for manufacturers to relocate to North Carolina. And with full-and part-time jobs available, it takes little else to persuade early retirees to relocate in a desirable place like North Carolina. This combination has placed North Carolina in the position of the nation's fifth most popular retirement state.

Progress has had little impact on the beauty of the state. Although increased population has opened previously isolated communities in the Blue Ridge and Great Smoky Mountains, they remain among the nation's scenic treasures. You'll agree with this if you ever see the Carolina mountains in October, when hardwood trees display a veritable explosion of color; brilliant reds, yellows, purples and lavenders and all the colors in between dazzle the eye while evergreens provide a vast background of green. Or try visiting in the spring, when the dogwoods, azaleas and mountain laurel trees are in full bloom. Winters are true winter, with regular snow in the elevations, but are mild enough that afternoons are always well above freezing.

University Triangle

The Carolina Midlands is a region of gently rolling hills, farms and hardwood forests. They're called the Midlands because they separate the flat coastal regions that roll toward the Atlantic Ocean from the high Appalachian plateau. The terrain is too rolling to be considered plains yet not hilly enough to be foothills. The Midlands present a unique combination of choices: from Beethoven to Bluegrass and from stock car racing to scholarly research, just about any kind of intellectual and recreational pursuit imaginable can be found here.

Three of North Carolina's best-known cities cluster together in the Midlands: Chapel Hill, Durham and Raleigh. Each contains one of the state's three top universities, which explains why this area is called the "University Triangle." The University of North Carolina is based in Chapel Hill, Duke University in Durham and North Carolina State in Raleigh. The universities—plus numerous research labs, think tanks and other academic institutions—attract intellectuals and technicians from all over the world. Per capita, there are probably more academics, PhDs and scientists living in the Triangle than in any other part of the country. Besides the three major universities, there are five four-year colleges and eight two-year colleges grouped within a few miles of each other, with more than 64,000 students. Among the better known schools are St. Augustine's College, Peace College, St. Mary's College and Wake Technical College. Education is big business in the Triangle.

Research Triangle Park: North Carolina's entry into the field of high technology and research got its start here in the Carolina

Midlands with Research Triangle Park. It's become one of the nation's major centers for industrial and governmental research as well as the largest research park of its kind in the United States. This enormous facility is located on a 6,800-acre wooded tract of land located between the three cities. It employs more than 30,000 people, including some of the nation's top scientists.

Since it's located within easy driving distance from any of the Triangle cities, employees, support personnel and associates live scattered throughout the three cities. You can imagine the impact this has on the economic and intellectual life as well as the social makeup of the community. People from all over North America and from all walks of life are represented in most neighborhoods. Some come here to teach or to work, then stay on to retire. Others come to visit academic friends and fall in love with the special dynamics of the University Triangle.

The universities and colleges profoundly influence lifestyles here, with a large percentage of the community either working for or with educational institutions, and others enjoy the many stimulating events connected with university life. Drama performances, lectures, sporting events and a host of other presentations are open to the general public as well as those involved with education.

A large number of retirees come from academic backgrounds, but those with no college experience at all find themselves getting into the whirl of things. "There are so many things to do, we wore ourselves out when we first moved here," said a retired couple from New York, who had moved to Chapel Hill. "Eventually, we slowed down and began to be more selective about which lectures we would attend or which sports events to watch. Through all of these activities, we've made some pretty solid friends. And, they're all dynamic, interesting people, every one of them."

Senior citizens can audit university classes on a space-available basis (as is the case anywhere in the state), and fees are minimal. For example: Duke University charges $90 for its continuing education program, which includes as many classes as you feel up to. Because of the unusual number of retired college graduates here, the interest in continuing education is very high. One group developed their own "free university" program in which retirees teach their own specialties to others. It's an exceptionally successful program, and, according to participants, it's in danger of swamping because of its phenomenal growth.

Raleigh: Raleigh is the state capital, founded in 1792 for the specific purpose of being North Carolina's capital. With 240,000 inhabitants, Raleigh is the largest city in the Triangle's metropolitan area, whose total population is fast approaching the one million mark. Visitors to the Greater Raleigh area will understand why two recent national studies named the Triangle as the number one place in America to live and to do business.

Home prices are predictably higher here than in other large North Carolina cities. Residential neighborhoods, such as the one surrounding the university campus, are absolutely upscale and lovely, but not cheap. This is not surprising in an area that is recession-resistant because of steady employment and high wage levels. This shouldn't put anyone off who is moving from a moderately expensive community in some other part of the country; chances are, they'll discover that prices are bargains compared to where they just left.

Chapel Hill: This city has adopted the nickname, the "Southern Part of Heaven," laying claim to having the best of small-town living in a unique cosmopolitan environment. They may be right. Certainly this is one of the most profoundly "college" towns in the country. With a population of 40,000, Chapel Hill is small enough to be intimately involved with academic life and the excitement of the university.

Chapel Hill's University of North Carolina was chartered in 1789 as the nation's first state university, thus beginning the Carolina Midlands' tradition of higher education. From one building, one hundred students and two professors, the university has grown to 22,000 students and more than 1,800 professors teaching in more than one hundred fields. The school is noted for its excellence in the arts, sciences and humanities and is an international leader in public health, medical research, business and computer technology.

The university's extensive campus is as beautiful as the school is prestigious. However, the main thing that impressed us was an overwhelming feeling of welcome and friendliness. No less than three times in a half an hour, as we strolled about the campus paths, gazing at ivy-covered halls and landscaped grounds, passing students misunderstood our starry gaze for bewilderment. They paused to ask if we needed help or directions.

Durham: Durham is the home of Duke University, well known as a center of higher learning and famous for its teaching hospital. For years the city was proud its nickname, "Tobacco Town"—in recognition of the economic importance of that product to the local economy and also because tobacco money played a big part in founding the university. Today it has a more politically correct nickname: "City of Medicine." This nomenclature is apt, because Duke University is world-famous for excellence as a medical school and research center, and the area boasts five major hospitals, including the Duke University Medical Center.

Duke has two impressive campuses. The West Campus has the beautiful, 55-acre Sarah Duke Gardens and gothic-style buildings populate the area. The East Campus (formerly Trinity College) is the site of the Duke University Museum of Art and its buildings are predominantly Georgian.

Recreation and Culture: Whether it's black-tie or blue jeans, ballet or beach music, the University Triangle area has something for everyone, with hundreds of concerts, cultural performances and exhibits each year. Entertainment includes a wide range of choices, everything from big-name performers at Hardee's Walnut Creek Amphitheater to classical ensembles in intimate performance halls and to outdoor music festivals with picnics on the grounds.

Visitors drawn to the visual arts can delight in the area's ethnic and native crafts, fine arts exhibitions and a thriving downtown artists' district of galleries in all three cities.

University theaters are the Triangle's answer to off-Broadway, with professional touring companies as well as students presenting jazz and dance, children's theater and more. North Carolina Theater is the state's only resident professional musical theater. It's acclaimed as "the best it gets this side of Broadway," as it brings productions of large-scale Broadway musicals to the area.

The North Carolina Symphony Orchestra is based in Raleigh, performing approximately 50 times a year in the city and another 150 times throughout the state. A variety of programming, including solo performances by acclaimed musical celebrities, has earned the symphony orchestra a national reputation.

Real Estate: Because of the schools, research labs and related industries, wages for academics and technicians are higher in the Triangle than in most of the Carolinas. This translates into higher housing costs and fancier homes in the more elegant sections. Homes in the $200,000-plus price range have no trouble finding buyers, yet homes in that price range seem like mansions compared to those in other parts of the country. We visited a couple who moved to Raleigh from New York City, from a small apartment into a spacious five-bedroom home on two acres of wooded grounds. "Our entire apartment could fit into this dining room, living room and kitchen," they said. "And never in our wildest dreams could we have afforded to *buy* an apartment there." Because they bought when interest rates bottomed out, the monthly payment on their $200,000 mansion in Raleigh is one third what they paid in rent for a tiny apartment in New York City.

Even though the cost-of-living and wages are somewhat above national norms, this is still the Southeast, a section not famous for excessively high wage scales. Workers not earning incomes paid to those with higher technical skills or academic standing earn only slightly more than typical North Carolina wages, so they simply can't afford to live in $200,000 homes. Therefore you'll find plenty of quality homes selling for less than $80,000. Some luxury condos start at $100,000; others, perfectly livable, are closer to the $50,000 range.

Medical Care: With a physician-to-population ratio five times greater than the national average, and two medical schools and two teaching hospitals here, it's not surprising that some of the nation's top-rated hospitals are in University Triangle. Residents are assured excellent medical care within reach. The university hospitals maintain specialties in every imaginable field, and private hospitals add to the caliber of care.

When Grandkids Visit: Take 'em to the Museum of Life and Science in Durham. Among the science displays is an interesting aerospace exhibit with a mockup of the spaceship Apollo 15. They'll also see Eros, the first U.S. spacecraft to orbit the earth. This is a hands-on museum that gets the kids involved. Also, the museum's Nature Center has an exhibit of native animals in their natural environment and a petting zoo where kids can pet animals in a farmyard setting.

Addresses and Connections

Chamber of Commerce: (Raleigh) 225 Hillsborough St., Suite 400, Raleigh, NC 27602-1879. (919) 834-5900, (800) 849-8499.
(Chapel Hill) 501 West Franklin Street, Suite 104, Chapel Hill, NC 27516. (888)968-2060.
(Durham) P.O. Box 2839, Durham, NC 27702. (919) 682-2133.
Internet: (Raleigh) http://www.ncnet.com/ncnetworks/ral-intr.html
(Chapel Hill) http://ncnet.com/ncnw/ch-intr.html
Newspapers: (Raleigh) *The Carolinian,* 649 Maywood Ave., Raleigh, NC 27603-2339. (919) 834-5558.
(Chapel Hill) *Chapel Hill News,* 505 W. Franklin St., Chapel Hill, NC 27516-2315. (919) 932-2000.
(Durham) *News and Observer,* 103 W. Main St., Durham, NC 27701-3638. (919) 687-0207.
Airport: Raleigh/Durham International Airport.
Bus/Train: Local bus services; Greyhound; Amtrak.

University Triangle Area

	Jan.	April	July	Oct.	Rain	Snow
Daily Highs	50	72	88	72	42 in.	1.8 in.
Daily Lows	30	47	67	48		

Pinehurst/Southern Pines/Aberdeen

The villages of Pinehurst, Southern Pines and Aberdeen, in the central part of the state, have long enjoyed the distinction of being premier golf destinations. Located within minutes of each other, this triangle of towns contains 35 superb championship courses within a 16-mile radius, some of which are among the most highly rated in the world. How did all this start?

In 1895, James Walker Tufts, a philanthropist from Boston who hated harsh New England winters, began to search the mid-South for a place to develop a health resort. He came across an area in North Carolina known by the descriptive name, "the Sandhills." The land had recently been timbered over and was rather bleak looking. Local people thought him foolish for buying 5,000 acres of the semi-barren land at the extravagant price of one dollar an acre.

The area was considered healthful because its sandy soil left few pools of stagnant water to breed malaria-bearing mosquitoes. He built a small hotel, a store and some cottages. He also planted a quarter of a million trees, plants and shrubs. The location was convenient for people from the North, because the main north-south railroad, from Florida to Maine, ran through the heart of the Sandhills. This was to become the escape route for New Englanders over the next century.

Frederick Law Olmsted, the designer of New York City's Central Park, was commissioned to create a New England-style village in the pines. Olmsted laid out the Village Green with an oval as the hub for spoke-like, winding roads and footpaths that radiated out in all directions. The trees are immense and lush today, and a short distance away, Pinehurst's main lodge looms above the tall pines.

Golf actually was an afterthought in Pinehurst. Original recreational activities included tennis, horseback riding, fox hunts, polo, trap shooting and croquet. Since golf was still in its infancy in America around the turn of the century, a merely experimental nine-hole layout was sculpted from the sandy hills in 1898. The game caught on; the hotel grew, expanded and kept expanding. Today, it's become almost monumental.

From Pinehurst's inception, people who came here for the winter thought kindly of the area when retirement time came around. They bought lots and constructed homes. The next logical step was subdivisions. Over the years more and more homes have been built among the pines and oaks, some with expansive, acreage-sized land, others on smaller plots, but always with elbow room.

Of course, membership in Pinehurst Club was mandatory for those who bought lots in the many subdivisions ringing the golf-tennis complex. So today, new buyers automatically inherit their memberships as part of the purchase price of their lots or homes. (They inherit the monthly fees, as well.) This is an important feature, since some golf club developments have a waiting list for membership.

Southern Pines is an offshoot development, separate from Pinehurst. Southern Pines is larger, with a population of 10,000 and a downtown area somewhat less touristy than Pinehurst's Village

Center. Southern Pines is basically a residential community, liberally endowed with golf facilities and shopping malls and a quaint town center. The homes we looked at were superbly designed to fit into the Sandhills' pine and oak ambiance. Many large estates here and around neighboring Pinehurst are of Georgian Colonial or Old English design. Mixed among the super-expensive areas are more moderately-priced neighborhoods, but we saw nothing particularly mundane.

Aberdeen, with 2,800 inhabitants, is the third village in this grouping. In its early days, Aberdeen was a bustling center of trade and commerce. Then came quieter years as the downtown saw businesses moving out. But Aberdeen has emerged from its down-time, and Main Street is lively once more, with its fine antique shops, boutiques and other shopping. Our impression of Aberdeen is that it's a place for more affordable housing, but still in the golf club circuit.

These golfing villages are located in the southern Piedmont region, between the Blue Ridge Mountains and the coast, and about 70 miles south of Raleigh. This has always been a convenient stopover place for vacationers on their way to Florida vacations. It's about halfway for many New Englanders and northerners, a logical place to break up the trip. They think, "Why not stay over a day or two and get in a few rounds of golf?" As retirement time draws nearer, folks naturally begin thinking more about Pinehurst and Southern Pines—and less about Florida. In fact, those 55 years and older currently make up 30 percent of the county's population.

Because the elevation here is higher than most of Florida, summers aren't quite as warm or humid. Furthermore, the 55-degree January days permit plenty of outdoor activities. "Any day it's not raining, I can golf, hike or ride horseback." said one retiree here. "When I lived in Florida, it was too hot and muggy in the summer to leave the house!"

The small-town atmosphere and lower-than-average crime rate lend themselves to a feeling of security. And because of the large percentage of out-of-state retirees, newcomers don't feel that they stand out as they might in some other small southern locations.

Recreation and Culture: Pinehurst is also known for tennis, which rivals golf for its reputation, with 28 courts in the area. Besides tennis, golf, horseback riding, hiking the miles of trails and all, what else could you want? If golf isn't your game, you could try sailing, waterskiing, fishing, trap and skeet shooting, hunting, bicycling and jogging. Croquet? Polo? Pinehurst even has a race track—not surprising since this is winter training quarters for thoroughbreds and trotters.

The Arts Council of Moore County, with 2,500 members, is at the forefront of a flourishing community of visual, literary and performing artists. The Performing Arts Center in Southern Pines sponsors the Sandhills Little Theater, which presents four productions a year and a host of other artistic, cultural and entertaining events. Dinner theaters provide both good food and good shows. Year-round Pinehurst-Southern Pines entertainment includes arts and crafts fairs, blue grass music in the park, film classics and jazz festivals.

Sandhills Community College offers an extensive adult education program. The school agrees to teach any course that can raise a minimum of 12 students—everything from painting to accounting, tailoring to real estate and handicrafts to creative writing. Since Pinehurst and Southern Pines are so close to Raleigh, Durham and Chapel Hill, it's no big thing to drive over for one of the major universities' sports events or for a particularly intriguing lecture.

Real Estate: After several days of touring the Pinehurst-Southern Pines area, I was tempted to fall back on the old cliché, "If you have to ask about real estate prices, you can't afford to live here!" However, I'm happy to say that after some investigation we found prices to be quite reasonable, considering what you'd be buying. In fact, people relocating from some of the more expensive sections of the country will find they can move up in quality of surroundings for a lot less than what they sold their old homes for. The median house in Pinehurst costs $152,000, in Southern Pines $81,000 and even less in Aberdeen.

Medical Care: More than adequate health care is covered by Moore Regional Hospital, a 397-bed facility with a medical staff of 135 physicians and 1,400 employees, assisted by 500 volunteers. A 24-hour mobile intensive-care unit provides up-to-date life support treatments. Moore Regional also has the largest, most comprehensive, hospital-owned and operated fitness facility in the state. A

smaller hospital, St. Joseph of the Pines Health Center, is primarily a
nursing hospital with 86 beds, which it uses in connection with its
retirement villas.

When Grandkids Visit: Remember when you could take a
train almost anywhere you'd care to travel? When airplanes were
only for long, cross-country trips? Passenger trains are almost extinct,
except for Amtrak, and even its existence is being threatened. Well,
chances are your grandkids have never been on a real passenger
train. Give them a treat and buy tickets on the Amtrak train that stops
off in Southern Pines. It doesn't have to be a long trip; you could go
to the next town and take a bus back. At least the grandkids will be
able to tell their grandkids that they once had a ride on a genuine
train.

Addresses and Connections

Chamber of Commerce: P.O. Box 458, Southern Pines. NC 28388.
(919) 692-3926.
Internet: http://www.sandhills.org/retire/comm/comm.htm
http://www.golflink.net/phurst
http://www.ncnet.com/ncnetworks/pin-intr.html
Newspapers: *Citizen News-Record*, 206 Sandhills Blvd. N., Aberdeen,
NC 28315-2412. (910) 944-2356.
The Pilot, 145 W. Pennsylvania Ave., Southern Pines, NC 28387-5428.
(910) 692-7271.
Airport: Raleigh International (70 miles), Charlotte International (98
miles). Limo service.
Bus/Train: Greyhound; Amtrak

Pinehurst/Southern Pines

	Jan.	April	July	Oct.	Rain	Snow
Daily Highs	55	74	91	75	50 in.	4 in.
Daily Lows	34	47	68	50		

Carolina Trace

Although Pinehurst and Southern Pines are golf course communities, most of their neighborhoods aren't protected by gates and
security guards. Basically, they're upscale residential areas with golf
courses conveniently located next door or nearby. The neighbor-

hoods are open; anyone can cruise through the streets without having to be residents.

We decided to investigate another kind of retirement community that's become extraordinarily popular, not only in the South, but also in other parts of the country: a private country club development. About 25 miles north of Pinehurst and Southern Pines, the Carolina Trace Country Club is an excellent example of this lifestyle.

For many, the term *private country club* carries the implication of elitism, snobbery and expensive property. What we found was something entirely different. When interviewing people living in "closed" developments like Carolina Trace, we asked how it felt to be "locked in," in an "us against the world" mode, rather than live in open communities like Southern Pines. First of all, residents say they love the feeling of security that comes from having an armed guard at the gate to keep strangers from wandering through the neighborhoods. They also like having their own security patrols. After interviewing several couples, we began to understand why they felt that way. Many came from high-crime areas—places like New York, Detroit and Chicago. These folks appreciate the meaning of the word "security," having been conscious of it all their lives. The second point is, residents have a real sense of belonging. People know their neighbors—they have dinner together at the clubhouse, they wave to each other as their pontoon boats pass on the lake, they play golf together. Since the club is a member-owned facility, they also sit down together and make decisions about how their community should function.

As for Carolina Trace being expensive—small lakefront homes start at $75,000. For someone moving from Long Island, that's a gift. Granted, some of the more elaborate layouts have been known to sell in the $400,000 range, but you can imagine what you get for that price! As for being elitist—the folks we interviewed came from ordinary middle-class backgrounds. They were fugitives from northern cold weather, but were also fleeing crime, high taxes and overpriced housing.

The centerpiece of the development is a sparkling lake that expands over 300 acres, with seven miles of shoreline stretching into every part of Carolina Trace's 2,500 acres. This means just about everybody has either a view of the lake or a place right on the water.

In all there are 17 small sections, or clusters of homes. Each section has its own swimming pool and tennis courts. This creates a series of neighborhoods within the community. These quiet little groups of homes are separated from each other by expansive woods of live oak, southern pine, holly and dogwood. In fact, half of the area is left in undisturbed forest. In 1997 *New Choices* magazine named Carolina Trace as one of the top 20 retirement communities in the country—the third year in a row it made this list.

Lest we forget golf—after all, this is a country-club development—we must mention the two 18-hole world-class golf courses that were designed by world-renowned golf course architect Robert Trent Jones, Sr., who also created Alabama's spectacular Golf Trail.

The history of Carolina Trace is not only interesting, but it also underscores what is happening today in similar developments around the country. Twenty years ago, Carolina Trace was a pioneer in planned communities. The developers built everything just right and promoted it well. In no time at all, the properties sold out to people, most in their mid-60s, from New Jersey, New York, Illinois and who knows from where else. Then they convinced their friends to buy the home next door. The residents got down to the business of managing their grounds, tennis courts, swimming pool, club house and so forth.

Twenty years later, the original purchasers are in their 80s. They have less interest in the golf, tennis or exercise facilities in the clubhouse. Many are moving back with family or moving into assisted retirement homes. New buyers are buying the homes reluctantly vacated by the original owners. But these aren't people in their mid-60s; these are young whipper snappers in their mid-50s. Once again the two golf courses are in use, and the tennis courts are bouncing. There's an expected 20 percent turnover in residents in the near future, which will change the entire composition of the club.

The big change is that the development is no longer be a "retirement community" in the strict sense of the word. Some new residents work full time; they live here because of the surroundings and they have no intention of retiring. Others live here part of the year, perhaps consulting or "telecommuting" by computer and modem, while holding down jobs in other parts of the country.

We predict that this will be a growing trend over the next few years. People will leave the workplace in their 50s instead of 60s. They will want to live in places like Carolina Trace, where they can live an active, vigorous life, yet be close enough to high-tech places like Research Triangle Park where they can keep their hands in the job market.

Carolina Trace's shopping destination is in the nearby town of Sanford (pop. 30,000). Sanford looks very much like other North Carolina towns of the same size, but there's something special there—the senior citizens' center. As mentioned earlier in this book, southern senior centers are often rather dreary places where the emphasis is on taking care of the community's less affluent elderly citizens. Sanford's senior center is a notable exception. Called the "Enrichment Center," this is one of the best senior centers we've encountered anywhere. While you'll see some "needy" clients here, the emphasis is on bringing all of Lee County's seniors into the program. (A tipoff is the number of Cadillacs, Lincolns and new Buicks parked in the visitors' parking lot.)

The county puts a lot of money and thought into this center, and it's geared to serving all spectrums of the community. As well as the usual dances, card parties and entertainment, the Enrichment Center organizes trips and excursions and lectures and plays. And seminars on financial planning, living trusts and how to manage stock portfolios aren't exactly educational courses for the impoverished. Other classes cover subjects such as: buying computers to get connected on the Internet, classical music appreciation and ballroom dancing.

Recreation and Culture: When you move to a country club community, your recreation and cultural activities are usually self-contained. With two Robert Trent Jones golf courses, more swimming pools and tennis courts than anyone can use, a lake full of fish and sandy beaches for swimming, what's left for recreation? By the way, the members put a welcome restriction on lake boating: only electric motors are allowed. That means no full-tilt waterskiing boats breaking the sound barrier on Sunday mornings when you're trying to sleep in.

Real estate: According to a local real estate company, lot prices in Carolina Trace range from $7,500 to $150,000. (These are large lots.) Homes are priced from $75,000 to over $400,000. New construction begins in the $55-per-square-foot range.

The town of Sanford has a nice mixture of older antebellum-style homes as well as newer neighborhoods catering to families involved with the growing Research Triangle Park area. This area is also a popular place for horse farms.

Medical Care: Hospital services are located in Sanford, at Central Carolina Hospital. The 180-bed facility is unusually large and well equipped for a town of Sanford's size. The facility offers 24-hour ambulance service as well as helicopter air lift service either to Central Carolina Hospital or to one of the hospitals in the University Triangle area. This is where some of the world's finest hospitals and medical specialists are found, at Durham's renowned Medical Center as well as excellent facilities in Chapel Hill and Raleigh.

When Grandkids Visit: Within Carolina Trace, activities the youngsters might be interested in include: swimming, golf, tennis and walking trails—in short a full range of activities on the lake. The only problem with having no gas motors on the lake (which encourages quiet fishing, sailing and rowing instead of zooming and roaring around the lake, full throttle, keeping deserving people from their naps) is when the grandkids want to go waterskiing. You'd better practice your rowing if you expect to get up to waterskiing speed.

Addresses and Connections

Chamber of Commerce: Sanford Enrichment Center, 1615 S. Third St., Sanford, NC 27330. (919) 776-0501.

Newspaper: *Sanford Herald,* P.O. Box 100, Sanford, NC 27331. (919) 708-9000.

Airport: Lee County Airport in Sanford (commuter connections); Raleigh International (70 miles). Limo service.

Bus/Train: County bus service; Greyhound in Sanford.

Asheville

Asheville is the queen city of North Carolina's western region, residing in the finger-like projection of the state that forces its way between Tennessee and Georgia. Nestled in the mountains where the Great Smokies and the Blue Ridge Mountains meet, Asheville sits at 2,340 feet above sea level. This elevation accounts for its pleasant summer weather as well as its brisk, but not harsh, winters.

Three North Carolina towns in this region form a triangle with Asheville as the apex and Hendersonville and Brevard forming the triangle's base. All three towns consistently receive praise as retirement locations in magazines, newspapers and retirement guides. Since there's only about 20 miles or so between one city and the next, it would seem they could be treated as one subject, but we feel they are different enough to deserve separate consideration. We are starting with Asheville, the best known of the three.

As the largest city in western North Carolina, Asheville (pop. 85,000) is the region's cultural and commercial center. This country is characterized by prosperous farms and forest-covered foothills, rounded and green, growing steeper toward the north. Its natural setting, surrounded by a million acres of national forest, combines with the convenience of city living to make Asheville and its environs one of North Carolina's most desirable retirement destinations. Not surprisingly, Asheville was famous as a resort town, attracting tourists and retirees, long before Thomas Wolfe described his hometown in his novel *Look Homeward, Angel*; even before George Vanderbilt thought about creating America's largest home here, the 255-room Biltmore House. Since the turn of the century, famous Americans, such as Henry Ford, his friend Thomas Edison, F. Scott Fitzgerald and William Jennings Bryan, enjoyed summers here. Many came for the summer and stayed on for retirement. They come in ever-increasing numbers, with a surprising number of "second-chance retirees" moving here after having tried Florida.

Because of its distance from a truly large metropolitan center, Asheville enjoys many services and amenities normally absent in a small city. No less than 16 shopping centers, four of them indoor malls, ensure wide selections of merchandise. Two interstate highways (I-40 and I-26) intersect in Asheville, as well as the Blue Ridge Parkway and ten other U.S. and state highways. This maze of freeways, plus an airport with daily flights and connections to several major cities, makes Asheville a transportation hub for this area.

The University of North Carolina at Asheville sponsors a unique resource for seniors living in the region. It's called the North Carolina Center for Creative Retirement. The Center consists of several programs designed to introduce retirement-age people to a wide variety of learning experiences as it integrates them into the community. The Center should be one of the first stops on your pre-retirement tour of Asheville, and, should you decide to move here, the Center should become part of your retirement scenario.

One of the center's programs is called "College for Seniors." Drawing on retirees' professional expertise and life experiences, curricula and classes are designed and taught by students as well as university faculty. Classes range from Chaucer to computers, from foreign affairs to opera. Another is the "Senior Academy for Intergenerational Learning," which matches retired professionals with university students to work as research partners, tutors and career mentors. The "Leadership Asheville Seniors" program brings seniors together to explore ways to link their talents and expertise with community needs. They work with civic leaders, social scientists, political activists and other experts to confront the community's past, present and future challenges. Lastly, the "Seniors in the Schools" program matches talented senior volunteers with public school students, where they tutor, present enrichment programs and organize special projects.

Recreation and Culture: Outdoor recreation here is enhanced by Asheville's proximity to some of the prettiest Appalachian country imaginable. Always within view, the Blue Ridge and Great Smoky Mountains soar to heights of 5,000 feet. Hiking, fishing, camping and winter skiing make for year-round outdoor recreation within walking or driving distance.

The mountains around Asheville provide a magnificent setting for golf, surrounded by scenic beauty and a pleasant year-round climate. Mountain golf is enhanced by lush fairways, sprawling bent grass greens, cool breezes and a gently undulating terrain. Eight public golf courses in the Asheville area challenge players with good weather in all but the two coldest months of the year. There are also nine private golf clubs. Within driving distance of a day's play, duffers have their choice of 32 different courses.

Lake Julian, a few miles south of Asheville, is always stocked with bass and bream. Canoes and picnicking are available. Lake Powhatan, in the Pisgah National Forest, has a sand beach, fishing, swimming, camping and picnicking. An abundance of well-stocked rivers and highland streams are within easy distance of Asheville.

In addition to a branch of the University of North Carolina, two other four-year colleges and several two-year schools serve the area. Residents, whether connected with the school or not, have access to the cultural events associated with universities. Retirees take advantage of the many non-credit courses offered by the university and community colleges. The unique "College for Seniors" program encourages retirees with special qualifications to join university faculty in teaching classes to mature adults.

The Asheville region cherishes a rich craft and folk heritage. Residents find many opportunities to participate in the fine arts: painting, dance, theater, and music, as well as mountain crafts. Entertainment in the area includes four little theater companies, Hendersonville Symphony Orchestra and Four Seasons Arts Council.

Real Estate: According to statistics, Asheville real estate sells at slightly above the national average. The west side of town offers more economical homes, with average selling prices around $84,000. The Haywood section, however, also on the west side of town, is one of the most expensive areas, with homes selling at almost double the price, averaging $164,000. Homes outside the city limits can be excellent buys and some are situated on acreage instead of lots.

Medical Care: A concentration of hospitals and related facilities firmly establishes the city as a medical center. The claim is that Asheville has more doctors per capita than anywhere else in the world. Whether or not this is accurate, the fact remains that health care here is outstanding. Memorial Mission Hospital is a locally-owned, not-for-profit medical center serving a 17-county region. It has nearly 500 beds, and more than 2,500 staff members and 400 physicians are actively affiliated with Mission. Virtually every specialty and subspecialty is represented.

St. Joseph's Hospital is a private, non-profit institution with 331 private rooms and is a regional leader in urology, oncology, orthopedics and laser-assisted and general surgery. The hospital has 360 physicians on staff, covering every medical specialty. Except for organ transplants and a burn center, the residents of Western North Carolina have the same major medical services that sophisticated university centers offer.

When Grandkids Visit: Take them to see the Biltmore House, a 250-room mansion built at the turn of the century by the grandson of Cornelius Vanderbilt. Of course the Vanderbilt family didn't live in all 250 rooms; they confined themselves to just 26 rooms on three floors of the mansion. The rest of the house was devoted to essentials like a bowling alley, swimming pool, servants quarters and the like. The art collection here is impressive, including works by Whistler, Renoir, John Singer Sargent and others. There's even a chess table that once belonged to Napoleon. If the grandkids aren't into art, take them to Sliding Rock, a natural 60-foot-long water slide, or take a float trip down the French Broad River (You might explain that the river was *not* named after a hussy from Paris, but because the river flowed toward what was French territory in those days).

Addresses and Connections

Chamber of Commerce: P.O. Box 1010, Asheville, NC 28802. (704) 258-6115.
Internet: ÿ20http://www.state.nc.us/Asheville/newcomer.htm
http://ncnet.com/ncnw/ash-intr.html
Newspaper: *Asheville Citizen-Times*, 14 O. Henry Ave., Asheville, NC 28802. (800) 800-4204.
Airport: Asheville Regional Airport.
Bus/Train: Local bus service; Greyhound.

Asheville/Hendersonville

	Jan.	April	July	Oct.	Rain	Snow
Daily Highs	46	68	83	69	47 in.	16 in.
Daily Lows	28	43	63	45		

Hendersonville

Just down the highway from Asheville, at a slightly lower altitude, the city of Hendersonville is cradled between two famous mountain formations: the Blue Ridge Mountains, which reach more than 3000 feet above sea level, and the Great Smoky Mountains looming 5,000 feet high in the west.

Every town seems to need an official nickname, so Hendersonville's is: "The City of Four Seasons." It lives up to its nickname, because it's situated ideally, enjoying a mild mountain climate and protected by the high mountain ranges from some of winter's worst weather. The barrier formed by the Great Smoky Mountains tends to hold back the flow of arctic air from winter storms that move down from Canada and blow across the Great Plains states and into the South. Even in winter's coldest weather, temperatures almost always rise above freezing in the afternoon. Zero-degree weather is extremely rare. Summers are in turn cooled by the 2,200-foot altitude and breezes flowing down from the mountain peaks. Well-balanced and adequate rainfall supports the county's bountiful flowers in spring, healthy crops in summer, rainbows of colors in fall, and relatively greenery in the winter.

This beneficial weather was the drawing card in the last century when Hendersonville was a favorite summer retreat for Low Country planters and merchants from Charleston and elsewhere. At the close of this century, it's becoming a favorite for those who once retired to Florida and but are seized by a desire to leave a boring climate and get away to the mountains.

Many advantages accruing to Asheville can be matched in Hendersonville, but on a smaller scale. The population here is less than 10,000, although at first glance the city looks much larger. Its downtown has undergone a tremendous rehabilitation program. By making the main street one way and adding lots of new parking spaces, they've slowed the pace and given the town center a pleasant, mall-like atmosphere. People of all ages, with a wide variety of interests, find the congenial surroundings the perfect place to raise a family or to get away from it all in their retirement years. The residential neighborhoods throughout the city and county offer quiet, traffic-free living with the advantage of being only minutes from shopping.

Money magazine recently rated Hendersonville among the 20 best cities for retirement in the United States. The primary criteria used in making the selections were a low crime rate, a mild climate, affordable housing, as attractive environment, proximity to cultural and educational activities, a strong economic outlook and excellent health care. A recent issue of *Where to Retire* also featured Hendersonville as a retirement haven.

Flat Rock: Seven miles from downtown Hendersonville, Flat Rock is a town rich with history. Flat Rock got its name from its vast outcropping of granite rock which is said to have been the site of Cherokee gatherings. Flat Rock was first settled by wealthy Charlestonians. The booming summer resort became known as the "Little Charleston of the Mountains."

Flat Rock's most treasured attraction is Connemara, home of the famous poet, historian, author and lecturer, Carl Sandburg. Sandburg found the perfect environment for thinking and writing in this home and farm that features a panoramic view of the Blue Ridge mountains, rolling meadows and mountain lakes. Just around the corner is the famous Flat Rock Playhouse, which has been officially designated State Theater of North Carolina and is one of the top ten summer theaters in the United States.

Recreation and Culture: You'll find five private golf communities and four public courses in Hendersonville and Flat Rock, and a couple more public courses in Brevard.

The Great Smoky Mountains National Park, which is easily reached from Hendersonville and encompasses 412,000 acres of breathtaking scenery viewable from miles of scenic roads and trails, and the even closer Nantahala National Forest both provide fishing, hiking and plenty of outdoor activities.

The 70-piece Hendersonville Symphony Orchestra performs five concerts a year, featuring guest artists from around the country. Since Brevard is just down the road, Hendersonville takes full advantage of Brevard's Music Center performances during its gala seven-week summer session. Nearby Flat Rock Playhouse draws sellout crowds, and Hendersonville Little Theater stages four productions a year.

Blue Ridge Community College annually enrolls approximately 2,500 students and serves 12,000 adults with both job-related and continuing education courses. Residents 65 and older are exempt from tuition for most classes.

Medical. Hendersonville is served by two modern, full-service hospitals, both of which feature advanced diagnostic equipment and specialized treatments. The Margaret R. Pardee Memorial Hospital has 222 beds and a 40-bed extended-care unit. Park Ridge has 103 beds, and has a general, acute- and surgical-care facilities.

Real Estate: Hendersonville offers housing choices for every budget and every lifestyle. At one time real estate was selling for very low prices, but over the last decade costs have been rising. The average selling price is about 15 percent above national averages. This isn't surprising; this is the fastest-growing area in western North Carolina. There are now 350 housing developments in Henderson county. One of our favorite areas in the Flat Rock area on the southern edge of Hendersonville. This is a scenic setting of foothills with desirable neighborhoods of homes in wooded, natural surroundings, sometimes with spectacular views.

Addresses and Connections

Chamber of Commerce: 330 North King Street, Hendersonville, NC 28793. (704) 692-1413.
Newspaper: *Hendersonville Times-News,* 1717 Four Seasons Blvd., Hendersonville, NC 28793. (704) 692-0505.
Internet: http://www.hendersonville.com/hendersonville.htm
http://wncguide.com/hend_co/downtown/Welcome.html
Airport: Asheville Regional Airport (20 miles).
Bus/Train: Greyhound.

Brevard

Even though Brevard has less than 6,000 inhabitants, it is the largest town in Transylvania County. Let me hasten to explain that this "Transylvania" has nothing to do with Count Dracula or vampires. The name originated in 1861, combining "Trans" for "across" and "Sylvania" for "the woods." The name is appropriate because Transylvania County contains 83,000 acres of the Pisgah National Forest as well as more than 5,000 acres of the Nantahala National Forest.

The county likes to call itself "The Land of Waterfalls," and rightly so, because of more than 250 falls in the forest. The waterfalls bear names like Looking Glass, Slippery Witch, Horsepasture, Turtleback and Rainbow Falls. The prize goes to the breath-catching 411-foot cascade of Whitewater Falls.

Like Hendersonville, Brevard is known for well-groomed residential districts and more than adequate shopping. Both towns routinely receive top recommendations by retirement writers. Both are comfortable-looking places with picturesque settings (especially the country around Brevard). Unlike Hendersonville, Brevard is in a dry county, so don't plan on a glass of beer with your anchovy-and-mushroom pizza; it'll be Pepsi-Cola.

Brevard is basically a residential community, quiet and tranquil. Although there are a few manufacturing firms in the area, there's no heavy industry. Homes in Brevard enjoy a natural setting of trees and mature shrubs.

Recreation and Culture. If you enjoy hiking and backpacking, camping and picnicking, canoeing, mountain climbing, golfing or biking, Brevard might be the place you'd like to call home. Local fishermen claim you'll find "trout heaven" as you explore Transylvania's trout-filled streams. Streams are stocked by the Pisgah North Carolina State Fish Hatchery, one of the largest hatcheries in the East.

Golf in Transylvania County can be relaxing and invigorating, regardless of your score. Beautiful mountain views surround you, and a variety of courses provide plenty of challenge for any skill level. However, of the dozen golf courses around Brevard, only two or three are public; the rest are private country clubs.

Brevard College hosts educational and cultural events on an ongoing basis and offers a wide choice of interesting courses tailored to seniors. Nearby Blue Ridge Community College provides tuition-free classes to seniors.

Each summer session, the Brevard Music Center brings guest artists to perform more than fifty concerts. What began in 1936 as a backwoods music camp is now considered one of the five major music festivals in the nation. The center supports four orchestras, two bands, a variety of chamber groups and an opera workshop. During the seven-week season, you can hear everything from symphony, pops and Broadway musicals to chamber music and opera. In past years, Brevard Music Center has hosted many great performers from Andy Williams and John Denver to Tony Bennett.

Real Estate: Real estate costs in Brevard are above-average to high. More than a third of the county is part of the Pisgah National Forest, and since much of the remaining land cannot be developed, land is expensive in comparison to surrounding counties. One nearby private community is on the extremely expensive side; it's not unusual to find homes priced well over $500,000. Average selling prices are in excess of $110,000.

Medical Care: The Transylvania Community Hospital is located in Brevard. It's a 64-bed acute-care facility, and is known to have a good coronary unit. For critical care, helicopter transport is available to the major hospitals in Asheville.

When Grandkids Visit: About five miles from downtown Hendersonville is a place called Jump-Off Rock. The legend says that an Indian chief and a Cherokee maiden frequently met here on the rock and did whatever Indian chiefs and Cherokee maidens customarily did when they met on a rock. When her lover was killed in battle (have you heard this story before?), the heartbroken maiden did what heartbroken Cherokee maidens always do in legends of this nature. However, I'm not going to spoil the story and give away the ending. If you want to know what the Cherokee maiden did at Jump-Off Rock, you and your grandkids will have to go there in person and find out.

Addresses and Connections

Chamber of Commerce: 2035 W. Main Street, Brevard, NC 28712-0589. (704) 883-3700.
Internet: http://webtelpro.com/~miniquilts/listframe.html
Newspaper: *Transylvania Times*, Broad St., Brevard, NC 28712. (704) 883-8156.
Airport: Asheville Regional Airport (33 miles).
Bus/Train: No public transportation—you'll need a car in Brevard.

Hendersonville/Brevard

	Jan.	April	July	Oct.	Rain	Snow
Daily Highs	48	69	84	69	48 in.	17 in.
Daily Lows	26	42	62	45		

North Carolina's High Country

Asheville sits in the foothills of the Blue Ridge Mountains, giving you just a taste of what is to the north and east. When you drive just a little way from Asheville, along the Blue Ridge Parkway, you'll see a dramatic change in scenery. The hills grow steep and craggy and turn into a classic Appalachian wonderland. Welcome to North Carolina's "High Country!"

The High Country is a scenic six-county region nestled in the lush Blue Ridge Mountains, stretching from Asheville to the Virginia border. There are no border crossings or dotted yellow lines to separate the High Country from the rest of the world, but you'll know when you're here. The air gets cleaner, the people get friendlier, the scenery becomes more spectacular, and you know it's time to relax.

This was Daniel Boone's country. In fact, local people claim that the famous wilderness pioneer was born and raised in Boone. True or not, he certainly did have a hunting cabin there at one time. He then set out in the late 1700s to lead colonists into Tennessee, Kentucky and Missouri, always looking for a place as pretty as North Carolina's Blue Ridge and Smoky Mountains. The High Country must have been a tough act to follow, for these mountains are truly gorgeous.

Driving the Blue Ridge Parkway is a great introduction to the wonders of this region and to gaining an understanding of the area's quiet natural beauty. Part of the National Park System, the Blue Ridge Parkway runs 120 miles through the heart of North Carolina's High Country. Views are enlivened by old farms with split rail fences, weathered cabins, gray barns and other bygone structures of the original "hill culture."

The idea of retirement in the High Country is not new. For over a century, wealthy families from all over the nation have traditionally used these mountains as part-time retirement locations, as summer hideaways and as secluded places where they could slip away for quiet time. Industrialists from Chicago and Pittsburgh, socialites from New York and Boston and southern aristocracy from Charleston, Charlotte and other affluent cities maintained summer retreats deep in the mountains. Places like Linville, Banner Elk and Blowing Rock were unknown to most of the country, but quite familiar to the wealthy.

The first resorts and retirement homes appeared on the scene in the 1890s, but it wasn't until the advent of the automobile and good roads that retirement began in earnest. Then, anyone who could afford a Chevy could visit and settle in these formerly exclusive areas. And settle they did. The High Country turned out to be a natural retirement haven, uncrowded, with inexpensive real estate, a mild climate and gorgeous surroundings. True, it's a little more crowded today, and real estate is no longer priced at giveaway values, but they can't take away the climate and surroundings.

Renewed interest in retirement began 20 or 30 years ago when developers began buying small valleys of wooded land to develop golf courses on building lots strategically arranged around the greens. The developers realized that golf was the irresistible bait that would lure northern buyers to these parts. Ski resorts also played a part in bringing people to the High Country and later bringing them back as retirees.

When you ask people why they chose the Blue Ridge Mountains for retirement, a major reason (right behind the area's beauty) is the mountain weather. Residents delight in contrasting seasons: mild summers, beautiful springs and honest-to-goodness falls and winters with soft blankets of snow creating a wonderland of beauty. Skiing draws visitors from Florida and other parts of the south, but although some Floridians visit here in the winter to enjoy winter sports, many other mountain retirees head for Florida to *escape* the snow. We interviewed several retired residents who regularly go to Florida from December through March. Some take RVs; others rent condos or houses on the beach. The wealthier folks own a second home in Florida; Vero Beach a popular destination for a winter reunion with their warm-weather neighbors.

Boone: The region's largest city, Boone, is located a few miles off the Blue Ridge Parkway. It's nestled in a breathtaking valley amidst some of the oldest, most scenic mountains in the world. Boone is the county seat of Watauga and likes to be known as the "Heart of the High Country."

Although Boone's population is just little over 13,000, it seems much larger because of its surprisingly large business district and extensive strip mall shopping areas. This is partly because Boone serves as the major commercial center for most of the surrounding towns, but also because of the large student population attending Appalachian State University; they double Boone's population with another 12,000 in the student body. Boone has grown from a small town into a small city over the years that we've been watching. The full-time resident population has increased by at least 30 percent, and university students by even more.

Nearby, you'll find numerous small towns and villages where you can blend into the daily routine and find yourself among friendly neighbors. The local folk, who proudly refer to themselves as "mountain people," are famous for their hospitality to "flatlanders." However, the large number of outsiders moving in from various parts of the country is growing larger every day. Before long, flatlanders could outnumber the mountain people.

Blowing Rock: Blowing Rock is the second largest town in the High Country, although, with a population of 1,200, it could be best described as a large village. Blowing Rock is an elegant place for all seasons; cool in the summer, dazzling in the fall, a Currier and Ives portrait in the winter and a festival of wildflowers in the spring. Perched atop the Eastern Continental Divide, Blowing Rock is known for its quaint shops, fabulous dining and charming accommodations. In short, it's become a tourist-oriented artists' colony. Visitors come by the droves—so many you'll have trouble finding a parking spot during the season. This extra traffic is the only downside we could find in Blowing Rock.

Banner Elk: Banner Elk is the hub of Avery County's energetic resort region, featuring premier ski slopes, outstanding golf courses and other recreational opportunities. Visitors to the Avery County area are thrilled by the beautiful mountain scenery. Several attractive residential areas have great retirement potential, with upscale developments as well as conventional homes.

An important yearly event, one you should treat your grandkids to, is Banner Elk's famous Woolly Worm Festival. Woolly worms of course, are caterpillars. Contestants raise woolly caterpillars for fame, fortune and winter forecasting.

Hound Ears: This is an example of the many gated communities gaining popularity with golfers and lovers of privacy and secruity. Despite its "down-home" name, Hound Ears is an example of an expensive and exclusive development, one of the area's earliest. The developer looked at this narrow valley and visualized a golf course spreading over its valley floor. After laying out beautiful greens and fairways and an attractive clubhouse, he quickly sold the lots he had·developed around the golf course. Buyers then demanded more land for retirement homes, so the developer began cutting roads through the woods and into the hills that overlooked his valley golf course. As fast as he could lay out a new section of lots, it sold out. Each new house seemed to be more luxurious than the previous one, with some homes valued well into the six-figures. We were told that one couple put $500,000 into construction, but before they could finish, someone offered them a million dollars for the house, as is.

Obviously, these places aren't for folks with ordinary pocketbooks. Security guards staff the entrances 24 hours a day, keeping out us uncelestial beings. In fact, one development (Linville Ridge) is said to be so exclusive that one can buy into the development only by invitation! (So far, the developers haven't invited us, so I suppose we won't buy. They probably wouldn't let us put it on our credit card, anyway.)

Linville: Inexpensive homes abound in North Carolina towns and villages alongside a few affordable country-club-type resorts. One example is the Linville Land Harbor development. An 18-hole golf course was laid out over an area that was originally a commercial shrub and tree nursery. The bluegrass fairways and bent grass greens are said to be some of the best in the area. A 65-acre lake is stocked with brown and rainbow trout, and a mile of the Linville River's rapids and pools pose a challenge to the fly fisherman. A large clubhouse, two tennis courts and an Olympic-sized pool complete the development.

This endeavor, which originally began as an RV park, marketed large-sized lots to vacationers. However, after putting in the resort's amenities, the developer declared bankruptcy. Fortunately, the lot-owners were able to buy the development out of bankruptcy and now own the property as joint tenants.

Because the lots were so big, some lot owners decided to build houses while others brought in mobile homes. Some RV owners have built extra rooms beside their cement pads, providing extra sleeping while they are parked plus extra storage while they are gone. Today, instead of a vacation park as originally planned, Land

Harbor is an interesting mixture of houses, mobile homes and RVs with most people living here year round.

Newland: Highways in this area are not for high-speed driving; they meander lazily around hill and dale. Every few miles turns up another surprise, another lovely town for retirement seekers. Each has its own personality and charm. The little town of Newland, for example, is a sleepy country town, unpretentious and quiet. A house set back from the road on several acres can still be found for less than $80,000, while cozy little homes in a friendly neighborhood could sell for even less. The most popular restaurant has an old-fashioned soda fountain and sells a lunch special for about three dollars. A public golf course—just as beautiful as the exclusive, private ones—provides sport for the duffers in the crowd.

Recreation and Culture: One of the major attractions for relocation in the High Country is the wide range of outdoor recreation. Golf courses, tennis, hunting, fishing—there are just too many to mention. Boone Golf Club is said to be one of the South's outstanding championship courses. Blue Ridge Country Club, near Linville Falls, is one of the newest semi-private championship golf courses, and Hawksnest Golf and Ski Resort near Banner Elk is another favorite. Downhill skiing is found at Appalachian Ski Mountain at Blowing Rock.

Even though the region is somewhat isolated from Asheville (a long hour's drive away), a surprising array of cultural activities are available to residents. Mayland College, located in Spruce Pine, sponsors extension class programs in many surrounding communities. This program, called Lifelong Learning, is associated with the Elderhostel Institute, which has as its purpose the fostering of continuing education among older people, regardless of their previous academic pursuits. Among classes offered are pottery, studio glass, mountain weaving, jewelry and iron working and sculpture/bronze casting. Elderhostel is an excellent way of meeting interesting people.

Real Estate: At one time I wrote that real estate in the High Country was one of the best bargains in the country. There are still bargains to be had, though you won't find them on every corner or back road. Popularity has caught up with the High Country: people with money have entered the picture once again.

However, all isn't for the rich. Enjoying the North Carolina mountains is practical because many affordable properties are available. You have to make your selection according to the heft of your wallet. Although some places may not be as costly, the view, the fresh air and the delightful weather do not depend on your bank accounts.

Medical Care: The city of Boone is the health care center for the Blue Ridge counties of Watauga, Ashe, Avery, Johnson and Wilkes. Watauga Medical Center, in Boone, a 127-bed primary and secondary care hospital, recently completed an $11 million expansion program. There's a new and expanded emergency department, a critical-care unit and a new outpatient surgical facility.

The Seby B. Jones Regional Cancer Center is located in a separate building on the Watauga Medical Center Campus. Founded in 1993, the new cancer center administers radiation (with a multi-energy linear accelerator) and chemotherapy treatments in a state-of-the-art facility that serves area residents.

The town of Banner Elk, in Avery County, is served by Cannon Memorial Hospital, a small acute-care facility.

When Grandkids Visit: Grandfather Mountain is the highest peak in the Blue Ridge Mountain range and is considered the most biologically diverse mountain in the East. After a climb to the top in the 1890s, John Muir, the father of America's national parks, wrote that he "began to jump about and sing and glory in it all."

Today visitors can actually drive to the summit and, along the way, enjoy spectacular scenery, endless vistas and intriguing rock formations. If lucky, you might photograph bears, panthers, deer, river otters and eagles in their natural wildlife habitats. Then, when you reach the top elevation, you can walk across the highest swinging footbridge in America.

Addresses and Connections

Chamber of Commerce: (Newland) 205 Cranberry St., Newland, NC 28657-8800. (704) 733-4737.

(Boone) 208 Howard St., Boone, NC 28607. (704) 264-2225. (e-mail : boonechamber@boone.net)

(Blowing Rock) 1038 Main Street, Blowing Rock, NC 28605. (800) 295-7851, (704) 295-7851. (e-mail: info@blowingrock.com)

(Banner Elk) P.O. Box 335, Banner Elk, NC 28604. (704) 898-5605. (e-mail: beacc@skybest.com)

Internet: http://ncnet.com/ncnw/bne-intr.html
http://www.boonenc.com
http://www.blowingrock.com/northcarolina/list-12.htm
http://www.grandfather.com
http://www.banner-elk.com
http://www.highcountryhost.com/n.carolina-mtns/index.html

Newspapers: (Blowing Rock) *The Blowing Rocket*, P.O. Box 1026, Blowing Rock, N.C. 28605. (704) 295-7522.

(Boone) *Mountain Times*, 2211 Highway 105, Boone, NC 28608. (704) 264-6397.

(Boone) *Watauga Democrat*, 747 W. King St., Boone, NC 28607-3423. (704) 262-0048.

(Banner Elk) *The Avery Journal*, P.O. Box 1130, Newland, NC 28657. (704) 733-2448.

Airport: Asheville.

Bus/Train: You will need an automobile in High Country.

Jefferson/West Jefferson

We discovered Ashe County and its twin towns more or less by accident. Jefferson and West Jefferson are slightly off the beaten track for relocation—almost a "best-kept secret." During a recent research trip through the Blue Ridge Mountains, we decided to make a short detour and pay a visit to McFarland & Co. Publishers, one of my publishers. Jefferson sits a few miles off the Blue Ridge Parkway near the Virginia state line. Previously, we had heard little about Jefferson as a potential place for Appalachian retirement, even though it's not far from some popular places like Boone and Banner Elk. We were pleasantly surprised to find Jefferson a good retirement possibility.

The town was established in 1803—the first town in America named for Thomas Jefferson. For over one hundred years, Jefferson remained the sole incorporated town in Ashe County. Of all the Blue Ridge country, Jefferson has probably changed the least since the Blue Ridge country was "discovered" by the outside world. The population boom hasn't struck as it has in other parts of the High Country. Since 1900, the populations of Jefferson and its twin community of West Jefferson have risen and fallen but changed little overall. Only about 10 percent of the county's residents live in town. The rest live on farms, in small crossroad communities or in one of two newly-developed golf course subdivisions. Combined, the twin towns muster a population of only 1,500, but this figure is misleading, since most retirees choose to live outside the town limits. Hardly a metropolis, the quaint downtown serves as the shopping center for the entire county of about 22,000 inhabitants, so all the facilities are in place, more so than in some other towns of this size. Jefferson's downtown, turn-of-the-century courthouse is a marvel of Victorian construction.

Local people say Jefferson reminds them of Boone, before Appalachian State University expanded and tourism took over to create traffic jams in the Appalachians. To be fair, this northernmost region isn't quite as hilly or as forested as some of the more popular places, but the degree isn't dramatic. One nice thing about Jefferson is that real estate prices haven't skyrocketed as they have in the Boone-Blowing Rock area. One couple told us, "When we retired from New Jersey, we first went to Florida. Then we decided we wanted to live in North Carolina, in the mountains. But we realized we couldn't afford to buy property in Watauga County, where everybody wants to live. Then we discovered Ashe County and Jefferson."

Recreation and Culture: Two excellent golf facilities are found in Ashe County. Mountain Aire Golf Club, in Beaver Creek, and Jefferson Landing, to the east of town, both have excellent 18-hole layouts. Since Jefferson Landing is a private development, golf privileges to non-residents may be restricted at some point in the future.

Like all of North Carolina's Blue Ridge country, outdoor recreation is convenient and varied. Many miles of trout streams flow through the region, and the abundance of game such as wild turkey, squirrel and deer can satisfy a hunter's dream. (One of the area's most famous hunters was the legendary Daniel Boone. In fact, Boone's descendants were among the first land owners in Ashe County.)

Wilkes Community College supplies Jefferson with a program for continuing education. Several classes designed for adults bring seniors together. The Ashe County Little Theater is an active part of the community, presenting a variety of plays throughout the year. The Ashe County Arts Council is another part of the cultural scene, coordinating special programs and sponsoring events like the Opera Carolina, the North Carolina Shakespeare Festival and the Appalachian Young People's Theater. The Ashe County Performing Arts/Civic Center, a multi-purpose cultural and meeting facility, is in the construction stage.

Real Estate: This is an area where folks take advantage of inexpensive land and acreage, with many preferring to be located away from the population center. Conventional homes, cottages and the ever popular log cabins are offered at affordable prices. We saw a few places on the market for less than $60,000. Inside the town limits, more homes are older, traditional brick construction. Homes in private golf course communities begin in the mid-$100,000 range.

Medical Care: Ashe Memorial Hospital takes care of a county population of 23,000, and is remarkably sophisticated for its location. The hospital has 76 acute-care beds, and the medical staff consists of 16 doctors in a wide variety of specializations. Ashe Memorial is a full-service hospital, with a wide range of services, from surgery to a cardiac monitoring and rehab center. There's also a 60-bed long-term nursing facility attached to the hospital. Ashe County is fortunate to have 18 doctors serving its people.

When Grandkids Visit: Try the New River State Park for some camping or canoeing adventures on the New River. Two areas of the New River Park are accessible by canoe only. Actually, the river isn't "new" at all. The river acquired its name by accident when a surveying party was mapping this region back in the late 1700s. When the maps were just about done, someone discovered a river they had overlooked. So the head surveyor penciled in the words, "new river," to remind himself where the stream should appear. However, he forgot to assign a name to the river before he sent the map off to Washington. New River it remains to this day.

Addresses and Connections

Chamber of Commerce: P.O. Box 31, West Jefferson, N.C. 28694. (910) 246-9550. (e-mail: ashechamber@skybest.com)
Internet: http://www.franklin-chamber.com

Newspaper: *Jefferson Post*, 203 S. Second St., West Jefferson, NC 28694. (910) 246-7164.
Airport: Bristol Regional, Bristol, TN (hour and a half drive).
Bus/Train: You'll need an automobile.

Blue Ridge Mountains

	Jan.	April	July	Oct.	Rain	Snow
Daily Highs	45	68	84	68	49 in.	18 in.
Daily Lows	25	41	62	44		

NORTH CAROLINA TAXES
North Carolina Department of Revenue
P. O. Box 25000, Raleigh, NC 27640 — Ph. (919) 733-3991
North Carolina's tax bills rank 31st among the least expensive in the nation

Income Tax

Single Individuals		**Married Filing Jointly**	
Taxable Income	Rate	Taxable Income	Rate
Not over $12,750	6.0%	Not over $21,250	6.0%
Next $47,250	7.0%	Next $78,750	7.0%
Over $60,000	7.75%	Over $100,000	7.75%

Personal Exemptions or Credits: Federal amounts, $4,000 per retiree*
Private Pension Exclusion: $2,000 per retiree*
Social Security/Railroad Retirement Benefits: Full exclusion
Standard Deduction: $3,000 single; $5,000 married, filing jointly
Medical and Dental Expense Deduction: Federal amount
Federal Income Tax Deduction: None
Other: One-third of federal credit for the elderly and disabled is allowed, with an additional credit for a fully disabled spouse, or dependent that varies with income and filing status.
*For pensioners with both public and private benefits, maximum exclusion is $4,000.

Sales Taxes

State 4.0%, **County** 2.0%, **City** None
Combined Rate Selected Towns
Charlotte: 6.0%, **Durham:** 6.0%, **Raleigh:** 6.0%
General Coverage: Food is taxed, prescription drugs are exempt

Property Taxes

Average assessment on a $100,000 home about $1,200 annually.
All real and personal property is subject to local taxation. The state imposes an intangibles tax on shares of stocks and bonds. In relation to personal income, property tax collections are in the lowest third among the 50 states.

Homestead Credit: Homeowners age 65 and older or disabled with disposable income below $11,000: Exempt on the first $15,000 assessed value
Disabled veterans: $38,000 assessed value exemption

Estate/Inheritance Taxes

North Carolina imposes an inheritance tax that ranges from 1% to 17%. The tax rate depends both on the value of the beneficiary's share and the relationship of the beneficiary to the decedent. A surviving spouse receives a full exemption. Certain other relatives (e.g., linear ancestors, descendants) receive a total credit of $26,150 that must be divided among these relatives (priority is given to minor children). This credit is equivalent to exemption of first $500,000. North Carolina also imposes a pick-up tax, which is a portion of the federal estate tax and does not increase the total tax owed.

South Carolina

European explorers touched foot on the shores of South Carolina as early as 1521. The leader of the expedition was the Spaniard Francisco Cordilla. Several attempts at colonization were unsuccessful until half a century later, when the British established the town that became Charleston. With an economy based on rice, indigo and cotton, the colony quickly became prosperous, as evidenced by large, stately plantation houses and elaborate "town homes" of wealthy planter families.

Fiercely independent, residents of South Carolina were at the forefront of struggles against British imperialism before and after the American Revolution. It seemed only natural that the state would again take the lead in agitating for secession from the United States before the outbreak of the Civil War. South Carolina was the first state to withdraw from the Union and initiated the first battle of the war by firing on Fort Sumpter in Charleston Bay.

The northern armies were particularly harsh to South Carolina; the Yankees blamed the state for starting the war and spread a broad path of destruction through the state. After the war, Reconstruction was equally vindictive, as South Carolina was further punished by a military

---

South Carolina
The Palmetto State
Admitted to statehood: May 23, 1788
State Capital: Columbia
Population (1995): 3,673,287; rank, 26th
Population Density: 121.7 per sq. mile: urban 69.8%
Geography: 40th state in size, with 31,189 square miles, including 1,078 square miles of water surface. Highest elevation: Sassafrass Mountain, 3,560 feet. Lowest elevation: Sea level, Atlantic Ocean. Average elevation: 350 feet.
State Flower: Carolina jessamine
State Bird: Carolina wren
State Tree: Palmetto
State Song: *Carolina, South Carolina on my Mind*

South Carolina

Cheraw

Aiken

Myrtle Beach

Georgetown

Columbia

Summerville

Charleston

Hilton Head

government that remained in power for another decade. Corrupt "carpetbaggers" from the North looted the state and drove it into bankruptcy. Recovery was slow and painful, finally breaking loose after World War II. The ensuing years brought industrial and agricultural prosperity, and today South Carolina is a model of charm and vitality. It's becoming the retirement and relocation target for many living in the northeastern and Great Lakes regions.

Like the other Atlantic coastal states, South Carolina can be divided into three regions. The first is the Coastal Plain, bordered by South Carolina's 2,800 miles of tidal shoreline, barrier islands and colonial cities. Next is the Piedmont region, whose rolling hills, rich farmlands and foothills comprise about two-thirds of the state's land. The third division is the Appalachians, with the highest elevation in the Blue Ridge Mountains, in the northwestern part of the state.

Grand Strand

Most of South Carolina's Atlantic Ocean coastline is sparsely populated lowland country, suitable for rice cultivation and sparsely populated. Generally, the major roads and highways run far inland, with occasional roads meandering toward the ocean. Except for Hilton Head, the Charleston area and a few isolated ocean-front towns, South Carolina's most logical beachfront retirement choices occupy a 60-mile stretch of spectacular coastline known as the "Grand Strand." It begins at Little River, on the North Carolina-South Carolina border, and stretches south to the Santee River, just beyond Georgetown. Myrtle Beach and Georgetown are the largest towns on the Grand Strand, but there are numerous smaller communities: Little River, North Myrtle Beach, Atlantic Beach, Surfside Beach, Garden City Beach, Murrells Inlet, Litchfield Beach and Pawleys Island.

Rice fields and timber plantations along the coast are being replaced by handsome residential resorts—places like Litchfield By The Sea, Heritage Plantation, Long Bay Club, Tidewater and other upscale developments. Golf seems to be the common denominator; some communities boast their own superb courses, while others offer privileges on spectacular links such as Marsh Harbour and The Legends.

Because the Gulf Stream's warm waters flow only 40 miles off-shore, the weather along the Grand Strand is mild, only two degrees cooler than the northern Florida coast. However, local residents qualify this by saying, "We do get some right smart cold spells from time to time." Our first visit was during one of these cold snaps, and I remember it vividly. A freezing north wind tortured me one morning as I tried to change a flat tire with numb, frozen hands (our only flat in more than 30,000 miles of research). However, by afternoon it had warmed up to the point that we were strolling the beach in our shirtsleeves.

Myrtle Beach

Myrtle Beach sits in the center of the accessible beach areas of the Grand Strand. With about 26,000 year-round habitants, Myrtle Beach doesn't sound like such a big place, but seasonal visitors can boost the population more than tenfold. The full length of the Grand Strand has a permanent population of about 58,000, a large percentage of whom are retired, but visitors expand the population by more than 300,000. Spring and fall have always lured golfers to enjoy the more than 90 golf courses along the Grand Strand. And summer traditionally draws crowds of vacationers to delight in beach sun-and-fun. Each summer seems to bring more and more tourists.

After we first researched Myrtle Beach about ten years ago, we described the town as South Carolina's equivalent of a Florida Panhandle resort: tourist-frenzied in the summer and somewhat relaxed in the winter. In fact, many restaurants and small businesses used to close shop when tourists deserted for the winter. Inexpensive homes were almost the rule and rentals were plentiful. I reported that after Labor Day, the town drops its frantic, super-hero role and changes to its mild-mannered, sleepy identity for the rest of the year.

Since that time, the population of the Grand Strand has doubled. All seasons are busy, partly because Myrtle Beach has become one of the South's premier golfing meccas. According to the chamber of commerce, Myrtle Beach has the greatest number of golf courses per square mile ·in the world! People who live in country-club developments in other parts of the South routinely organize excursions to play golf on the Grand Strand. Besides golf courses, you'll find an assortment of golf schools, golf shops and a wide range of golf vacation packages, should you decide to come here to test the water (or the sand traps for that matter).

A proliferation of country-western entertainment centers, modeled after Missouri's Branson and Tennessee's Grand Ol' Opry, have joined golf to make full-tilt tourism a year-round business. Adding to the momentum are events like the annual Harley Davidson motorcycle rally and the Sun Fun Festival. The increased tourism is nice for commerce, but it creates traffic congestion and additional strain on summer-season facilities, already under pressure. With an increased work force and long-term visitors competing for housing, bargain real estate is out of the picture today.

Despite the aforementioned drawbacks, folks are still coming here to retire in droves. A look around tells why. Between Myrtle Beach's main thoroughfare (which used to be Highway 17) and the ocean, several blocks of beautiful homes on spacious, well-landscaped ·lots provide neighborhoods of gracious living, and other equally nice choices are found away from the business centers. Other choices are golf course communities and upscale subdivisions as well as more modest homes between the main street and the Highway 17 bypass.

Myrtle Beach doesn't come off well in the FBI's crime statistics, ranking higher than the national average in offenses. No surprise here; crime rates always rise when a city gets more than its share of tourists. Theft of cameras, luggage and golf clubs from tourists' cars and burglaries of hotel rooms boost crime statistics, yet these crimes have little to do with permanent residents. Local law enforcement officials assure us that the crime rate in residential neighborhoods is at or possibly below the norm for South Carolina as a whole. And that's not bad.

Recreation and Culture: It goes without saying that golf is the major reason people choose to relocate along the Grand Strand. Golf is practically a religion here; the 90 championship courses were designed by such golf "deities" as Palmer, Nicklaus and Fazio. With so many courses available within a half-hour drive, your problem will be deciding which layout to play next. Deep-sea and surf fishing also rank high in outdoor sports, and freshwater angling is available nearby in rivers, lakes and tidewater creeks.

Live entertainment has found a home in Myrtle Beach, which now offers seating for more than 20,000, with nightly cascades of stars rivaling Branson and Las Vegas. As one travel writer commented, these entertainment emporiums are "popping up like prairie dogs in a cloudburst." The new 40,000-square-foot, state-of-the-art Gatlin Brothers Theater at Fantasy Harbor plays host to the Grammy Award-winning trio, as well as other popular performers (recent guests include Lee Greenwood and the Charlie Daniels Band). For country music fans: the Carolina Opry, Dolly Parton's Dixie Stampede and Alabama Theater should keep you entertained.

Real Estate: Average housing costs have been reported to be $105,000 for mid-range, three-bedroom homes. In the main part of Myrtle Beach, an older section of elegant homes lying between the main thoroughfare and the ocean manage to maintain a semblance of the quiet, upscale neighborhoods it was famous for. Away from the beach, less-costly neighborhoods of newer houses provide homes for relocation. But the growing trend is toward gated or semi-private subdivisions with golf courses or park-like surroundings as the key attraction.

Medical Care: Myrtle Beach's major health care centers are the 160-bed Conway Hospital, the 172-bed Grand Strand General Hospital and the 130-bed Loris Community Hospital. There's also a U.S. Air Force Base hospital located here.

When Grandkids Visit: There is so much beach fun to be enjoyed here, that you will have no problem entertaining the grandkids. But if they haven't had their fill of water fun, you might take them to the Myrtle Waves Water Park. The 20-acre park has a variety of water slides, a wave pool, some surfing rides and a "lazy river" ride—in all, 30 rides and attractions. Those over 55 years of age or below 48 inches in height get discounts on their tickets. (Who knows, there might be extra discounts for people who are over 55 years of age and below 48 inches in height.)

Addresses and Connections

Chamber of Commerce: P.O. Box 2115, Myrtle Beach, SC 29578.
   (800) 356-3016.
Internet: http://www.myrtlebeach-info.com/mbl.html
   http://www.myrtlebeachlive.com/tidelands
Newspaper: *Myrtle Beach Herald,* P.O. Box 7116, 2105-B Farlow
   Street, Myrtle Beach, SC 29577. (803) 626-3131.
Airport: Myrtle Beach Airport.
Bus/Train: City bus service; Greyhound.

Myrtle Beach/Georgetown

	Jan.	April	July	Oct.	Rain	Snow
Daily Highs	60	75	89	75	51 in.	2 in.
Daily Lows	40	53	71	53		

Georgetown

At the end of the Grand Strand, halfway between Myrtle Beach and Charleston, the small city of Georgetown delivers a fascinating snapshot of its colonial and antebellum past. Actually, Georgetown's rich history goes back even further than colonial times. Many readers will be surprised to know that Winyah Bay was the site of the earliest European settlement in North America. Colonists from Spain established a settlement at Winyah Bay in 1526, a century before the Pilgrims landed on Plymouth Rock. The Spanish, however, failed as farmers, found no gold and after a year were driven away by disease and hostile Indians.

By the mid-1600s, both the English and the French had established outposts to trade with Indians along the coast. Placid inland rivers served as highways, graced with live oaks dripping with moss and magnolias abundant with fragrant, white blossoms. At first, agriculture was difficult; swamps and rivers were infested with alligators, poisonous snakes and mosquitoes, and bordered with impregnable tangles of vines and cane. It wasn't until the early 1700s that the Carolina tidelands were tamed and the Native Americans were forced to withdraw.

In 1729 Georgetown was established as a shipping port for the highly successful indigo and rice plantations in the region and for inland traders. Barges and flatboats floated down-river loaded with cargo. However, the intricate labyrinth of inlets, hidden bays and barrier islands made ideal hideouts for pirates, who attacked slow, heavily laden merchant ships headed for England. Some of the more famous pirates who lurked offshore carried names like: "Blackbeard" and "Caesar."

By the time of the American Revolution, Georgetown was an important city with a well-developed class of prominent and influential planter families. Thomas Lynch Jr., one of Georgetown's most vocal patriots, was a signer of the Declaration of Independence. Another area planter, Christopher Gadsen, is remembered for the flag he designed: "Don't Tread on Me!" Georgetown resident Francis Marion was the legendary "Swamp Fox," who led a ragged band of followers to handily defeat the British in this area.

I hate to use the timeworn cliché "a town where time stood still," but the saying fits Georgetown perfectly. This is a virtual treasury of colonial, antebellum and Victorian architecture. You can't help but feel humble as you tread silent, tree-shaded streets past historic homes, each one older than the last, some more than 250 years old. It's easy to picture men wearing three-cornered hats and ladies dressed in long skirts and petticoats, ambling along the streets. You begin to wonder how life in South Carolina must have been before the American Revolution, before the Civil War, before the invention of automobiles, electricity and miniature golf.

The panorama from the high bridge coming into Georgetown leaves little to the imagination as to why Georgetown County is called "the Tidelands." Rivers flow gently to empty into the blue-green Atlantic Ocean eleven miles away. The harbor shelters a shrimp boat or two, and the oldest fish-house in the state sits on the banks of the Sampit River.

With a population of 11,000, Georgetown is small and soft-spoken, yet immensely proud of its historic business district, another gem of preservation. The city recently spent $4.5 million dollars on further restoration. Front Street faces the harbor and has an Old-World appearance with ancient buildings in rows of pastel calico. A harbor walk leads along the river where tall-masted sailing ships once came to the bustling seaport with goods from all over the world. The town clock tower sits atop the old Market Building, dating from 1842. Today the Market Building houses a museum depicting the days of rice, indigo and slavery.

Although Georgetown is technically located on the Grand Strand, it isn't on the ocean. The town's waterfront is Winyah Bay; the nearest ocean beaches are found at Pawley's Island, some 22 miles away. Pawley's Island is one of the oldest beach resorts in the country, having been used for recreation since the late 1700s. It also has the distinction of being one of the few South Carolina sea islands where original antebellum and Victorian beach homes have survived the occasional hurricanes that bruise the coast.

This is a place for people who used to like the old-time atmosphere of Myrtle Beach, but who are appalled at the changes in population density and proliferation of highway mall businesses. Folks who've relocated here, from Ohio, Long Island and elsewhere, feel protective of their discovery, they don't want to spoil their piece of utopia. To protect the town from tourist clutter, Georgetown has some strictly enforced zoning laws that should guard against glitz and sleaze.

One advantage of relocating here is that friends and relatives like to visit; it's convenient for those going to or from Florida on vacation. "We moved here eight years ago," said one couple, "and after sending out our Christmas card list the first year, with a Georgetown postmark, we've seen more family and friends than when we were next-door neighbors."

Recreation and Culture: Sitting in the midst of a water wonderland, intimately in touch with creeks, rivers, inlets, bays and ocean, it's no surprise that outdoor recreation often involves water-related activities. Boating and canoeing are enjoyed year round on miles of coastal marsh and creeks. Surf and deepwater fishing are great and freshwater fishing for largemouth bass, bream or catfish is very productive. And it used to be common to haul in sturgeon as long as automobiles, weighing 500 pounds. That's why Georgetown was once the nation's center of caviar production. Unfortunately the slow maturity rate of sturgeon helped place them on the endangered list, and in the 1980s a moratorium was placed on sturgeon fishing.

Tasty blue crabs are harvested by an unusual piece of tackle: panty hose. Fishermen tie a fish head or chicken neck in a piece of panty hose and attach it to their line. When a crab snags the bait, the hook-like parts of the claws tangle in the fine mesh of the hose. The hapless crab can't let go until the guy is safely in your net.

Georgetown County has a dozen excellent golf courses, with another 50 championship courses in the Myrtle Beach area just 30 miles away. Public and private tennis courts are also plentiful.

Several artists' associations promote the arts in the county. They include: Georgetown Watercolor Society, Winyah Arts Association, Dreamkeepers Community Center and others. The Swamp Fox Players are widely recognized for their numerous theatrical productions. The group invites anyone with a yen to participate in live theater to work with the Swamp Fox Players and have the opportunity of learning by doing.

Real Estate: Gracious townhouses and churches lie hidden in the historic district. At one time, homes in the historic district were give-aways, but in the past 10 or 15 years, most have been snapped up and restored. Real estate in general is affordable, however; according to county records, an average home in other parts of Georgetown costs $75,000. Upscale homes and condos are found in Litchfield and Pawley's Island area; the average cost is $125,000, but many sell for over $300,000. Construction costs are ranked among the lowest in the United States, and the county has more than 25 contractors involved in building single-family homes and renovating houses in the historic district. Some mid-rise condominium construction is underway.

Medical Care: Georgetown Memorial Hospital, a 142-bed facility, utilizes the latest technology. More than 50 physicians and 20 surgeons staff the facility, most of whom also maintain private practices A recent multi-million-dollar addition houses a 24-hour trauma center, chemotherapy and other services.

When Grandkids Visit: For sure, pick up a self-guiding tour map from the chamber of commerce and take the grandkids on a trip into history as you view the fascinating old homes. Another interesting-sounding adventure is a cruise either to the barrier island that protects Winyah Bay or down the Plantation River. I'm not necessarily recommending these tours, because I've never been on them, but they sound intriguing.

Addresses and Connections

Chamber of Commerce: 1001 Front Street, P.O. Drawer 1776, Georgetown, SC 29442. (800) 777-7705.
Internet: http://www.georgetown-sc.com
Newspapers: *Coastal Observer,* Wacammaw Park, Pawleys Island, SC 29585. (803) 237-8438.
Georgetown Times, 615 Front St., Georgetown, SC 29440-3623. (803) 546-4148.
Airport: Myrtle Beach International (30 miles), Charleston International (55 miles).
Bus/Train: Greyhound.

Charleston

After its settlement in 1670, Charleston quickly became one of the most prosperous cities in the 13 colonies. Charleston was the standard against which people measured other cities in terms of beauty, culture and riches. Located in what today is called the "Low Country," the land was rich and fertile. Planters, acquiring wealth from fantastically productive rice plantations, began designing mansions as lavish as money could provide. They built with such loving attention to detail and such devotion to quality and style that future generations of Charlestonians have resisted all temptations to exchange those prizes for new fashions. At least 240 homes are known to have been built before 1840 and 76 pre-date the Revolution, with some dating back to the 1720s. Hundreds more date from the time of the Civil War and Reconstruction.

Today, Charleston vies with Savannah for the title of most beautiful city on the Atlantic Seaboard. Each scores high marks and each claims to be the "cultural center of the South." It's difficult to choose between them.

In 1989 the nation watched in horror as television news showed Hurricane Hugo ripping into Charleston. We watched winds tear away trees and rip roofs from the historic old buildings. We felt as if we were witnessing the destruction of an old friend. But high winds had scarcely subsided when plucky residents rolled up their sleeves and started to work. They began trimming damaged limbs from trees, repairing slate roofs and straightening the disorder. Charleston citizens are justifiably proud of the recovery. "Within six months," said one resident, "we had things cleaned up and repaired as good as before."

This episode was just another in a long string of dramas played on Charleston's stage. Like Scarlet O'Hara in *Gone with the Wind*, Charleston has endured more than her share of tragedies: fire, earthquake, hurricanes, enemy cannon bombardments, occupation by hostile troops, urban blight and assault by profit-hungry developers. Charleston always stood firm, protected herself when she could and repaired damage and treated wounds when she couldn't. To people here, Hurricane Hugo was just another challenge.

The city limits of Charleston contain 96,000 inhabitants, but the cultural focus is on the downtown section. This picturesque area is so steeped in legend and history that a walk through its downtown streets is an adventure in time travel. It's easy to imagine fine carriages jaunting along the cobblestone streets or fashionably dressed women and nattily attired men strolling the sidewalks, past cobblestone alleys and intricate wrought-iron gates. A pause in front of a home built in the 1700s evokes a feeling of humility as one mentally recreates the setting—almost three centuries past. In California, where we live, any building over one hundred years old is considered a priceless antique.

Charleston has scrupulously—almost jealously—maintained her southern traditions and gracious architecture for three centuries. She is proud of her southern neoclassical architectural styles: Georgian, Federal, Greek Revival as well as Victorian. Homes built in the 1920s sit near homes built two centuries earlier. Like an aristocratic southern belle who appreciates the finer points of chivalry and good manners, Charleston has rejected the unspeakably common intrusion of colored-glass buildings and towering condominiums. She refuses to replace tradition and history with glitter and quick profits. The result is a treasury of historical architecture unmatched anywhere in the country. The city is not simply a collection of historic buildings, but a living museum of the traditions, cuisine, architecture and gracious manners of the Old South. Charleston is a way of life.

Built on a narrow peninsula, Charleston's downtown section isn't very large. The peninsula is so narrow that it's almost an island between two rivers that empty into the ocean at the city's east end. Charleston's emphasis is on private homes rather than on commercial activity, but the most important enterprise (from my standpoint as a lover of seafood) in this old section is the superb collection of fine restaurants. As major tourist attractions, Charleston's restaurants fully live up to their reputation for excellent seafood and southern gourmet dishes of all descriptions. We cannot possibly pass through Charleston without a pause for our favorite culinary delight: she-crab soup. It's creamy, made with the roe and meat from the female blue crab, and laced with a spot of sherry and some subtle spices.

Many old mansions in Charleston's Historic District were long ago converted to apartments, which at one time rented at unusually affordable rates—given the enchanted, historic atmosphere. Carriage houses behind the mansions had been remodeled into studio apartments or charming cottages with lofts converted into upstairs bedrooms. However, as Historic District real estate becomes more and more valuable, more homes are being restored to their days of antiquity, and prices for rentals have risen to match the more expensive housing.

Should you become ambitious and want to own your own historic mansion, you'll no longer find bargains here, but whatever you pay, properties in the old district will hold their resale value. But be aware that the purchase price of a "restorable" old mansion isn't the end of the investment. You have to be prepared to spend a bundle of money on restoration.

Charleston living isn't for everyone. It can be terribly formal, paced with a tempo of southern society, intellectual pursuits and traditional manners. We've been told that it's sometimes difficult to be accepted in the upper echelons of society. But even if you aren't into buying historic mansions and entering the social whirl, you could do as the old-time planters did: live in Charleston for the season and somewhere else the rest of the year.

All is not lace curtains and fresh paint in old Charleston. As in many cities, the curse of urban blight hovers. Not very far from the prosperous streets described here, you'll find rows of abandoned houses, so old and uncared-for that they look as if they might collapse from old age and decay. These neighborhoods seem tawdry and run down. It's unfortunate that there's not some way to preserve these old mansions. Some stand three stories high, with beautifully crafted balconies and balustrades rising the full facade. Porches, high columns and carved woodwork add to the impression of museum pieces from an irretrievable past. Within a decade these will probably all be gone. Most neighborhoods bordering the downtown area do not look to be appropriate retirement places for the average couple.

Over half of the city's population lives in West Ashley and James Island, which lie just to the west of the peninsula. West Ashley and James Island are a mixture of old and new; older neighborhoods with brick homes and graceful oak trees settle in with newer subdivisions and commercial centers.

If you don't care to live in or near a city center, or if you can't afford one of the historic places, you should check the outskirts of Charleston or one of the outlying towns, where you can live outside the city but visit Charleston for dinner or a play any time you feel like it. Nearby places where people choose to retire are Charleston's islands or nearby towns such as Summerville (described in a later section).

Charleston's Islands: A network of rivers meet at Charleston: the Stono, Ashley, Cooper and Wando rivers make Charleston Harbor and the surrounding coast a virtual cluster of islands. Many are uninhabited, overgrown with thick brush, only a few feet above high-tide level. But others are popular residential areas.

Just east of Charleston, bordered by the Atlantic Ocean and the Intracoastal Waterway, two semitropical islands and one luxurious resort community are popular places for relocation. Miles of sandy beaches, pastel homes and warm friendly people make relocation pleasant. The inspiration of nature combined with the passion of history in nearby Charleston enthralls those who live there.

The Isle of Palms is a classic family-oriented beachfront community offering a wide variety of accommodations and recreation options. Wild Dunes, located on 1,600 acres at the northeastern end of the Isle of Palms, is a premier resort community with championship golf and tennis facilities, a full-service marina and a full selection of homes and villas for sale.

Sullivan's Island is the Isle of Palms' sister island. More of a residential beach community, Sullivan's Island is located just south of the Isle of Palms, across Breach Inlet. There are beautiful beaches and an impressive selection of homes on this island. Natives describe the difference between the two islands this way: Isle of Palms is "more of a resort island," while Sullivan's Island is "more of a beach town."

Sullivan's Island offers much more, however, than a quiet beach-town atmosphere. Here you'll find a quaint restaurant area, historic Fort Moultrie, a working lighthouse, public tennis courts and an old-fashioned community playground complete with a grandstand gazebo! Of course, Sullivan's Island offers all the natural amenities you could want: wide, sandy beaches, fishing, swimming, boating, sunning and more.

Johns Island, more rural in character, combines an intricate network of waterways with fertile farmland, residential property and limited commercial development. Daniel Island and the Cainhoy Peninsula, which lie east and north of the peninsula, are among the most recently annexed areas of the city. The pristine Daniel Island, a full 4,500 acres in size, is just beginning to reflect the thoughtfully planned, environmentally sensitive community mapped out in the Daniel Island Master Plan. It is sure to be the future's complement to Charleston's historic downtown.

Recreation and Culture: Golf heads the list here for many people, with 117 holes on 24 golf courses in the area. Naturally this is a year-round sport. And all the water in the area, both salt and fresh, you can be sure that fishing, crabbing and shrimping also rank high among outdoor sports. Exploring the inlets, islands, creeks and rivers is done with everything from kayaks to canoes, from sailboats to fishing boats.

For nature lovers who prefer long stretches of unspoiled marsh and beach, Charleston's nearby resort islands prove an irresistible lure. Kiawah Island's 10,000 acres, for example, include 10 miles of pristine beach and give sanctuary to an abundance of wildlife.

Throughout its history, Charleston has stood as a cultural capital of the South. The performing arts are well represented; a symphony orchestra, community theater groups and several local ballet companies perform regularly. The Gibbes Museum of Art and numerous art galleries, along with the abundant examples of architectural excellence and craftsmanship, expose residents and tourists to the visual arts. The listing of Charleston's museums, theaters and special places to visit would fill a book.

In addition to all that Charleston offers every day, special events provide a perfect excuse to bring residents downtown. One of the biggest draws is Spoleto Festival U.S.A. According to the *Washington Post,* this is "the world's most comprehensive arts festival"; it's held from late May through early June. The agenda includes opera, chamber music, symphonic music, drama, ballet, modern dance and the visual arts.

Real Estate: Since properties in the downtown section of Charleston are trendy and expensive, most people choose to locate within a short drive from the city center. Any number of towns and communities within a few miles of downtown Charleston are excellent choices for relocation. Mount Pleasant, James Island, Goose Creek, Johns Island and others are logical places to investigate. Several resort-type retirement developments offer Charleston living in country-club environments. Some of them are the Elms of Charleston, Ladson and Fairfield Ocean Ridge. Price ranges run from inexpensive to prohibitive, depending on your ways and means.

Medical Care: Charleston's medical facilities are among the finest in the country. Five major hospitals, Charleston Memorial, Roper, Bon Secours-St. Francis Xavier, Veterans' Administration Medical Center and Medical University of South Carolina are concentrated in an eight-block medical district on the Peninsula. The Medical University is a leading biomedical, teaching, patient-care and research center. Its specialized treatment programs include the Children's Hospital, the Storm Eye Institute and the Institute of Psychiatry. In addition to the major hospitals, Charleston has a number of nursing homes and hospice-care and convalescent centers.

When Grandkids Visit: Across the bay at Patriots Point Naval and Maritime Museum, the USS *Yorktown* is tied to its permanent retirement dock. Even if you weren't old enough to have fought in WWII, "the Big One," you'll enjoy visiting the amazing floating city-warship that carried the nickname "Fighting Lady." You and the kids will have fun visiting the ship's bridge, flight deck and gun emplacements and viewing the continual movies about the carrier's exploits. There's a great display of navy bombers and fighters, the same ones you watched in the newsreels at the Saturday afternoon matinees when you were your grandkid's age.

Addresses and Connections

Chamber of Commerce: P.O. Box 975, Charleston, SC 29402-0975. (803) 577-4853.
Internet: http://www.lowcountry-sc.com/
http://cristaldi.com/jrc/sc.htm
Newspaper: *Post & Courier,* 134 Columbus St., Charleston, SC, 29403-4800. (803) 577-7111.
Airport: Charleston International Airport.
Bus/Train: City bus; Greyhound; AmTrak.

Charleston

	Jan.	April	July	Oct.	Rain	Snow
Daily Highs	61	78	90	77	49 in.	.04 in.
Daily Lows	38	54	71	55		

Summerville

Summerville, a small city of 25,000 people, is about 20 miles from Charleston—near enough to take advantage of all that the southern jewel offers, yet far enough away not to be bothered by the frenzy of the city. Located on a relatively high, pine-encrusted ridge, the town was first inhabited in the late 1700s. Traditionally, from May to September, families along the nearby Ashley River and from coastal Charleston fled the malarial lowlands to enjoy their forest colony. Since they spent every summer here, what more logical name could it have than Summerville?

After the Civil War, the town gained a reputation as a health center and winter resort. Today it is gaining favor as a place for retirement. Much of its charm derives from the natural beauty of the historic architecture—with 700 buildings on the National Historic Register—and the profusion of azaleas, camelias and wisteria that line the streets and provide seasonal blooms. Its rambling streets, which deliberately wind around large pine trees to avoid destroying them, also add charm to Summerville.

Early on, Summerville realized that these pines were among the town's biggest assets. So when the village incorporated as a town in 1847, elected officials passed a law that prohibited the cutting of trees without permission and fined offenders severely. The town's motto was born, and still holds strong today: Sacra Pinus Esto—"The Pine is Sacred." The ordinance is one of oldest of its kind in the United States, and is still on the books.

Summerville's special hometown feeling bubbles over during the Christmas holiday season. A special tree lighting ceremony in the town square starts things off, and every Thursday until Christmas, the town enjoys strolling carolers, late evening shopping, free hot cider and cookies, free gift wrapping, Santa in the Square and horse-drawn carriage rides through the historic district.

Recreation and Culture: Summerville is the site of four golf courses, one of which is considered the area's premier layout. Altogether, there are about 37 golf courses within an hour's drive or less from Summerville.

Built along the banks of the historic Santee Canal, Old Santee Canal State Park has miles of boardwalks and nature trails along limestone bluffs and scenic freshwater habitats, occupied by multitudes of birds, flowers, cypress and 300-year-old live oak trees.

Cultural opportunities in Summerville include live theater productions as well as various concerts. The Flowertown Players stage four to five dramatic productions annually. The Flowertown Players, a nonprofit organization, recently purchased and restored the old Summerville Community Theater with the help of the community. The Charleston Symphony presents the Summerville Concert Series three or four times each year and during the summer months concerts in Azalea Park are given every other week.

Real Estate: Plenty of lovely homes sell for in the $80,000 to $90,000 range, probably average for similar communities. There are also more upscale homes going for $150,000 to $350,000, but these palatial homes give full value for the dollar. What we found interesting during our research visit was the number of really old homes on the market. One was a plantation house build in 1852, on five acres, with outbuildings, for $350,000. A home in town, built in

1850, was on the market for $280,000 and a home built in 1819, on 1.4 acres with five fireplaces and a carriage house for $400,000.

Medical Care: In 1993, Columbia Summerville opened as a 94-bed full-service hospital and brought a whole new range of services to the community, including maternity, intensive-care and cardiac-care units, medical/surgical care and same day surgery to the citizens of Summerville and Dorchester County. In addition, several key patient areas at Columbia Summerville have been identified as Centers of Excellence. With Charleston only 20 miles away, the total health care package in Summerville is more than adequate.

When Grandkids Visit: Make sure they go on a walking tour of Summerville's private historic homes and gardens. A map and brochure can be obtained from the chamber of commerce. The map contains a six-block route to homes dating from the 1820s to the early 1900s. Also, since Charleston is so close, all of the attractions of that city are available for your grandkid's enjoyment.

Addresses and Connections

Chamber of Commerce: P.O. Box 670, Summerville, SC 29151. (803) 875-4464.
Internet: http://edisto.awod.com/gallery/sville/demo.html
Newspaper: *Summerville Journal Scene,* 104 E. Doty Ave., Summerville, SC 29483-6300. (803) 873-9424
Airport: Charleston International (20 miles).
Bus/Train: Greyhound bus; Amtrak in Charleston.

Hilton Head Island

Hilton Head Island is one of the East Coast's most popular vacation havens, as well as a preferred retirement destination for those who can afford it. Situated in South Carolina, 40 miles north of Savannah, Georgia, Hilton Head Island is the East Coast's second largest barrier island. It's probably the most attractive, too. The semitropical island is defined by its tidal rivers and streams and unspoiled forests of moss-draped live oak, magnolia and palmetto. Twelve miles of white, sandy beaches, quiet lagoons, meandering creeks and expanses of sea marsh symbolize the romance and mystery of the Carolina Coast.

Hilton Head Island was discovered in the 1600s and through the years managed to preserve its natural heritage because of the residents' sensitivity to the island's pristine beauty. Development has been a model for forward-looking planning, conservation and sensitivity to the environment. Custom homes and villas are interspersed with open areas and wildlife preserves. Commercial zones are free of garish signs and billboards, and the beaches are pristine and clean.

As you can imagine, Hilton Head's upscale resorts, world-class tennis and championship golf facilities are irresistible for tourists and vacationers. More than a million visitors come here every year, yet the island is refreshingly tranquil. Traffic, commercial and recreational facilities are coordinated to allow visitors and residents to coexist nicely.

The island is divided into eight gated developments called "plantations" (after the southern farms they replaced where indigo, rice and cotton once grew). Each plantation is centered around active living. Golf, tennis and social club memberships are included with ownership of some properties and optional with others. The four main resort communities are: Port Royal Resort, Palmetto Dunes, Sea Pines and Shipyard Plantation. Between these four you'll find 22 golf courses with a total of 360 challenging holes.

Hilton Head Island has two delightful shopping areas: Shelter Cove Harbour, with a waterfront promenade, and Harbour Town, with its distinctive hexagonal lighthouse. Residents and tourists alike patronize the chic shops and boutiques and dine at restaurants whose menus offer the best in seafood and distinctive Low Country cuisine. The island's list of gourmet restaurants is impressive. According to the chamber of commerce, more than 200 restaurants, cafés and fast-food emporiums serve everything from stand-up pizza and eggrolls to haute cuisine.

Recreation and Culture: Golfers love the 425 holes of golf spread over 12 locations on Hilton Head Island and nearby Daufuskie Island. For tennis buffs, there are more than 250 courts ranging from major complexes that host national championships to one or two courts adjoining a condo or apartment complex.

Five hundred acres on the island are reserved as a forest preserve, hosting an astonishing 260 species of birds, alligators, deer, raccoons and wild turkeys. (A three dollar gate pass is required to enter. Wild animals enter free of charge.) Hiking, shrimping from the shore, biking and boating fill out the menu of outdoor activities.

Real Estate: Hilton Head Island has a wide variety of neighborhoods (none of them cheap). Developments with private beach access are Sea Pines, Shipyard, Palmetto Dunes, Port Royal and North and South Forest Beach. Marina neighborhoods include Sea Pines, Wexford, Shelter Cove, Long Cove, Windmill Harbour and Moss Creek. Some neighborhoods are gated; some are not.

The island is one place where condominiums are plentiful. They range in price from $65,000 at Forest Beach to $200,000 plus at Sea Pines. Conventional homes come in all price ranges. At the time of our research trip, nice homes ranged from $150,000 up to whatever your bank will lend you.

Medical Care: Hilton Head Island supports a large community of doctors, dentists and other health care professionals. The local 68-bed Hospital Medical Campus has a medical staff that represents over 30 specialties and subspecialties, a number frequently found in hospitals five times its size. Among the hospital's most recent additions are a 15-bed sub-acute, skilled-nursing unit, a physical rehabilitation clinic and a diagnostic cardiac catheterization lab.

When Grandkids Visit: Nearby Pinckney Island National Wildlife Refuge has 4,000 acres of salt marsh and island that are accessible by 14 miles of trails. The University of South Carolina's Coastal Zone Education Center, free by appointment on weekdays, offers fascinating insights into marine science studies. Also, Victoria Bluff Heritage Preserve, with its wildlife observation points and trails, is a great place for nature walks.

Addresses and Connections

Chamber of Commerce: P.O. Box 5647, Hilton Head Island, SC 29938-5647. (803) 785-3673.
Internet: http://www.islandpacket.com/hhi/index.html
http://www.welcomecenters.com
Newspaper: *Hilton Head News*, 111 W. Bay St., Savannah, GA 31401-1108. (912) 236-9511.
Airport: Savannah International Airport (45 minute), Hilton Head Island Airport with commuter flights.
Bus/Train: Amtrak at Savannah (one hour).

Hilton Head Island

	Jan.	April	July	Oct.	Rain	Snow
Daily Highs	59	76	89	77	49 in.	.5 in.
Daily Lows	38	55	71	57		

Sun City Hilton Head

The governors of southern states interested in retiree recruitment programs are looking at Del Webb's Sun City Hilton Head development, as an alternative to expensive tax and land concessions that states grant to attract industry. The Sun City Hilton Head is patterned after the original Sun City development near Phoenix. South Carolina officials are counting on the project to start a new wave of economic development and perhaps set a pattern for the future. The projected 8,000-home enclave, which was launched in 1994, is estimated to have brought 4,000 jobs to the area. It would take an enormous number of smokestack industries to match this economic benefit. The state's investment was merely adding an off-ramp to the interstate.

The Sun City concept has been extremely successful in the Southwest, where Sun Cities have become synonymous with retirement living. But this is the first experiment in the Southeast. The advantage to this type of retirement—besides quality surroundings and excellent facilities—is the carefully planned social structure that's in place when newcomers move in. They find instant involvement in bridge clubs, golf foursomes, hobbies, travel clubs and much more. It eases the effort of making new friends in the adopted community. Everything is in place, ready to start a new life.

Sun City Hilton Head is located a convenient 13 miles from Hilton Head Island and 20 miles from historic Savannah, Georgia. The area surrounding Sun City Hilton Head is rich in history and has a multitude of old churches, plantations and museums. Therefore, it's no accident that the Village Center, the heart of the community, is a "recreation campus" designed to resemble a traditional southern town square, complete with a picturesque clock tower. The Village Center offers an indoor/outdoor tennis club, bocci courts, a bowling center, a fitness complex and a putting course.

Sun City Hilton Head promises people 55 years of age and older the allure of an active lifestyle in a four-season climate, the quiet charm of southern hospitality, the power and beauty of the nearby Atlantic Ocean and the never-ending challenges of a true golfer's paradise. Can it keep these promises? It looks like it's going to be a success.

Recreation and Culture: Rustling palmettos and stands of pines surround the 18-hole golf course, and future plans call for another 18-hole course as well as a 27-hole course. The first course, Okatie Creek, was designed by PGA Tour Pro Mark McCumber and offers five different tee boxes on each hole.

A fully equipped crafts center contributes to the flavor of this active community, where residents can participate in clubs and hobbies from photography to ceramics. Part of the attraction of an organized community such as Sun City is the plethora of social activities available to all. The arts and cultural life includes live theater, dance and a variety of galleries. The well-respected Savannah Symphony and other cultural delights of Savannah are a short drive away, and those of Hilton Head Island even closer.

Real Estate: In keeping with Del Webb's Sun City tradition, Hilton Head offers 15 different models designed to satisfy various requirements for a dream home. With four groupings, Sun City Hilton Head's has 15 well-designed models. Prices run from the low $100,000s to the middle $200,000s.

Chamber of Commerce: 12 Sun City Lane, Bluffton, SC 29910. (800) 978-9781.

Aiken

Aiken (pop. 25,000) is a genteel, Old-South town, located in the western corner of South Carolina's Piedmont region, with the majestic Blue Ridge mountains a short drive away. Aiken is another of those southern gems that managed to escape the torch of vengeful Union soldiers. It was a narrow escape. General Sherman had dispatched a detachment of cavalry with orders to burn the cotton mill and the town. But General Wheeler's troops took up positions in Aiken and bluffed the federal forces into thinking the

Confederates had more troops than were actually present. The Yankees retreated to rejoin their main force and went on to ravage Charleston and Columbia.

From its inception, Aiken was known as a health resort. Wealthy people from Charleston and the coastal plantations came here to escape the sultry, lowland summer heat and malaria-bearing mosquitoes. By the 1890s, Aiken entered a new golden age when wealthy northerners, seeking pleasant, quiet places for their winter homes, "discovered" the town. Aiken became established as a rich man's playground, a haven for wealthy Yankees from New York and Connecticut. These northerners became known as *winter colony*.

At an altitude of only 527 feet, the region's mild climate permitted year-round grazing for horses—a perfect place for the wealthy to raise thoroughbreds and polo ponies. Before long, the rich, the filthy rich, and the disgustingly filthy rich began buying old mansions and building new ones of their own designs. They bought farms for their race horses and enclosed pastures with white fences. In 1893, they established the Palmetto Golf Club—the fifth oldest in the nation—and were soon slicing drives into the piney woods and losing golf balls in the lake.

These newcomers brought prosperity to Aiken and, with it, a return to a genteel lifestyle that had disappeared with the Civil War. Despite Yankee accents and customs, Aiken's old, aristocratic families accepted the winter residents into local society. This established a tradition of openness and hospitality that has characterized Aiken as a town with a legacy of hospitality and friendliness.

Aiken is a good candidate for retirement for a number of reasons, not the least of which is its beautiful, gracious setting. Huge mansions and cute little cottages are shaded by enormous trees on meticulously landscaped lots, in country club settings and golf course communities. The natives are ingrained with notions of politeness and southern chivalry, all adding immeasurable charm to the setting.

One way Aiken differs from most southern towns is that so many out-of-state people have moved here that distinctions between natives and newcomers have blurred. Where did these outsiders come from? Initially people came to work for the Department of Energy's high-tech, atomic energy facility in Aiken. The department imported engineers, physicists, technicians, bricklayers—you name it—from all over the country.

When the energy project was finally up and running, many workers moved elsewhere to new jobs. Others—some nearing retirement anyway—elected to stay. The word soon got around about this beautiful little city with mild winters, friendly people and low real estate prices. This brought even more outsiders into Aiken. The result is an eclectic collection of people from all over the country.

Aiken isn't all single-family homes, mansions and honeysuckle. Modern condominiums, apartments and gated communities are home to many families. Away from town, you'll find small farms and homes on acreages for horses or garden hobbies. Luxury communities—Kalmia Landing, Woodside Plantation, Midland Valley, Cedar Creek and Houndslake—offer country-club retirement accommodations and an atmosphere of studied elegance.

Its robust business district makes Aiken look larger than it actually is, because it's the shopping and employment center for a large area. Aiken County has about 133,000 people. Yet the large city of Augusta is only 17 miles distant for heavier shopping and additional cultural and entertainment opportunities.

When we were doing our research it was not unusual to have many local boosters for a community. But Aiken had an unusual number of out-of-state people who highly recommended their retirement choice. A couple formerly of Columbus, Ohio, said, "We took our time and looked at retirement locations in seven states before we made our decision. Aiken clearly came out on top in our selective process. There was no single reason for selecting Aiken, but rather, the combination of climate, cost-of-living, medical and educational facilities, recreation and most importantly, the friendliness and charm of the area."

Recreation and Culture: Aiken has some of the South's premier golf facilities, with 19 golf courses within a 20-mile radius of the city. Several feature senior citizens' clubs. The famed Masters Tournament for professional golfers is held each spring only 17 miles west of Aiken in Augusta. Within the city, golfers can play at Palmetto Golf Club. There's also Highland Park, founded in 1903.

As if 19 golf courses aren't enough for Aiken's sports menu, the town has five polo fields! As you might guess, in an area with so many horses polo is a popular sport. No reason you can't try it. (Perhaps your spouse will help you get on the horse.)

From its local ballet to the grandeur of the Etherredge Center, Aiken's cultural opportunities are not easily surpassed. The city offers its residents and visitors a wide array of annually scheduled events in the visual and performing arts. The Aiken Center for the Arts functions as the nucleus of the downtown's cultural activities to bring art, drama, music, dance, and film events into the community.

The University of South Carolina-Aiken (USCA) has a tremendous cultural impact on Aiken, and it ranks as one of the finest public institutions in the Southeast. The university sponsors the "Academy for Lifelong Learning," a program specifically designed for adults over 55, with short courses on a variety of topics from financial planning to gardening to history. Adults over the age of 60 can attend USCA undergraduate courses tuition free on a space-available basis.

Real Estate: Aiken's housing comes with all imaginable price tags. We've seen properties selling the mid-$60,000 to mid-$600,000 ranges. Since average selling prices are under national averages, you can expect to get top value for your dollar. The selling price for a home in a nice area is $107,000 and from $175,000 up in an elegant area.

Medical Care: Aiken Regional Medical Center (ARMC) is a large six-story facility with 225 beds and 117 physicians on staff. There's also an office complex with 38 doctors maintaining practice. The Carolina Cancer Center and other specialty practices are located here. Seventeen miles away, in Augusta, you have a choice of nine hospitals with a total of 4,000 beds. Military retirees and dependents have Veterans' Administration hospitals in both Columbia and Augusta.

When Grandkids Visit: The Aiken County Historical Museum is located in the estate of Richard Howe. You'll get a chance to peek at late 18th- and early 19th-century life in Aiken County. Exhibits include American Indian artifacts, a drugstore replica from the former town of Dunbarton and a handmade miniature circus featuring 1,700 pieces. USCA offers a planetarium, and Hoplands Gardens is always a popular place with children.

Addresses and Connections

Chamber of Commerce: 400 Laurens St., NW, Aiken, SC 29801.
   (803) 641-1111.
Internet: http://www.aiken.net/lifestyles/retirement.html
Newspaper: *Aiken Standard,* 124 Rutland Dr., Aiken, SC 29801-4006.
   (803) 648-2311.
Airport: Bush Field in Augusta (20 miles).
Bus/Train: City bus service; Southeast Stages intercity.

Aiken

	Jan.	April	July	Oct.	Rain	Snow
Daily Highs	56	77	91	77	43 in.	1 in.
Daily Lows	33	49	69	50		

Cheraw

Cheraw is one of South Carolina's oldest and most picturesque inland towns. Named for the Cheraw Indians, whose main town was nearby, Cheraw began as a small trading post. Joseph and Eli Kershaw were granted most of the town at some point after 1768, and shortly thereafter laid out the present wide streets and the Town Green. The area of the original plan is now the nucleus of a 213-acre historic district, listed in the National Register of Historic Places, and is rich with gardens, trees and parks and the architectural legacy of more than 200 years.

Cheraw was as far upriver as steamboats could travel on the Great Pee Dee River and was the scene of busy steamboat traffic in the 19th century. Thus Cheraw was an important commercial center, boasting the largest bank in South Carolina outside of Charleston. Unfortunately, Cheraw's business district was destroyed when General Sherman's army visited the town during his tour through South Carolina, but fortunately no homes or public buildings were burned. Fine homes from this period still grace wide lawns and gardens.

Cheraw is located on the edge of the Carolina Sandhills that stretch from Pinehurst, North Carolina, to Warm Springs, Georgia. The town is located less than two hours from Columbia and Charlotte, three hours from the mountains, two hours from Myrtle

Beach and one hour from Pinehurst. Today Cheraw is a beautiful, prosperous town of close to 6,000 people who take pride in taking the best of the past and making it an important part of the future.

Citizens here have been involved in preservation efforts for almost a century. Well known for its trees for more than 150 years, Cheraw has been named a "Tree City" by the state tree-preservation program every year since the program's inception.

In the early 1960s, the town planners put in the infrastructure needed to attract and sustain modern industry, and Cheraw today boasts a stable and varied economy that includes a Fortune 500 company as well as several foreign companies.

The head of Cheraw's newcomer welcoming committee says, "We welcome newcomers and are proud of our wonderful retirees who have become a vital part of our community. The town's people are committed to the arts, recreation, good schools and government." She went on to point out that in Cheraw, as in many small southern towns, the best way to immediately become involved in the community is by joining a church. Cheraw is home to almost all denominations, and any congregation is delighted to welcome new members. Joining Cheraw's chamber of commerce also provides a good chance to meet the community at the bi-monthly Business After Hours.

Recreation and Culture: The Cheraw area offers numerous opportunities for all kinds of recreation. In town there are 115 acres of park land and 50 miles of public right-of-ways with thousands of trees, four parks, two recreation centers, a theater, five tennis courts and plenty of walking trails. A public landing for the Great Pee Dee River is located in town, providing access to great fishing, hobby diving and boating in a lovely park setting. Additional water recreation is offered at the three lakes within 30 miles of Cheraw.

Cheraw State Park is South Carolina's oldest and one of the largest. With 7,361 acres, the park offers a 332-acre lake with canoeing, fishing and swimming and towering cypress trees at the upper end. Cabins and lakefront camping are available for overnight stays. Hiking trails and a boardwalk around the lake make exploring this park a pleasure. The park's newest addition is a 6,928-yard, championship 18-hole golf course laid out among the rolling hills, woodlands and wildlife, with a full-service pro shop. Just across the way Cheraw Country Club offers more golf with a 6,459-yard, 18-hole course. The Country Club also has a clubhouse, a swimming pool and tennis courts. There are 13 more courses within a 30 mile area.

Sandhills State Forest and Sandhills National Wildlife Refuge, not far from town, provide public hunting, fishing, hiking trails, ponds and picnic sites. Hunting is also possible in nearby game management areas.

The state forest also provides mountain bike trails, primitive camping and horse and carriage trails. There's even a mini-mountain to climb! The wildlife refuge has photography blinds and wildlife viewing areas. All together there are more than 96,000 acres of public land in Chesterfield County.

Chesterfield-Marlboro Technical College offers a variety of adult classes, and both Francis Marion University and Coker College are nearby. The Cheraw Community Center houses an art gallery, meeting facilities, art classrooms and a teen center. The Chesterfield County Library regularly offers discussion groups and speakers, and Cheraw State Park hosts various nature and craft programs. On occasion, a community choir and a little-theater group perform for special events and there is an occasional square dance. The Recreation Department also offers aerobics and line dancing classes, and both short and long trips to places of interest.

Real Estate: Cheraw has beautiful antebellum neighborhoods as well as newer subdivisions. Prices here are about average for similar size towns in South Carolina. A typical, three-bedroom home in an ordinary neighborhood sells for around $75,000. A bargain home might go for $50,000. A really nice house in a more expensive neighborhood would sell for $125,000 to $175,000. There is only one set of condos in Cheraw, and they sell for $35,000.

Medical Care: Chesterfield General Hospital, a 72-bed facility with a 24-hour, physician-staffed emergency room, inpatient and outpatient surgery, intensive-care and cardiac rehabilitation units and state-of-the-art diagnostic technology, serves Cheraw's local needs. Regional medical centers in Columbia, Florence and Charlotte are also quite close by. Cheraw's award-winning rescue squad responds to emergencies, and 26 physicians provide family and specialized care. Should the need arise, there are three nursing homes.

When Grandkids Visit: When grandkids come to visit, Sugarloaf Mountain makes a great outing. Twenty miles from Cheraw in Sandhills State Forest, Sugarloaf is a child-size mountain rising one hundred feet above the surrounding terrain, a remnant of the oldest mountain chain in North America. April and May are particularly good times to visit, when the mountain laurel is in bloom. Cheraw State Park's boardwalk, dam and swimming area are also popular spots for kids and the lake offers paddle boats and canoes.

Addresses and Connections

Chamber of Commerce: 221 Market Street, Cheraw, SC 29520. (803) 537-7681, (803) 537-8425.
Internet: http://www.discoverypress.com/aarc/cheraw.html
Newspaper: *Cheraw Chronicle,* 191 Cheraw, Cheraw, SC 29520. (803) 537-4518.
Airport: Cheraw has a local airport for private planes. The nearest public airport is in Florence, SC (45 miles). Larger airports are slightly less than two hours away in Charlotte, NC, and Columbia, SC.
Bus/Train: Pee Dee Regional Transportation provides intercity bus service; Amtrak connection is at Hamlet, NC, (20 miles).

Cheraw

	Jan.	April	July	Oct.	Rain	Snow
Daily Highs	52	74	90	74	43 in.	3 in.
Daily Lows	29	46	67	48		

Columbia

Here in the heart of the South, there's a city that combines all the graces of a rich past with the vibrancy of the emerging Sunbelt. Columbia, South Carolina, is a center for military, academic, government and business life. With a population of 110,000, Columbia is a city, yet small enough to feel like a hometown.

Many "Old South" grew haphazardly, with roads and streets going in random directions, without planning of any sort. But Columbia is different. The British needed a capital city for South

Carolina, so in 1686 they designed one of the first planned cities in the Colonies. The city's broad boulevards and architectural gems attest to its early beauty. Robert Mills, one of the pioneers of U.S. architecture, designed several buildings here as well as many in Washington, D.C. (One of his more famous works is the Washington Monument.)

Columbia suffered tragically during the Civil War when General Sherman's troops, on their infamous March to the Sea, burned the city, destroying as much as of it as they could. Comparing photos taken after this holocaust and after Reconstruction makes one appreciate the meticulous efforts to reconstruct Columbia as it was before the war.

One of Columbia's advantages is its strategic location—literally in the heart of South Carolina. The mountains and the ocean are each a little more than a two-hour drive away, making Columbia accessible to the best of both worlds. The city is situated at the point where the coastal plain meets the beginning of Piedmont country. At the western edge of the city, the rolling foothill country begins, and at the opposite edge, the country is flat all the way to the ocean. The streets are shaded with tall trees, and there's a quiet charm that comes with ordinary people living in ordinary neighborhoods. Yet, Columbia has its sophisticated side as well—a cosmopolitan feeling that goes with being a university town.

Columbia's mix of people, places and events offers something for everyone. People who like to live near a college or university can be assured that, with no fewer than nine institutions of higher learning, there's always an intriguing course, lecture series, exhibit or cultural event to enjoy. The University of South Carolina, with 28,000 students, is Columbia's focal point of cultural enrichment. Along with a nearby two-year college, the school attracts academics from around the nation, many of whom later decide to join the ranks of Columbia's retired. A surprising number of academic-oriented northerners have found this to be a great place for retirement. By the way, Columbia claims to have a higher percentage of retirees living here than anywhere else in the state.

This is also a popular retirement location for military families because of nearby Fort Jackson and the obvious advantages of retiring near a military installation—health care, post-exchange and golf privileges. During World War II, thousands of GIs were stationed here, awaiting shipping orders to join their comrades in Europe. Many fondly recall the mild winters and friendly South Carolinians; these memories are bringing the ex-GIs back to Columbia for their retirement careers. These two out-of-state groups, academic and military, contribute toward making the Columbia area heterogeneous, with open, accepting feelings toward newcomers.

We found several retirees who had started out intending to retire elsewhere, but somehow wound up happily retiring in the Carolinas. For example, one retired couple admitted that they had always planned on retirement in Florida. "Every year, as we made our annual trip to Florida, we broke our trip up with a stopover in Columbia," they explained, "and again on the way back. Then, one day, just before retirement, we realized that we really liked Columbia better than Florida!" They decided to rent an apartment, just to "see how Columbia feels." They found low living costs and friendly, cultured neighbors. "We never made it to Florida," they said with satisfied smiles. "We still go there for vacations, though."

I asked the husband how he felt as a Yankee moving into a "Deep South" town. Did he find any prejudices? "To tell you the truth, I haven't noticed anything like that," he said. "My neighbors are just as nice as the ones we had back home, but they're definitely more friendly. Other northerners warned us, 'They'll be neighborly, yes, but they'll never invite you to their daughter's debutante party unless you were born in Columbia.'" He shrugged his shoulders and said, "That's a relief to me, because the last place I'd want to be invited would be to some teenager's debutante party! I'd have to invent an excuse why I couldn't go."

Columbia's real distinction is its ability to grow and thrive while maintaining an easy, friendly spirit and a lifestyle that works for people of all ages. Mayor Robert D. Coble, known to his constituents as "Mayor Bob," puts it nicely: "Here in Columbia, we have found what others are still searching for."

The Congaree Vista, a historic (and developing) 600-acre area, once a warehouse district on the Congaree River, is now an upscale section featuring some of the city's best bistros and shops, antique stores and art galleries. Pre-war buildings along Main Street are being redeveloped for town house and loft living.

Recreation and Culture: Ten golf courses invite play in the Columbia area. If you're planning a visit to check out the town, you can get a combination golf-motel package through the chamber of commerce. The motel and four hours of golf come at nice discount. For spectator sports, Columbia has a minor-league baseball team, the Bombers.

Open-air concerts and festivals are held at Finlay Park. The Town Theatre, the nation's oldest community theater, presents plays for theater-going audiences. This year the Columbia Museum of Art, home to the impressive Samuel H. Kress Collection of Baroque and Renaissance art, is scheduled to move into its downtown building, which will accommodate its growth and provide an optimal environment for its collections.

Of course, with several universities in Columbia, you may be confident of finding year-round entertainment and interesting events in for form of plays, lectures, and musical presentations. All South Carolina state colleges and technical institutes waive tuition for residents over 60 years of age (on a space-available basis), providing retirees with lots to do. Retirees can also take full advantage of this benefit at regional campuses in Beaufort, Lancaster, Allendale, Sumter, Union, Aiken, Conway and Spartanburg. Also, special low-cost spring and summer residential academic programs are available exclusively for senior citizens.

Real Estate: Columbia is almost circled by country clubs and golf course communities, places very popular with retirees. The Irmo area just west of Columbia combines recreation on Lake Murray with golf and country living. Homes located on or near the 500 miles of lake shoreline northeast of Columbia are within a 30-minute trip to downtown. Several retirement developments located nearer the city center are drawing retirees, with upscale patio homes and non-assisted living complexes. According to the chamber of commerce, many ex-Floridians are moving here. The Columbia area is 12 percent below national averages, with nice, three-bedroom homes starting around $90,000 and golf-course homes at $150,000.

Medical Care: Columbia offers excellent medical care; the metropolitan area has 13 hospitals, the major ones being: Baptist Medical Center, Lexington Medical Center, Providence Hospital, Richland Memorial Hospital and Dorn Veterans Hospital. Military retirees can take advantage of Fort Jackson's health facilities.

When Grandkids Visit: Columbia is a city where you almost have too many choices of where to take the grandchildren. You can visit the State House, whose western wall is marked to show where cannonballs struck during Sherman's fiery march, then you can tour a space-travel exhibit honoring the state's home-grown astronauts at the South Carolina State Museum. They'd probably also like to see the high-tech F-16, the world's most sophisticated fighter jet, at McEntire Air National Guard Station. If none of the above suits them, you can always fall back on the nationally acclaimed Riverbanks Zoo and its new 70-acre Botanical Garden.

Addresses and Connections

Chamber of Commerce: P.O. Box 1360, Columbia, SC 29202. (803) 733-1110.
Internet: http://www.columbiasc.net/city/city1.htm
http://www.gcbn.com
Newspapers: *South Carolinian,* 2321 Main St., Columbia, SC 29201-1955. (803) 254-8362.
Southern Free Press, 540 Saint Andrews Rd., Columbia, SC 29210-4500. (803) 798-1860.
Airport: Columbia Metropolitan Airport.
Bus/Train: Local buses; Greyhound; Amtrak.

Columbia

	Jan.	April	July	Oct.	Rain	Snow
Daily Highs	50	72	88	72	43 in.	5 in.
Daily Lows	32	50	69	50		

SOUTH CAROLINA TAXES
South Carolina Tax Commission
P. O. Box 125, Columbia, SC 29214 — Ph. (803) 737-5000
South Carolina's tax bills rank 12th among the least expensive in the nation

Income Tax

Not over $2,250	2.5%	$6750 - $9,000	5.0%
$2,250 - $4,500	3.0%	$9,000- $11,250	6.0%
$4,500 - $6750	4.0%	Over $11,250	7.0%

Standard Deduction: Federal amount
Public Pension Exclusion: $3,000 for retirees under 65 if elect to claim, $10,000 for re-
tirees age 65 or older
Private Pension Exclusion: Same as Social Security/Railroad
Retirement Benefits: Full exclusion
Standard Deduction: Federal amount
Medical and Dental Expense Deduction: Federal amount
Federal Income Tax Deduction: None
Other: Tax credit (maximum of $300) for amounts paid to an institution providing skilled
or intermediate care. Married persons filing jointly are allowed a tax credit up to $210.

Sales Taxes

State 5.0%, **County** 1.0%, **City** None
Combined Rate in Selected Towns:
Charleston: 6.0%, **Columbia:** 5.0%, **Greenville:** 5.0%
General Coverage: Food is taxed, prescription drugs are exempt.

Property Taxes

Average assessment on a $100,000 home about $2,500 annually.
All real and personal property is subject to tax. In relation to personal income, property
tax collections are in the middle third among the 50 states.
Homestead Credit: Age 65 or older, blind, or permanently disabled: $20,000 of fair mar-
ket value. Paraplegics and disabled veterans: Total exemptions of dwelling house and lot
not to exceed one acre

Estate/Inheritance Taxes

South Carolina does not impose an estate tax nor an inheritance tax. It imposes only a
pick-up tax, which is a portion of the federal estate tax and does not increase the total tax
owed. Credit amount is state tax.

Index to Places